Music and Discourse

JEAN-JACQUES NATTIEZ

Music and Discourse
Toward a Semiology of Music

TRANSLATED BY CAROLYN ABBATE

PRINCETON UNIVERSITY PRESS

PRINCETON, NEW JERSEY

Published by Princeton University Press, 41 William Street,
Princeton, New Jersey 08540
In the United Kingdom: Princeton University Press, Chichester, West Sussex

First published in Paris, France, 1987 as *Musicologie générale et sémiologie*.
Copyright © 1987 by Christian Bourgois Editeur

Library of Congress Cataloging-in-Publication Data

Nattiez, Jean-Jacques.
[Musicologie générale et sémiologie. English]
Music and discourse : Toward a semiology of music / Jean-Jacques
Nattiez ; translated by Carolyn Abbate.
p.   cm.
Translation of: Musicologie générale et sémiologie.
Includes bibliographical references and index.
ISBN 0-691-09136-6
ISBN 0-691-02714-5 (pbk.)
1. Musicology. 2. Musical analysis. 3. Semiotics. I. Title.
ML3797.N3713   1990   781'.1—dc20   90-37225

This book has been composed in Baskerville and Weiss

Princeton University Press books are printed on acid-free paper
and meet the guidelines for permanence and durability of the
Committee on Production Guidelines for Book Longevity of the
Council on Library Resources

Printed in the United States of America

10 9 8 7 6 5 4 3 2

Designed by Laury A. Egan

TO JEAN MOLINO

It is quite normal, in the course of our daily
work, that we avoid direct contact with that work's
foundations. But it is equally clear that the
moment must arrive when we should reflect upon
the objectives we are pursuing, and the paths we
take towards them.

LEO TREITLER, 1967

Contents

Preface

THIS BOOK is based upon a hypothesis that I shall immediately state: the musical work is not merely what we used to call the "text"; it is not merely a whole composed of "structures" (I prefer, in any case, to write of "configurations"). Rather, the work is also constituted by the procedures that have engendered it (acts of composition), and the procedures to which it gives rise: acts of interpretation and perception.

These three large categories define a total musical fact (I use "total musical fact" in Mauss's sense of the "total social fact"). They can be called the neutral or immanent level, the poietic level, and the esthesic level. To say that the work—whether score or sound waves—cannot be understood without knowing either how it was composed or how it is perceived might *seem* terribly banal, but is in reality just the opposite. We should think, for example, of the traditional assumptions of various types of musical analysis. In conventional analysis, the musical work may be reduced completely to its immanent properties. This, broadly sketched, is the structuralist position—yet it is also, in what is only ostensibly a paradox, the position taken by a great number of musicologists and music theorists. For others, the work is of no interest except in its relation to an act of composition or to a set of conditions surrounding its creation. This is, obviously, a composer's point of view, but it has wider currency as well. Still others regard the work as having no reality except as perceived. This is a popular position, and is indeed the "common sense" view of the matter.

If, however, musical analysis shows *how a work of art functions*, it is impossible to reduce that work to only one of its three dimensions. The work's immanent "configurations" do not harbor the secrets of compositional processes or of perceptive behaviors. Knowledge of history or culture does not suffice to explain why the work is what it is; the work can no longer be shrunk to that which we perceive in it. The *essence* of a musical work is at once its genesis, its organization, and the way it is perceived. For this reason, musicology, music analysis, and even approaches to musical interpretation that are less specialized or "scientific," require a theory that deals with the practical, methodological, and epistemological results of this holistic vision of music. I shall call this general theory *musical semiology*.

Stated thus, musical semiology may well seem ambitious. True, each of the three points of view defined above springs from particular (and often limited) biases of the various specialists. The music historian is scarcely concerned with perception. Work done by a theorist of achronic bent, or an experimentalist inclined toward perceptive mechanisms, may seem questionable when no appeal to history is made. My deep conviction, however, is that the problems and contradictions endemic to discourse about music, and particularly to the various types of music analysis, stem from the fact that its practitioners rarely bear in mind the coexistence of the three levels. I therefore consider it crucial to encompass through a large-scale synthesis all the results of this tripartitional conception of semiology as applied to "thinking about music."

I have adopted a particular organizational strategy in this book—one that is, I think, fully justified by the complexity of the problems explored here. Chapter 1 is an introductory chapter that lays out the tripartitional model of semiology, which I have borrowed from Jean Molino (from whose benign authority I have not, I hope, gone far astray). Given the rich history of semiology as a discipline, I have not reviewed each and every semiological theory currently on the market, nor have I tried to evaluate their applicability to music. From studies in the field of general semiology, I have kept only what I considered indispensible if the reader (musician or nonmusician) is to grasp the shape of my arguments, among which are Peirce's concept of the interpretant, as well as Granger's. I compare the theory of the tripartition to theoretical work (the most familiar in the field) done by Jakobson and Eco, in order to define one unique aspect of the stance taken in this volume: that *semiology is not the science of communication*.

Part I (Chapters 2–5) is intended to demonstrate the relevance of a tripartitional conception of the musical fact by examining basic concepts, as well as classic areas of musicological study: the concept of music, that of the musical work, the status of the sound-object in electro-acoustic music, and the nature of musical symbolism. In passing, I touch upon sensitive questions such as the universals of music and the diverse orientations of musical aesthetics.

Part II (Chapters 6–8) is intended to define the semiological status of discourse about music, since—if the theory of the tripartition may be applied to all human activities and endeavors—metalanguages can serve as the object of a similar approach. This survey constitutes the theoretical basis of certain music-analytical problems to be taken up in future volumes.

In a concluding section (Chapter 9), I attempt to explain how musical theory and musical analyses are *symbolic constructions* (as I define the term throughout this book). I refer to the example of harmonic theory, and demonstrate how abstract theoretical concepts introduced in Parts I and II can be applied to interpreting multiple analyses of the Tristan Chord.[1]

Throughout this book I shall appeal to certain concepts critical to my conception of musical semiology; among them are the concept of *plot*, borrowed from the historian Paul Veyne, and the notion of *autonomization of parameters*, adopted from the work of musicologist Leonard Meyer.

This book constitutes the first volume of an extended study of musical semiology, and deals (as the title suggests) with a general theory of both musical discourse and discourse about music. Further volumes will evaluate different analytical models, both in Western music and ethnomusicology, and propose various concrete semiological analyses, derived from the tripartitional model set out in this book. I shall above all attempt to demonstrate how analysis of the *work* and of *style* involves the three semiological levels—poietic, neutral, and esthesic. The properly music-analytical part of the next volume will present a critical examination of important writers of the twentieth century: Schoenberg, Schenker, Réti, Forte, Meyer, Lerdahl and Jackendoff. I will conclude with reflections on the epistemological nature of musical analysis, and the affinities between musical semiology and hermeneutics.

To the readers of my previous book, *Fondements d'une sémiologie de la musique* (1975), I should point out that this is a completely rewritten work. I wanted to take account not only of my own intellectual evolution, but also of a rich variety of research that has been brought to

---

[1] The French edition, published in 1987 by Christian Bourgois, contained a third part, a French translation of articles on melody, harmony, rhythm, and tonality that were originally written for the *Enciclopedia Einaudi*. On the suggestion of the American publisher and my translator, these sections were omitted from the present volume, since English-speaking readers (unlike French and Italian-speaking readers for whom the articles were originally conceived) have access to entries on these topics in works such as the *New Grove* or the *Harvard Dictionary of Music*. It was our collective opinion that anglophone readers would be much more familiar with the variations in, and the difficulties of, defining such parameters, and that the new concluding Chapter 9, which in some ways anticipates future volumes by demonstrating the concrete applications of concepts introduced in Volume 1, would be more appropriate for this audience.

my attention since 1975. I have occasionally adopted certain passages from my earlier book; these are indicated in the notes. As for the remainder of this book, certain sections are heretofore unpublished, while others are adapted from articles published in various places over the past ten years.

In the process of reworking my original ideas, I have also taken into account the numerous reviews of the *Fondements*.[2] Though these reviews occasionally displayed a certain epistemological sectarianism, though they sometimes made obvious interpretive errors (which I shall address), these exhaustive discussions (conducted, for the most part, on a very high level) have allowed me understand the context of many misunderstandings. I have by no means taken offense at being misunderstood—indeed, it would be in every way contrary to the spirit of semiology as I practice it to react in such a way; as Popper wrote, "it is impossible to speak in a manner that is *never* misunderstood" (1981: 48). I would like to thank all those who, having taken the time to scrutinize my writing, inspired me to better formulation of my thoughts.

My thanks are due equally to those who, in the past fifteen years, have shared in discussions of my concerns, too numerous to be mentioned here. I would like, however, to mention those who have played major roles in my decision to undertake this project, especially Craig Ayrey, Patrick Carnegy, Rossana Dalmonte, and Jonathan Dunsby. Pierre Boulez, Irène and Célestin Deliège, Jean-Claude Gardin, Gilles-Gaston Granger, Georges Mounin, Nicolas Ruwet, and Paul Veyne have in their various ways influenced the unfolding of the book. I wish to express special thanks to Jean Molino, to whom the book is dedicated, for the numerous conversations, suggestions, and comments he has tendered during the twenty years in which I have been involved with musical semiology. Finally, however, I should not close this English edition without thanking both Carolyn Abbate, who not only played a decisive role in the book's acceptance for English-language publication, but also undertook a difficult translation with skill and finesse (and in some places greatly improved my original text), and Walter Lippincott, director of Princeton University Press, who has supported the project from the beginning. The list of acknowledgments, together with my bibliography, bears witness (I hope) to my aspirations: I perceive myself as making a synthesis, and entering into a dialogue with my colleagues. I hardly need to say that

---

[2] Cf. Boilès 1975; Dunsby 1977, 1983; Godzich 1978; Hatten 1980; Imberty 1976; Laske 1977; Lidov 1978; Lortat-Jacob 1976; Malson 1976; Merkelbach 1977; Noske 1979; Osmond-Smith 1976; Schneider 1980; Scruton 1978; Stefani 1980; Subotnik 1976; Tarrab 1976.

I do not pretend to have answers for all the questions raised by a semiology of music. Yet by orienting those questions around Molino's theory, I hope at least to measure up to expectations that I have sensed, time and time again, in the numerous anonymous interlocutors that I have encountered over the years.

One evening, watching a performance of Kawan Kyulit[3] by the students at Wesleyan University, I was amused to hear the puppets perform the following dialogue:[4]

"What are you studying?"

"Ethnomusicology."

"What courses do you have to take?"

"A survey of world musics, techniques of transcription and field methods, history of ethnomusicology . . ."

"Huh! and what else?"

"They're having me learn a little information theory, a little linguistics, a little anthropology."

"That's a really interesting combination. What else?"

"Musical semiology . . ."

"Huh? What's musical semiology?"

"To tell the truth, I'm not always sure."

I hope that this book will enable that student at Wesleyan to find an answer to his question—but if that proves impossible, then I hope at least to have provided material for a new comic sketch the next time they perform.

Montréal, November 1989

[3] Javanese shadow-puppet theater, with gamelan accompaniment.

[4] In Kawan Kyulit, the actual musical sections are articulated by spoken and improvised dialogue, often dealing with local events.

Translator's Note

THE AUTHOR has taken the occasion of the English translation to introduce a number of revisions, both large and small, into the published French text; readers who compare the two versions will therefore discover that they sometimes diverge. A preliminary version of portions of Chapter 9 appeared as "Plot and Seriation Process in Music Analysis," *Music Analysis* 4 (1985), translated by Catherine Dale. Though I consulted Dale's felicitous rendering, I have made my own original translation of the material.

A word about one particular decision: I have throughout, retained the words *musicologie* and *musicologue* (musicology, musicologist) to refer respectively (as does Nattiez) to the investigation of all aspects of music and to any individual interpreting musical facts. French is more generous than English in this respect, allowing those whom our scholarly institutions prefer to separate—music historian, critic, theorist, analyst—to coexist fruitfully within the embrace of a single concern. This is a small gesture, but it expresses my conviction (as someone whose own work has resisted institutional taxonomies) that a Balkanization of musicology into history, criticism, theory, and analysis must be avoided. This unhappy separation serves only to limit dialogue and to foster misunderstanding—and as such is foreign to the spirit of a rich and engaged musical hermeneutics.

Introduction

1

A Theory of Semiology

1. The Sign

ALL THEORIES of semiology, general or applied, are based upon a definition of the sign. In my preface, I stated that I would neither rehash general treatises on semiology nor provide lengthy discussions on the nature of the sign. For present purposes it seems adequate to examine two approaches to the sign suggested by modern semiology.

The most famous definition is that of Ferdinand de Saussure, in the *Cours de linguistique générale*:[1] "the linguistic sign unites not a thing and a name, but a concept and a sound-image. The latter is not the material sound—a purely physical thing—but the psychological imprint of the sound, the impression that it makes on our senses: the sound-image is sensory, and if I happen to call it 'material,' it is only in that sense, and by way of opposing it to the other term of the association, the *concept*, which is generally more abstract" (1922: 98; English trans. 1959: 66). "I call the combination of a concept and a sound-image a *sign*, but in current usage the term generally designates only a sound-image, a word, for example (*arbor*, etc.). One tends to forget that *arbor* is called a sign only because it carries the concept 'tree,' with the result that the idea of the sensory part implies the idea of the whole. Ambiguity would disappear if the three notions

[1] As chance would have it, the works of the two founders of modern semiology, Saussure and Peirce, remained incomplete. The *Cours de linguistique générale* of Saussure was written by two of his students, Bally and Séchehaye, who based their text on the notebooks of students who attended his lectures over the course of several years, from 1907 to 1911. The standard edition is that of 1922; we had to wait until 1968 for the publication of the complete edition of the students' notes (thanks to the labors of R. Engler).

involved were designated by three names, each suggesting and opposing the others. I propose to retain the word *sign* to designate the whole, and to replace *concept* and *sound-image* respectively by *signified* and *signifier*; the last two terms have the advantage of indicating the opposition that separates them from one another and from the whole of which they are parts" (1922: 99; trans. 1959: 67).

There has been a great deal of discussion of what is known as Saussure's "psychologism," discussions inspired in particular by his notion of the "sound-image." For areas of studies devoted to Saussurian thought per se, this question may well still be of crucial interest. On the whole, however, posterity has preserved only one facet of this debate: the idea that the sign results from the union of the signified and the signifier, the latter being "a purely physical thing." This was especially true in the wake of Hjelmslev's reinterpretation of Saussure in his *Prolegomen to a Theory of Language* (1943), where the work of "depsychologization" was accomplished through a change in basic terminology: the signified becomes the "content" and the signifier becomes the "expression."

Saussure's definition is quite remarkable in that it implies two characteristics that tend to recur in all definitions of the sign:

(a) A sign is made up of two entities. That Saussure gave them particularly evocative names is one of his great merits.

(b) The relationship between these two entities is characterized by a process of *referring* [renvois]. Often this process is given the name *semiosis*.[2] The notion of referring connects modern semiology to the tradition of scholastic definitions of the sign, such as that of Augustin: *aliquid stat pro aliquo*.

(c) By making the sign a union of the signifier and the signified, Saussure conceived of the relationship between the two "faces" of the sign as stable and bi-univocal. Beyond this, the relationship is *arbitrary*:

> The idea of "sister" is not linked by any inner relationship with the succession of sounds "s-ö-r" which serves as its signifier in French; that it could be represented equally by just any other sequence is proved by differences among languages and by the very existence of different languages: the signified "ox" has for its signifier "b-ö-f" on one side of the border and "o-k-s" (*Ochs*) on the other. (1922: 100; trans. 1959: 67–68)

[2] According to the term popularized by Morris (1938: 1): "The procedure according to which something functions as a sign can be called *semiosis*."

(d) The following, however, is one of Saussure's most difficult ideas, because it is the most abstract: that the sign is characterized by its *value*. It does not exist within a *system* of signs except by opposition to and difference from the other signs in the same system. "Language is a system of interdependent terms in which the value of each term results solely from the simultaneous presence of the others" (1922: 159; trans. 1959: 114). Saussure applies this idea of *value* both to the signified "face" and the signifier "face" of the sign. As soon as he writes that "phonemes are above all else opposing, relative, and negative entities" (1922: 164; trans. 1959: 119), he sets himself up as the precursor of phonology, and, by extension, of *structuralism* itself, even though the word "structure" never appears in the *Cours de linguistique générale*. In the Saussurian edifice, the notion of *value* demands that of interdependent relations. This is why Saussure is led to separate the synchronic from the diachronic (i.e., there is a *system* of language that is explicable independently of language's history), *langue* from *parole* (this system is embodied not on the level of individuals but in a linguistic collectivity), external from internal elements of language (the system exists only as relationships between internal elements).

(e) Finally, we can see that, in Saussure's view, structure is not possible in language unless the relationship between the signifier and the signified is stable.

Can we, however, rest content with this "static" conception of the sign? An example can be drawn, for the moment, from the realm of verbal language: forcing the signifier "happiness" to correspond to *one* signified, whose description could embrace the thing that all English-speaking individuals associate with the word "happiness" in every possible situation where the word might be used, would seem a difficult task indeed. We shall see presently that this reservation about the "static" sign is especially relevant to music. I have preferred for this reason, at an early stage in my argument, to employ both a conception of the sign proposed by American philosopher Charles Sanders Peirce, and that proposed in 1968 by Gilles-Gaston Granger (of Aix-en-Provence, currently professor at the Collège de France), a philosopher whose special field is symbolic systems. In his excellent book *Essai d'une philosophie du style*, he undertakes an examination of Peirce's semiotic triangle in the context of a discussion of formal and natural languages. Peirce's triangle, according to Granger, offers "perhaps the most suggestive schema for the functioning of linguistic signs, and signs in general" (1968: 113). According to Granger, who follows Peirce in this respect, a sign or "representamen" is "a thing which is connected in a certain way to a second sign, its 'object,' in such a way that it brings a third sign, its 'interpretant,' into a relationship with this same 'object,' and this in such a way that it brings a fourth sign into a relationship with this same 'object,' and so on ad infinitum" (1968: 114). Granger represents this graphically as in Figure 1.1. As Guy Bouchard has pointed out (1980: 342–43), Granger essentially proposes an amalgam of section 2.92 of Peirce[3] and other passages in which "things" are designated "signs." (cf. 2.228 and 2.94, as follows)

Rummaging through the *Collected Papers* for the years 1897 to 1906, I was able to turn up no fewer than twelve different definitions of the sign and the interpretant. (Nattiez 1979–1980)[4] To follow the arguments made below, we need only examine three of these definitions in some detail:

(1) "A sign, or *representamen*, is something which stands to somebody for something in some respect or capacity. It addresses somebody, that is, creates in the mind of that person an equivalent sign, or perhaps a more developed sign. That sign which it creates I shall call the *interpretant* of the first sign. The sign stands for something, its *object*" (2.228).

(2) "Genuine mediation is the characteristic of the *Sign*. A *Sign* is anything which is related to a second thing, its *object* in respect to a quality, in such a way as to bring a third thing, its *interpretant*, into relation to the same object, and that in such a way as to bring a fourth into relation to that same object in the same form, ad infinitum" (2.92).

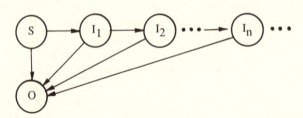

Figure 1.1

[3] During his lifetime Peirce published only a small number of articles. His papers have since been collected into eight volumes, the *Collected Papers* of 1931–1935 and of 1958. His paragraphs are designated in the specialist literature by volume number, followed by the number of the actual paragraph. A critical chronological edition of Peirce's writings is currently being assembled.

[4] For an even more detailed study, the reader might consult Bouchard 1980: 343–54; Bouchard, with no pretense to exhaustiveness, studied twenty-one definitions of the sign in Peirce's writings, and organized them into a paradigmatic classification in three categories.

(3) "In consequence of every sign determining an interpretant, which is itself a sign, we have sign overlying sign" (2.94).

Peirce's thought is so complex, and so often contradictory, that reconstruction of *the* coherent Peircian doctrine seems at the present nearly impossible. Despite this, the various definitions of the sign and the interpretant—even in their very diversity—remain most suggestive. I shall derive one interpretation and one possible application of the "sign" from his ideas, yet—and clear understanding of this point is critical—neither the interpretation nor the application can correspond absolutely to any single, stable state of Peircian thought.[5]

The following characteristic points in Peirce's definition of the sign should, then, be kept in mind:

(a) Peirce's "sign" is clearly analogous to Saussure's "signifier." This should remind us that in current usage—as we saw from the preceding—the word "sign" designates only the "sound-image."

(b) Peirce inscribes himself into the scholastic line: for each individual, the sign refers to something other than itself.

(c) Peirce's first and greatest original idea is his notion that the thing to which the sign refers—that is, the interpretant—is also a *sign*. Why?

(d) Because (and this is another aspect of his originality) the process of referring effected by the sign is *infinite*.

(e) Though Peirce never states it explicitly, this leads us to conclude that the object of the sign is actually a *virtual* object,[6] that does not exist except within and through the infinite multiplicity of interpretants, by means of which the person *using* the sign seeks to *allude to* the object.

We might try grounding this discussion in the concrete through a small empirical experiment, returning to the example of the word "happiness." For each reader, the word will instantly "make sense." But what happens if we try to explain its content? In attempting to do this, a series of new *signs* occur to us—"bliss," "satisfaction," "contentment," "fulfillment," and so forth—*signs that vary from one reader to the next, according to the personal experiences of each.* For this reason it would be preferable, if possible, to substitute a *spatial* image in which interpretants appear to be caught in a web of multiple interactions, for the more conventional *linear* representation of an "infinite chain" of interpretants.

The thing to which the sign refers is thus contained within the *lived*

---

[5] A recent study by Pierre Thibaud (1983) seems to advance as far as possible toward a reconstitution of the organization of Peirce's thought, and does so with all necessary prudence.

[6] Jean Molino; personal communication with the author.

experience of the sign's users. To the extent that we accept the sign as a "worldly thing" (to speak philosophically), itself belonging to our lived experience,[7] we can endorse a definition of the sign, proposed by Molino: "the sign is a fragment of actual experience, which refers to another fragment of actual experience that remains in general *virtual*, the one being the sign or the symbol of the other" (1978: 21).

The consequences of Peirce's dynamic conception of the sign are incalculable, both empirically and epistemologically. If I make his idea axiomatic to accommodate my conception of musical semiology, I do so because every component of this volume—whether the basic theory of the tripartition (which I shall discuss shortly), my critique of other concepts of musical semiology, or my music-analytical propositions—is grounded in the Peircian notion of the infinite and dynamic interpretant.[8] Since the rest of the book is, in a sense, both a defense and an illustration of the Peircian concept of the sign, I will postpone for the moment any further discussion of it.

A brief working definition of the sign can, however, be extracted from the preceding discussion: *a sign, or a collection of signs, to which an infinite complex of interpretants is linked, can be called* A SYMBOLIC FORM.[9]

2. Meaning

The concept of the interpretant allows us at this point to specify what we mean when we speak, as follows, of the essential (if controversial) notion of *meaning*.

Ogden and Richards were able to devote an entire work, *The Meaning of "Meaning,"* to an examination of different concepts of meaning, and to assemble up to sixteen definitions. (1970: 186–87) Quine (1961) had no hesitation in limiting questions of meaning to the study of metaphysics. A problem is not, however, solved by suppres-

---

[7] The Saussurian concept of the signifier as an acoustic image is already far more comprehensible if one associates it with the lived experience of the user.

[8] One can find elsewhere in Peirce's writings a much more static conception of the sign and the interpretant. Yet given that Peirce never established a final version of his theories, one has the option of choosing from among his definitions one that seems to correspond most closely to the reality of things—in much the same fashion as Morris, who was able to search for a behaviorist notion of the sign among the other Peircian definitions.

[9] My use of Cassirer's term is deliberate, despite the fact that the objection might be raised that this term was never explicitly defined (see Freund 1973: 146). In the final section of the Introduction (Part 7), I shall suggest a more precise definition of the "symbolic form," based on the theory developed in the course of the Introduction.

sion. As Galileo reportedly said, "eppur si muove": we must acknowledge that such a thing as "meaning" exists, whatever its true nature may be.

Beyond this: if we take a minimal (but sufficient) definition of semiology to be the study of domains constituted by signs—that is, of "objects that, to somebody, refer to something"—in the course of a semiological investigation (whether general or specifically musical in character) we cannot evade questions about the nature of meaning.

Now, musical meaning might be assigned some verbal translation (a certain gesture may mean "the prolongation of the dominant" or "the moment of the protagonist's death"), but it cannot be *limited* to that verbal translation. The temptation to do so is often difficult to resist, doubtless because we are never so *aware* of what the meaning of something in a nonlinguistic domain may be as when we attempt to explain that nonlinguistic domain in verbal terms. Imberty has written lucidly on the dangers of this temptation: "the musical signifier refers to a signified that has no exact *verbal* signifier . . . musical meaning [sens], as soon as it is explained in words, loses itself in verbal meanings, too precise, too literal: they betray it" (1975: 90–91).[10] For music, it is paramount not to define meaning solely as a reflection of some *linguistic* meaning.

The following *general* definition of meaning—a relatively simple one—might be proposed: *An object of any kind takes on meaning for an individual apprehending that object, as soon as that individual places the object in relation to areas of his lived experience—that is, in relation to a collection of other objects that belong to his or her experience of the world.*

A few refinements to the terms used in this definition should be made: "Object" refers to *words* (that is, the "props" of meaning) as well as to concepts per se, concrete or abstract things, individual behaviors, and social facts. I speak of an "individual" because precise understanding of what goes into the functioning of symbolic objects must be predicated upon the study of that functioning as it exists in the individual, prior to any analysis of the phenomenon's manifestations in an interpersonal transaction or at the level of a collectivity. I write of "apprehending" rather than either "producing" or "perceiving," so that it will be clear that the meaning of an object exists not only for the person who receives it, but also for its producer.

"Meaning" in this sense is allowed by any number of philosophers. "Meaning" may be defined by a formula more lapidary still; *meaning exists when an object is situated in relation to a horizon.*

---

[10] We shall return in some detail to this question in Volume 2, in the chapter devoted to musical semantics.

Granger (1968), because he conceived of meaning as the *residue* of a process of formalization, assigned a somewhat different sense to the concept of meaning. His work—and this is what makes it valuable to us—is nonetheless grounded in Peirce's notion of the interpretant. What is essential for Granger is that there is a proliferation of interpretants when an object of any kind is placed for the individual relative to his or her lived experience. The meaning of an object of any kind is the constellation of interpretants drawn from the lived experience of the sign's user—the "producer" or "receiver"—in a given situation.

At this point we can propose a framework for approaching the complex links between symbolic form and interpretants.

3. *The Semiological Tripartition*

I owe to Molino a striking empirical example, one that he used in one of his first public lectures dealing with conceptions of semiology. (1975b)

The example takes the form of a literary parlor game, popular in the eighteenth century (though the surrealists would not have scorned it). One plays it by making a statement in the following form: A is to B as X is to Y, with the letters replaced by terms picked at random.

We thus get statements such as:

The toothbrush is to God as Verdi is to the Italians.

Schenkerians are to musicology as flowerpots are to the city of London.

Ravel's "Boléro" is to frogs as safety valves are to confectioners.

Clearly, these statements are absurd. They are, however, unequivocally in English, like Chomsky's famous "colorless green ideas." Even beyond the fact of their Englishness, there is "something else there"—it would be hard to insist that the phrases make *no* sense whatsoever. As Molino points out, they are structured on the model of a clear, logical proposition, and because of this we can infinitely draw out the interpretants that could be associated with "toothbrush" and "God," or "Verdi" and "Italy,"—interpretants that, being common to these terms taken two by two, permit us to *construct* a plausible parallel. For example, one might imagine that God has as much need of a toothbrush as the Italians do of Verdi, or that a toothbrush is an attribute of God, just as the Italians' love of Verdi is a characteristic of their nationality. (I refuse to enter upon a potentially perilous exegesis of the statement about Schenkerians!) Farfetched as these glosses might be, at least they are *possible*.

What conclusions can be drawn from our little parlor game?

(a) We know that the choice of the four terms is random. In this specific case, then, we can be sure that no intention to create meaning is *behind* any given statement; that is, that *from the producer's vantage point,* the statement makes no sense.[11] The statement has, nevertheless, been produced according to an explicit "rule of the game" ("to produce a statement in the form A is to B as X is to Y") without which the statement would not exist *as it is* in its material form.

(b) It is possible to assign a meaning, even many meanings, to the statement that has been produced. The meaning of a text—or, more precisely, the constellation of possible meanings—is not a producer's transmission of some message that can subsequently be decoded by a "receiver." Meaning, instead, is the *constructive* assignment of a web of interpretants to a particular *form*; i.e., meaning is constructed by that assignment. The assignment is made by a producer (in many cases), or by a "receiver" or "receivers," or by both producer and "receiver(s)," but it is never guaranteed that the webs of interpretants will be the same for each and every person involved in the process. With greater clarity than most scientific investigators, Pirandello has described this phenomenon: "the sad thing is that you will never know (and I can never tell you) how I interpret what you say to me. You have not spoken in Hebrew, of course not. You and I, we use the same language, the same words. But is it our fault, yours and mine, that the words we use are empty? . . . Empty. In saying them, you fill them with the meaning they have for you; I, in collecting them up, I fill them with the meaning I give them. We had believed that we understood one another; we have not understood one another at all" (Pirandello 1972:147).

(c) In confronting a group of statements produced according to the indicated "rule," even without knowing the "rule," it is possible—despite the arbitrary nature of the interpretants that might be attached to those statements—to assign an identical formal description to the statements, to deduce solely from observation the formula *A is to B as X is to Y*. These statements are thus proven to be at least partially *analyzable*—analyzable even in the case where intentional meaning is absent and apparent sense is absurd.

Three dimensions of this symbolic phenomenon thus emerge:

(a) *The poietic dimension*: even when it is empty of all *intended* mean-

---

[11] In the following discussion, "sens" and "signification" are used more or less interchangeably. [Translator's note: I have, in general, used "sense" for the former, and "meaning" for the latter.]

ing, as it is here, the symbolic form results from a *process of creation* that may be described or reconstituted.

(b) *The esthesic dimension*: "receivers," when confronted by a symbolic form, assign one or many meanings to the form; the term "receiver" is, however, a bit misleading. Clearly in our test case we do not "receive" a "message's" meaning (since the producer intended none) but rather *construct* meaning, in the course of an active perceptual process.

(c) *The trace*: the symbolic form is embodied physically and materially in the form of a *trace* accessible to the five senses. We employ the word *trace* because the poietic process cannot immediately be read within its lineaments, since the esthesic process (if it is in part determined by the trace) is heavily dependent upon the lived experience of the "receiver." Molino proposed the name *niveau neutre* [neutral level] or *niveau matériel* [material level] for this trace. An objective description of the neutral level can always be proposed—in other words, an *analysis* of its immanent and recurrent properties. This is referred to throughout this volume as "analysis of the neutral level."[12]

Before proceeding, we should explain the terminology that Molino proposed.

(a) We can find the distinction between "poietic" and "esthesic" in the inaugural lecture of Paul Valéry for the Collège de France in 1945. (see Valéry 1945) Valéry, without using the term "poietic," aimed nonetheless to define certain characteristics of poetics.

(b) The word "esthesic" was Valéry's neologism, coined in the same lecture; he prefers it to "aesthetic" in order to avoid possible confusions, and on sound etymological grounds: the ἄισθησις was indeed the faculty of perception. Enjoying, contemplating or reading a work, musical performance, as well as scientific and analytical approaches to music,[13] are, de facto, situated on the side of the esthesic.

(c) The poietic. For Gilson (1963), from whom Molino borrowed this term, every work endowed with empirical existence, with reality, is the product of an act of making, of a labor. With "poietic" (from

[12] Not "neutral level of analysis," in order to avoid ambiguities, and the controversy surrounding certain malapropisms in the *Fondements*. Some very attentive readers of the original volume noticed, however, what was at stake: Imberty, for instance, quite rightly defined the neutral level as being "the level of the work, as object, considered independently of its conception or execution" (1976: 338). The neutral level is a level in the work, a level whose poietic or esthesic aspects have been *neutralized*. On the "neutrality" of the *analyst*, see the more detailed discussion in Chapter 6, section 3.

[13] Does the performer complete the "poietic" aspect when he is the first interpreter of a given work? This question will be addressed in Chapter 3, Section 1. Chapter 7, Section 3 qualifies the question of analytical and musicological interpretation in certain critical ways.

ποιεῖν, to make), Gilson understood the determination of the conditions that make possible, and that underpin the creation of an artist's (or a producer's or an artisan's) work—thanks to which something now exists which would not have existed, except for them. For Gilson, the poietic is divided into three elements:

(1) deliberations on what must be done to produce the object;
(2) operations upon external materials;
(3) the production of the work.

Molino, redefining the field of inquiry delimited by Gilson, points out how "poietics" is applicable to the special case of poetry:

(1) the study of techniques and rules which, at a given moment, for a given form, define the state of the resources and procedures used by the poet (for example, the techniques of formulaic style in the realm of oral poetry; or techniques of rhetoric or poetics in written poetry); (2) analysis of particular strategies of production which, from evidence and clues left by the author, or from characteristics of the work itself, serve to furnish a model for the production of the work . . . ; (3) study of the intentions of the author, who in the plastic arts or in literature often wants to communicate or express something about the work; (4) finally, reconstructing the expressive meaning, conscious or unconscious, which might be found within the work." (Molino 1984b, 9–10)

Each of Molino's propositions demands more extensive explanation and discussion (which will be undertaken in the next volume, in the chapter on "poietic" analysis)—particularly since some of the terms used ("author's intentions," "conscious or unconscious meaning") are in effect epistemological bombshells.

(d) The following primary definition of "analysis of the neutral level" can be proposed: *This is a level of analysis at which one does not decide a priori whether the results generated by a specific analytical proceeding are relevant from the esthesic or poietic point of view. The analytic tools used for the delimitation and the classification of phenomena are systematically exploited, until they are exhausted, and are not replaced by substitutes until a new hypothesis or new difficulties lead to the proposition of new tools. "Neutral" means both that the poietic and esthesic dimensions of the object have been "neutralized," and that one proceeds to the end of a given procedure regardless of the results obtained.*

Before going farther, we might illustrate the theory of the tripar-

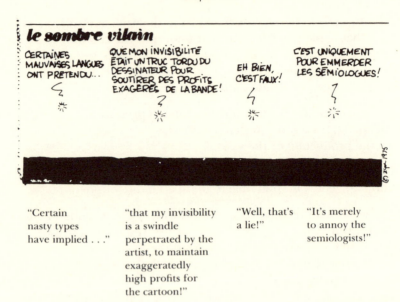

| "Certain nasty types have implied . . ." | "that my invisibility is a swindle perpetrated by the artist, to maintain exaggeratedly high profits for the cartoon!" | "Well, that's a lie!" | "It's merely to annoy the semiologists!" |

tition with an example slightly less radical than the literary parlor game described above, borrowed in this case from a cartoon strip.[14]

For the reader the message is "clear." The artist zyx, no doubt a bit tired of the semiological exegeses of cartoons prevalent in the 1970s, wants to get a rise out of the semiologists by reducing his character to nothing, making him impossible to analyze. As it happens, however, I know the true story of why this particular cartoon was invented: it is actually an "inside joke," which the artist intended for Jacques Samson, a former student of mine, who wrote an article called "Pour une approche sémiologique de la bande dessinée" (1975).

Now: would the "ordinary reader" be *wrong* to interpret the cartoon in the way suggested above? Of course not. I simply wish to emphasize that, from the *poietic* point of view, the "private joke" may well be an integral part of the artist's intentional meaning, but it is nonetheless inaccessible from the *esthesic* coign of vantage. Proof of this lies in the fact that we cannot fully judge the "poietic" aspect without interrogating the artist about his work. The reader *contructs* a plausible, logical sense that, in this instance, transcends the specific "intentional meaning" of the author.

But the story of the "sombre vilain" teaches us something else as

[14] I should like to thank both the author, Jacques Hurtebise, for allowing me to reproduce his cartoon here, and Jacques Samson for the information he provided me concerning the cartoon's "poietic" aspects.

well: the artist may indeed have wanted to annoy the semiologists, but his cartoon, nonetheless, is still "analyzable." What the artist drew on paper is a formal object that one can describe and comment upon. There is an anonymous landscape, a person whose presence (despite his invisibility) is pinpointed by the star, and a written text. This "trace" reveals a coherent style when it is compared with other cartoons by the same author: the person always appears in the background of the landscape; the story is never divided into more than four successive images or boxes. Between the poietic process and the esthesic process there exists a *material trace*, not in itself the bearer of an immediately decipherable meaning, but without which meaning(s) could not exist: a trace that we can analyze. *Semiology is not the science of communication. However we conceive of it, it is the study of the specificity of the functioning of symbolic forms, and the phenomenon of "referring" to which they give rise.*

The semiological "program" that we shall adopt thus has three *objects*:

(1) the poietic processes
(2) the esthesic processes
(3) the material reality of the work (its live production, its score, its printed text, etc.)—that is, the physical traces that result from the poietic process.

Three families of analysis correspond to these three *objects* (Molino's poietic, esthesic, and neutral levels)—families of analysis through which we attempt to understand the specific features of the symbolic.

(1) poietic analysis
(2) esthesic analysis
(3) analysis of the work's immanent configurations (of the *trace*); that is, analysis of the neutral level.

Two observations:

(a) Poietic and esthesic phenomena are *processes*; immanent configurations are organized into *structures* or *quasi-structures*.[15] The result

[15] Throughout this book, I have tried to avoid as much as possible the word "structure." In the strictest sense, there are no structures except mathematical structures—that is, a series of symbols that are related within a system. To speak of structure in a work of art in particular—referring to the interdependence of parts in a whole—is already more metaphorical. To say of an entire work that it is a "structure," meaning thereby that the work has an existence independent of the historical circumstances of its creation, seems to me a clear abuse of language. At this stage, I have retained the term simply in order to provide a sense for the opposition in kind between the "work"

15

of this distinction is a complex epistemological and methodological disparity between poietic and esthesic analyses on one hand, and analysis of the neutral level on the other.

(b) To distinguish between the level of the *object* and the level of the *analysis* is paramount, in order specifically *not* to confuse the *trace* itself with the *analysis* of that trace.[16] The trace remains merely an amorphous physical reality, until it is entrapped by analysis. In French, for example, one speaks of the poietic and the esthesic in the masculine (du poiétique, de l'esthésique) to refer to poietic or esthesic activities or facts, and of both in the feminine (de la poiétique, de l'esthésique) to refer to these two modes of analysis.

4. Semiology and Communication

Semiology—once again—is not the science of communication. This radical affirmation will, perhaps, be found shocking; certainly this particular aspect of my semiological theory has in the past encountered a lively resistance,[17] doubtless due to the force of certain received notions that dog the history of semiology. For this reason, we should linger a bit over accepted notions of communication.

We might suppose that Molino (albeit using a different set of terms) was merely recovering a classic schema for "communication":

$$\text{"Producer"} \longrightarrow \text{Message} \longrightarrow \text{Receiver}$$

and the "process." The term "quasi-structure," as unwieldy as it may seem, seems to me more correct, and will be justified in stages in the course of my argument.

[16] The *Fondements* did not, perhaps, distinguish clearly enough between the neutral level as the object of an analysis, and the analysis of the neutral level (cf. note 12). If I continue to insist upon this distinction, it is to facilitate understanding of this critical point.

[17] See, for example, the critique by David Lidov, that the tripartition "discards so lightly the distinction between communicative and noncommunicative use of symbols. To me this distinction is paramount" (1978: 17). In the remainder of his commentary, Lidov establishes a connection between the noncommunicative aspect of the theory of the tripartition, and what he claims as Molino's manifestation of merely lukewarm interest in problems of meaning and signification (ibid.: 17–18; 21). Molino, it is true, expresses many reservations about possibilities for a successful "science" of semantics. The position of "meaning" in his general theory of symbolism is nonetheless absolutely central; besides this, his insistence upon the purely formal aspects of analysis in his own empirical work stemmed from certain immediate considerations regarding the state of research in literature and literary criticism (cf. Molino et al. 1974; Molino-Martin 1981; Molino 1979b).

This is not at all the case. For this traditional schema we need to substitute the following diagram, one that makes no sense except when connected to the theory of the interpretant:

Poietic Process   Esthesic Process

"Producer" ———▶ Trace ◀——— Receiver

Here, the arrow on the right—and this makes all the difference—has been reversed.

The semiological theory of Molino implies, in effect, that

(a) a symbolic form (a poem, a film, a symphony) is not some "intermediary" in a process of "communication" that transmits the meaning intended by the author to an audience;

(b) it is instead the result of a complex *process* of creation (the poietic process) that has to do with the form as well as the content of the work;

(c) it is also the point of departure for a complex process of reception (the esthesic process) that *reconstructs* a "message."

The esthesic process and the poietic process do not necessarily correspond. As Molino often states in discussions of the matter, the poietic is not necessarily destined to end in communication. The poietic cannot leave traces in the symbolic form per se; if it does leave such traces, they cannot always be perceived. In the realm of music, the most obvious example is doubtless the Schoenbergian tone-row—not to mention Webern's or Boulez's self-conscious musical structures. The experiments of Francès (1958) clearly demonstrated that quite unambiguous poietic "activities," such as using a subject and a countersubject in a fugue, are not necessarily identified by the "receiver." On the other hand, the listener will project configurations upon the work that do not always coincide with the poietic process, and do not necessarily correspond to what Deliège[18] happily dubbed "realized intentions." (For instance, the thematic material upon which a work is constructed may be intended by the composer and leave a trace in the work, but not necessarily be perceived by the "receiver," who may have other ideas about what constitutes the work's themes.)

Molino's theory is not a negation of communication. It is, instead, a theory of symbolic functioning that deems communication no more than any *particular case* of various modes of exchange, only *one* of the possible results of the symbolic process. Musicologists, music theorists, analysts, critics, and musicians often have a different view of the matter: for them, there *must* be communication between the com-

---

[18] Personal communication with the author.

poser and the listener. Deryck Cooke, in his famous and controversial book *The Language of Music*, wrote that "the listener makes direct contact with the mind of a great artist" (1959: 19). In Coker's more recent book *Music and Meaning*, we read: "It is expected of the composer that he conceive the music's gestures and attitudes because he wishes to affect the behavior of performers and listeners, and he knows these gestures affect him when he adopts the attitudes of other interpreters. Such role-taking is needed for musical communication on the composer's part . . . Music is, above all, addressed to us as listeners or performers, and intended to affect us" (1972: 149-50; 151). A German semiologist of music writes, "a pregnant association is engendered between the intention, the structure of the work, and the expectations of the listener" (Stockmann 1970: 254).

These positions—more normative than empirical—do not, I fear, correspond to the realities of the situation. They bypass what seems to be the essential characteristic of human activities approached from a semiological viewpoint: their dynamic and constructed aspect.

This same myth of communication may be found among many semiologists, and not only among the less famous. We might recall Jakobson's celebrated schema:

Context

Message

Addresser   Contact   Addressee

Code

As Jakobson explained the diagram, "the addresser sends a message to the addressee. To be operative the message requires a *context* referred to ('referent' in another, somewhat ambiguous, nomenclature), seizable by the addressee, and either verbal or capable of being verbalized; a *code* fully, or at least partially, common to the addresser and the addressee (or in other words to the encoder and decoder of the message); and finally, a *contact*, a physical channel and psychological connection between the addresser and the addressee, enabling both of them to enter and stay in communication" (Jakobson 1963: 213–14). The two key words here are "code" and "communication," because a code common to the addresser and the addressee (that each might possess a different code is admitted only as an exception that proves the rule) is the thing that permits communication. The schema is epistemologically essential for Jakobson, since this very schema justifies the *structuralist* approach to language and poetry: if there are no disjunctions between producer and receiver, the semiological analysis of "systems of communication" can be rooted in studies of the immanent structure of languages and texts.

Structure, code, and communication are also key words in Umberto Eco's semiology—and Eco's ideas deserve a particularly close reexamination.

As noted previously, this book does not recapitulate the general history of semiology; for this reason, no systematic, critical explication of various semiological theories has been presented. We must, however, make an exception for Eco, who is at this time the only living semiologist to give us, in his many works, an original synthesis of the varied currents in semiological thought. His work, which is accessible in Italian, German, French, and English, has beyond this an international scope and position that few other semiological theories have attained. To many scholars and students, semiology today *is* Eco, for the success of *The Name of the Rose* has accelerated the spread of his theoretical work. Not to examine the main outlines of his conception of semiology, not to situate it in relation to the theory adopted here, would indeed be unthinkable.[19]

Eco's semiologcal works are numerous, and the tale of their translation and republication is complex. *La struttura assente* was translated into French in 1972 (as *La structure absente*); this book had in turn an Italian complement, *Le Forme del contenuto* (1971), that included certain additional chapters available in *La structure absente* but not in *La struttura assente*; these extra chapters are also published in English in *The Role of the Reader*. (1979b) For his English-language readers, Eco revised and reorganized the whole congeries in *A Theory of Semiotics* (1976), which also appeared in an Italian equivalent, *Trattato di semiotica generale*. (1975) *Lector in fabula* (1979a) offers a concrete application, in the form of literary readings, of the theoretical views expounded in the previous books. *The Role of the Reader* also included a selection of chapters from *Lector in fabula*. *Semiotica e filosofia del linguaggio* (1984)—the English translation, *Semiotics and the Philosophy of Language* appeared in the same year—was a reorganization and revision of five articles that appeared in the *Enciclopedia Einaudi*. (1976–1980) Yet across these various books, their translations, and their reworkings, and across the years between 1968 and 1984, Eco's basic viewpoint has not changed. For this reason, the following discussion concentrates on *La Structure absente* and its close descendent, *A Theory of Semiotics*.

---

[19] Two reviewers of the *Fondements*, Godzich (1978) and Schneider (1980), examined Eco's ideas in their reviews, although the *Fondements*, written in 1975, did not involve any theoretical borrowings from *La struttura assente*.

Eco's general semiology has a distinctly ecumenical character. He attacks no one, except those *hors combat* (Morris) or inaccessible (Lévi-Strauss),[20] and manages to recuperate a quasi-totality by absorbing concepts purveyed by various semiological theories: *langue*, *parole*, code, message, denotation, connotation, interpretant, structure, isotopy, and so forth. His critical agenda is to define the limits of semiology, with the aim of constituting semiology as an autonomous and separate discipline. At the same time, he proposes a theory that aspires to unification of the various currents of thought—a theory founded on the notion of the code. What, then, is this theory?

(1) The theory proposes a "logic of culture" (1976: 3) that will "make semiotics into a general theory of culture, and, in the final analysis, replace cultural anthropology with this theory of culture" (1972: 28). For Eco, the elements of culture are semantic units included in a web of communication. (ibid: 24)

(2) To speak of logic is to speak of structure. Culture, apparently, is a heterogeneous medley. But the function of the notion of "structure" is to enable us to bring order to this jumble: "structure is a model, constructed by means of certain simplifying operations, operations that enable quite diverse phenomena to be made uniform according to a similar viewpoint" (ibid.: 53).

(3) These structures have a *subjacent* character; we can describe them by identifying *codes*. An extensive critique of Eco's work would ideally inventory all his definitions of the word *code* and all the examples given to illustrate it, in order to determine whether they contradict one another. For present purposes, two of his propositions will suffice:

(a) "One hypothesis of semiotics is that underpinning every process of communication there exist rules or codes, which rest upon certain cultural conventions" (ibid.: 13).

(b) "The code institutes a correspondence between a signifier and a signified" (ibid.: 4).

Eco, in an extremely lucid passage, summarizes his entire argument on "communication": "semiotics studies all cultural processes as processes of communication; it sets out to show how *systems* exist beneath cultural *processes*; the system-process dialectic leads to affirmation of the code-message dialectic" (ibid.: 30–31). Everything depends, obviously, upon knowing *what* those subjacent codes, those "systems," actually are.

---

[20] Lévi-Strauss stated on Canadian television, "I never read my reviewers. If they do not agree with me, that makes me angry, and if they do agree, it is certainly due to misunderstanding."

Eco's main claim to originality is his strong stance against certain classic givens of structuralism: he distances himself from Jakobson's model by insisting that "the codes are multiple, and are not common to the producer and the receiver" (ibid.: 54; see also 119, 166). For Eco, this same fluid situation also characterizes the realm of *meaning* in contradistinction to the realm of *signal*, which is properly dealt with by the model of information theory. In his sensitivity to this "fluidity," Eco is on the right track: in effect, he recognizes the fundamental discrepancy between the poietic and the esthesic.

He does not altogether abandon this fruitful tack. The codes may be different for producer and receiver; but beyond this, there can be codes and subcodes for the same individual, or within the same group. "The multiplicity of subcodes which runs through a culture shows how the same message can be decoded from many points of view, in recurring within different systems of conventions. Thus for a given signifier, we can perceive the basic denotation attributed to it by the producer, yet we may also assign it different connotations, because the receiver [in decoding it] follows a path that is not the same as the path set by the code that the producer used as his reference [in producing it]" (ibid.: 114). To the extent that Eco takes account of the fact that the producer's code and the receiver's code may be mutually exclusive, he drifts very close to putting his finger on the notion of the neutral level; "the message is presented *as an empty form, to which one can attribute many possible meanings*"[21] (ibid.: 117). This is a form "empty of sense, yet nonetheless has—from the vantage point of internal logic of signifiers—a precise organization" (ibid.: 118).

Eco goes even further in his conception of multiplication of meanings; he recognizes as a fundamental precept the existence of interpretants in the Peircian sense: "the notion of the interpretant, in its richness and imprecision, is a fruitful one precisely because it shows us how communication . . . circumscribes these cultural units asymptotically, without ever 'touching' them—cultural units are thus continually being proposed by communication, and are its object. While this vision of a continually interrupted circulation might seem despairing, it is nonetheless the normal condition of communication. Rather than being repudiated by some metaphysics of the referent, this 'interrupted circulation' must be analyzed for what it is" (ibid.: 6–7; cf. also *A Theory of Semiotics*, 71, for a rephrased version of this paragraph). Here Eco, with his "cultural units defined asymptotically" arrives at a

---

[21] Emphasis is mine.

notion of the object of the sign as *virtual object,* similar to that discussed previously.

So far, so good; indeed, it may seem odd that I am undertaking a negative critique of Eco's theory. But things become somewhat dubious when he attempts to determine the *nature* of the famous "codes." For Eco, the codes have for quite some time been nothing more than *structures,* and a "convention that stabilizes the modalities of correlation" (1978: 275).

To understand the implications of this, we must take a small detour into the question of the concepts of *denotation* and *connotation*—or, more specifically, the denotational and connotational codes. Returning to a classic distinction in linguistics,[22] Eco associates a "hard" meaning with denotation, while connotations are secondary and discretionary; these latter Eco considers "subcodes" (ibid.: 55). But it is, perhaps, worthwhile to examine carefully his definition of denotation: "by 'denotation' we should understand the immediate reference which a given term engenders in the message's receiver. Since we have no wish to appeal to mentalism, denotation should be defined simply as *the immediate reference which a code assigns to a given term in a given culture. There is one possible solution: to say that an isolated lexeme denotes a certain position in a semantic system.* The lexeme /Baum/ [tree] in German denotes this position, this semantic 'valence' which determines that /Baum/ is the term which is set in opposition to, say, /Holz/ [wood as a material], and /Wald/ [forest]" (ibid.: 87). In recapitulating Hjelmslev's famous example, Eco tumbles into the aporias of structural semantics, *and they will not let him escape their clutches.*

Eco's flight into a *structural* theory of the semantic field results in an epistemological earthquake that jolts the reader at page 73 of *La structure absente,* or, in much the same terms, at pages 71–72 of *A Theory of Semiotics.* To cite the former, "a cultural unit is not merely characterized by the 'flight of interpretants'; it is defined as a 'place' within a system of other cultural units which are opposed to it, and which delimit it. Cultural units do not exist, cannot be defined, except in their potential opposition with other units of value" (1972: 73). In short: to give semiotics a "method," Eco believes that the existence of structures—or at least "local" structures—must be maintained: "Saussure plus Lévi-Strauss plus Hjelmslev plus Propp provide a method (that we can assume is coherent)—and that method is structuralism" (ibid.: 328). This act of allegiance is unambiguous. Eco has seen quite clearly that the notion of the interpretant blocks any structuralist theory of communication: "Even if one cannot identify these cultural

---

[22] See, for example, Martinet 1967.

units (signifieds) except through a process of infinite semiosis . . . we can at least claim *that* the assignment of a signified to a signifier is made on the basis of the codes, not *how* that assignment is made" (ibid.: 73). But meaning cannot simultaneously be both the relationship between the signifier and the signified (the first step in a chain of interpretants) *and* a fixed, stable position within a *system*.

We might think that in Eco's theory the interpretant has been relegated to the level of connotations, and that connotations escape from the prison-house of structuration. This is not, however, the case: "To know the signified connoted by a signifier within a given context is equivalent to knowing the choice exercised by the producer or the receiver; that is, to have identified their different but complementary positions within various semantic fields" (ibid.: 95).

The description of codes and subcodes will thus consist of a collection of semantic fields, analyzed from the structuralist perspective; that is, along the axes of opposition that make apparent a "general system of the form of the content" (ibid.: 75). Eco's example is the following:

/Mus/ can connote a "living thing" in reference to the axis "living" vs. "not living"; it can connote "rodent" in reference to a zoological field, it can connote "pest" in connection to the axis "pest" vs. "nonpest" or "not tame" vs. "tame" and so forth, continuing into the most complex definitional signifieds, and into legendary or fairy-tale connotations. (ibid.: 95)

Here one question immediately occurs to us: *how many codes must be brought forth to describe the coupling of signifier-signified at work in a system of communication; at what point does their number cease to grow?* In the infinite chain of interpretants, it is precisely a sign that refers to another sign (Peirce's definition in 2.300; cited by Eco 1972: 66)—that is to say, a signifier/signified coupling that refers to a signifier/signified coupling, and so forth. Given this fact, we are forced to inventory as many codes as there are identifiable pairings of interpretants. The types of codes that Eco identifies (for the visual realm, for instance) are nothing more than classifications of interpretant pairings. As Eco writes, "it is important to note that in many cases the 'codes' [note the quotation marks] would probably be *connotative subcodes*, or even simple *repertories*. A repertory does not structure itself within a system of oppositions [like a code], but simply establishes a list of signs which divide themselves according to the laws governing a subjacent code" (ibid.: 217). He could not state more clearly that there will be a different code for every new pairing of signifier and signified.

If this is true, the codes would be as infinite in number as the in-

23

terpretants: *and this is a contradiction in terms if one wishes to propose a structural theory of "codes."* (This is what I termed Eco's "epistemological earthquake.") The notion of the code is in effect only useful from the structuralist perspective, the Saussurian and Hjelmslevian perspective that trusts in the stable signifier/signified pairing. As soon as the codes collide with the multiplicity of interpretants, we can no longer clearly see what their methodological efficacy might be.

At this point, I could be asked how I account for the distinction between denotation and connotation. Many of us indeed harbor an intuitive feeling that there exists a level in "meaning" shared by everyone, a level that Martinet identified (not without a certain peril) with the definition of the dictionary, as opposed to this dust cloud of personal and affective associations that, compared to the hard kernel of meaning, seems quite secondary. If the Peircian interpretant represents at once an atom of meaning and an idea that serves as a point of departure for an account of semiosis as a phenomenon—which I believe, and which Eco also admits—then what we ordinarily call denotation designates a *constellation of interpretants that are common to the poietic and the esthesic*. As long as an interpretant is situated, in isolation, on either the poietic or the esthesic side, then we have entered into the sphere of connotation. A conception of the *autonomy* of the poietic and the esthesic can thus take account of one idea suggested by Osgood's work (1957), an idea in fact cited by Eco: that we cannot establish a priori criteria for the distinction between denotation and connotation. Even as we must recognize the importance of this dichotomy, we must realize that it cannot be resolved except empirically, on a case-by-case basis.

If I belabor this point, it is because this problem, here approached from the theoretical angle, will rebound with some force when we come to deal with certain areas of musical semantics.

Eco is too subtle a thinker not to be conscious of the contradiction that weaves through *La struttura assente*. He states it explicitly in concluding:

> Two types of discourse have been sketched over the course of this book. On the one hand, there is a call for a description of semiotics as "closed systems," rigorously structured, seen in a synchronic overview. On the other, there is the proposition of a communicative model of an "open" process, wherein the message varies according to the codes, the codes intervene according to ideologies and circumstances, and the entire system of signs continually restructures itself on the basis of an experience of

decoding which the process initiates, as "semiosis in progress." (ibid.: 404)

How can we escape the contradiction? Eco maintains that the two aspects are not opposed. To do this, he must attempt to reconcile the proliferation of interpretants with maintenance of local structures, by making "the semiological process a *succession* of closed and formalized universes" (1972: 406). In reality, Eco wishes to assume the mantle of two heritages, that of Saussure and of Peirce. Semiological events, however, cannot be simultaneously open and closed. The entire book is thus shot through with restrictions, defensive postures, and calls for cautiousness. Structure is a hypothesis that collapses disparity into a "single model of communication" (1972: 321, cf. also 338). "Within semantic systems, the constitution of a complete code *must continue to be a regulating hypothesis*"[23] (ibid.: 112). "Semantic fields are merely *postulated* as heuristic devices, in order to explain the signifying oppositions within a given group of messages"[24] (ibid.: 84). "The notion of the code is a sort of umbrella term . . . the system of rules . . . is actually so complex that we see no other solution for the moment than to call them all codes" (ibid.: 113). "Every time a structure is described, something is generated within the universe of communication which deprives that structure of part of its credibility" (ibid.: 113).

One might consider this equivocation to be elementary epistemological prudence and genuine skepticism. But if semantic fields and structures prove themselves untenable, why retain them at all? Eco has in his theoretical arsenal all the elements he would need to turn his back on structuralism: the tripartition, interpretants, and above all the concept of *circumstances of communication* (borrowed from Katz and Fodor), on which Eco bases his discussion of the role of circumstances in determining meaning. (57, 101–2, 112, 116) He appears to believe, nonetheless, in the possibility of a "formalization of circumstances of communication" (117), even though it has become readily apparent that the number of situations that affect communication is as infinite as that of interpretants. Does determination of the circumstances under which a message is stated permit the creation of a structure? Eco seems to believe in the possibility. (112) He has realized nonetheless that the most sophisticated of the semantic models that he offers, that of Quillian, "is based on a process of unlimited semiosis" (107) and that "the entire sequence of interpretations, according to which the process of semiosis animates and makes possible

[23] Emphasis is mine.
[24] Emphasis is mine.

the lexeme, rests upon connotation" (91). This is no doubt why he renounces "any pretensions that structural semantics may make to absolute objectivity" (85).

Eco, in tackling Lévi-Strauss's structuralism, demonstrates brilliantly in the final part of *La struttura assente* that the idea of *a* universal Structure, which effects some sort of invariant organization of the human mind, is an epistemological impossibility: "if the ultimate Structure exists, it cannot be defined; no metalanguage can ever capture it—because if it can be discovered, it is no longer ultimate" (ibid.: 383). But "Structure"—the "absent structure" of his title—is not merely absent on this global level. It is absent locally as well. Eco's critique of Lévi-Strauss cannot possibly be reconciled with one of his own definitions of "code," in which the "code" becomes in essence a metacode for all codes and all possible structures:

> When one speaks of a "language" as a "code," one must think of a huge series of small semantic systems (or fields) which pair with the signifying system in diverse ways. The code now begins to appear as (a) the system of signifying units and the rules governing their combination, (b) the system of semantic systems and rules of semantic combinations that govern various units,[25] (c) the system of possible semantic couplings of various units and the rules governing the transformation of one term into another,[26] (d) a repertory of cirumstantial rules which admit the diverse contexts and circumstances of communication, which correspond to the diversity of possible interpretations. (110)

Just as the Lévi-Straussian structure annuls itself in emptiness and the absolute, Eco's "code" breaks up into the infinitely small. (By now it should be clear why I have decided not to make use of the concept of "code.") Eco is an antistructuralist structuralist, and if I were to publish an "Introduction to Semiological Research" (which is the subtitle of Eco's book), I would probably call it *Il codice assente* (*The Absent Code*).

Eco, nonetheless, has all the artfulness of a professional magician. There is a crack in the mass of ideas brought together in *La struttura assente*, a crack that will permit his escape from the aporias of structure. Eco rightly remarks of Greimas's structural semantics that "if the semantic fields are numerous and contradictory, their choice depends on the particular hypothesis that governs an individual reader of the text" (1972: 85). Later, Eco writes that "if semiotics . . . cannot

[25] The code of the code . . .
[26] The code of the codes of the codes . . .

tell us what happens to the message once it is received, *then psycholin-guistics can, nonetheless, tell us what the receiver projects upon the message in a given set of experimental circumstances*"[27] (393). The attempt to account for meaning through structure is nullified by this simple sentence, which throws its lot in with the mentalism from which structure was to free us; it acknowledges that structural semiology is checkmated in any attempt to identify meaning from the receiver's perspective; it substitutes psychological experimentation for the hypothetical investigation of codes.

A Theory of Semiotics led us in 1976 "toward a logic of culture" on the basis of a "theory of codes." More recently, in *Semiotica e filosofia del linguaggio*, Eco has undertaken a rather timid self-criticism of his concept of codes (1984: 256) that in the end merely recuperates the term—now far more metaphorical. Historical justification and the "constant struggle between order and adventure [avventura]" are meant to justify this usage. (302) In practice, the internal contradiction of his conception becomes theoretically untenable, and Eco was left with no other option than to turn to the reader, the "receiver." This, of course, is what he did in *Lector in fabula*. (1979a) The English title is more telling: *The Role of the Reader*. (1979b) It is significant that within this collection of articles an essay on the "open work" originally published in 1959 should reappear, along with a more recent and quite stimulating study, which appeared in 1976, on Peirce's interpretant as a semiological foundation of "openness." The entire book deserves separate consideration. We can, however, simply note that this new flight to the reader's perspective means (in my opinion) that Eco has implicitly recognized, without theorizing, the impossibility of grounding a semiological theory of meaning in the immanent level alone.

A whole generation has in fact embarked on the same intellectual journey as Eco.[28] The flight from structure, characteristic of post-structuralism, involves turning away from the immanent, in order to rediscover the author and the reader. At the same time, post-structuralism is still confronted by the question that the advent of structuralism had declared closed, but that haunted Eco's thinking nonetheless: if there is a proliferation of interpretants, "why do we not realize that an art work requires a hermeneutic interrogation more than a structural definition?" (1972: 333).

Faced with the impasse reached by Eco, there are two options. The

---

[27] Emphasis is mine.

[28] With his *Semiotics of Poetry* (1978) and *La production du texte* (1979), Riffaterre also directed a theory of literature toward the dialectic of text and reader.

first is to retrieve the past, to burn the antiquated structuralist library, and start again with the fine old tradition of controlled exegesis. The second is to consider that, all in all, structuralism was not wrong in recognizing some level of material immanence in the text—a level that cannot be outlined, and that is not exclusive. This insight is worth retaining, even when pure structuralism has proven unworkable.

In thus dissecting Eco's thought, I had no desire to give myself over to the easy game of assassination; the examination was intended to emphasize instead how Molino's vision of the tripartition seems to open up a means of overcoming difficulties that a whole generation born during the heyday of structuralism has now begun to encounter. How can we reconcile formal and hermeneutic description, the analysis of a neutral level, and a material trace, with the web of interpretants? This, indeed, is the fundamental question posed by the present state of semiological research, by research guided (like this volume) by application of Molino's general principles to the special case of music. The whole of this book is an attempt to answer this question.

My detour into Eco's work will enable me to show that my particular theory of reference situates itself within a specific moment in the history of semiology and of the humanities. At this point, then, it seems proper that we be more explicit about the connections between Molino's tripartition and certain important ideas in contemporary humanistic studies.

5. *Situating the Tripartition*

Where does Molino's concept of the *niveau neutre* originate? Very likely in structuralism. If structuralism's flaw is its claim to explain man's works solely on the level of their immanent configurations, its historical merit was showing that a literary text (to take one example) possessed a dimension beyond its biographical or historical origins.

Molino recognized—and this is one of the specific points of his theory—that one must go beyond the immanent structures of the object of study. I would nevertheless claim that the principle of his analysis of the neutral level inscribes itself within an epistemological filiation that originated in Saussure, since the distinctions between external and internal linguistics and between *langue* and *parole* in the *Cours de linguistique générale* enable us to identify the internal and immanent, "a specific domain of research and existence, which cannot merely be reduced to external conditions" (as Molino has put it in a personal communication).

It is easy to see why models from structural linguistics should thus occupy a favored position when we are dealing with the analysis of the neutral level. There is nevertheless an essential difference between the classic structuralist approach and our "analysis of the neutral level." Structural description of an object as an organized whole cannot, after nineteenth-century historical linguistics, avoid passing through some systematic phase. Yet equally impossible today would be an attempt to maintain that *knowledge* of the traces left by man can be reduced solely to the immanent level. Analysis of the neutral level inherits from structuralism this basic insight: messages manifest a level of specific organization, that must be described. But this level is not sufficient: the poietic lurks under the surface of the immanent; the immanent is the spring-board for the esthesic. *The task of semiology is to identify interpretants according to the three poles of the tripartition, and to establish their relationship to one another.* Even when the *analysis of the neutral level* is (as we shall see) often the easiest analysis to undertake, *that analysis constitutes only one part, one chapter in the semiological program suggested here.*

Phonetics is one sector within modern linguistics that has demonstrated a need for recognizing three dimensions within the phenomena it examines; it was doubtless one of Molino's sources for the tripartition. As Molino reminds us in one of his articles (1975a: 48), the discipline is divided into three areas—articulatory phonetics (poietic analysis), acoustic phonetics (analysis of the neutral level), and auditory phonetics (esthesic analysis). The three families have not, of course, developed with equal richness within the discipline—yet it is worth noting that phonetics as a science has refused to insist that physical description of sounds inevitably corresponds to either the manner in which the sounds are produced, or the manner in which they are perceived.[29]

[29] Lidov is critical of taking phonetics as exemplary for the tripartition: "there is one salient truth, which Molino seems determined to ignore: the social fact of language has contrived a system of agreement between the two fields . . . in this agreement lies the possibility of communication, and in the actuality of communication, the *raison d'être* of our studies. In the agreement—the code—poietic and esthesic are united, imposed on in such a way that they need not always be distinguished either from each other or from the code itself" (Lidov 1978: 18). There are two problems here. First, Lidov confuses phonetics with phonology: the first is the study of the fact of *parole*, distinct from one individual to another; the second is the study of the facts of language (*langue*), common to all readers within a community. It is perfectly true that phonological unities transcend the poietic/esthesic distinction, but beyond this we must explain *why*. (Cf. the theory of short and long circuits in communication that will be discussed in Volume

We can now acknowledge that, within "human works," the phenomena of production, the traces that result, and the facts of perception do not necessarily coincide. Having acknowledged this, we can move toward an important *application* of the semiologic perspective defined here: a critical reading of methodologies in the human sciences during this century. Here, a few brief examples must suffice to suggest the potential scope of this critique. The first thesis of the Prague Circle of Linguistics states that as soon as one analyzes language as expression or as communication, then the explanation that seems most natural, and occurs most easily, is the *intention*[30] of the speaking subject. Here, the level of immanent description is declared to be related to the poietic. Lévi-Strauss's structuralism has, similarly, been understood as a "logic of esthetic perception" (Simonis 1968: 312–33). The phrase restates, in different terms, Simonis's conclusion that the "immanent" structures that structuralism uncovers actually correspond to esthesic categories. The Chomskyan concept of "linguistic competence," we can now see, mixes up the poietic with the esthesic, since "competence" is simultaneously the faculty of producing (poietic) and of understanding (esthesic) sentences that have never previously been spoken or heard. As for the history of musicology as a human science, one aim of this work is to demonstrate that various fields of study within musicology urgently need to take account of the tripartition and its implications.

Molino feels that praxis in the human sciences constantly confuses the poietic, neutral, and esthesic levels, such that scholars appealing to the same matrix of thought can reach divergent, contradictory, and arbitrary conclusions: "we cannot advance in our knowledge unless we keep these three dimensions separate. There will come a time when we can put them together again, and offer a synthetic construction; after this advent there will never again be such confusion as once there was. Before, there is confusion. After, there is synthesis. Between the two, there has been descriptive analysis" (Molino 1975b). Of course, the tripartition is easier to imagine than to realize; nothing guarantees that we have at our disposal the powerful tools necessary for analysis of the three dimensions. I often undertake, for this reason, to suggest the *limitations* of music analysis.

Molino, of course, is not the first to allude to a certain discordance

---

2.) Second, is it legitimate, when poietic and esthesic correspond, to speak of a "code"? (see the discussion in Section 4) Lidov's refusal to take the tripartition into consideration causes him to miss the constructive dimension of symbolism, the fact that the esthesic process *reconstructs* the message: it encounters the poietic, it does not "receive" it.

[30] Emphasis is mine.

between the poietic and the esthesic; similar remarks may be found scattered through the literature on the subject of interpretation. The following survey is culled at random from my reading:

> Kant, instead of seeing the aesthetic problem from the point of view of the artist's practice (of the creator), meditated on art and beauty only from the "spectator's" point of view, and in so doing, inexplicably introduced the "spectator" into the concept of "beauty." (Nietzsche on Kant, cited in 1974: 275)
>
> For the musical event, there are three points of view: the author's, the performer's, and the listener's. Their relation to one another is varied in the extreme, sometimes contradictory, sometimes confused. (musicologist André Souris, in Souris 1976: 47)
>
> In fact composer, performer, and listener can without undue exaggeration be regarded not only as three types or degrees of relationship to music, but also as three successive states of specialization. (composer Roger Sessions, cited in Sessions 1962: 4)
>
> Sonorous events fill an intermediary role between the producer's side, and the side of those who perceive them: they serve as a vehicle for communicative connections. (musicologist Doris Stockmann, in Stockmann 1970: 76)

In this last citation the distinction among the three levels is once more lodged within the framework of classic communication theory (cf. ibid.: 77).[31] Beyond this, none of our authors, even when they recognize the existence of three levels, has drawn conclusions about their consequences for analysis.

All the original force—but also all the difficulties—of Molino's concept resides in its demand for an "intermediary" analysis, the analysis of the neutral level. Analysis of the neutral level is (as Laske 1977: 221 happily phrased it) a *methodological artifact*. Understanding this is, at this stage, absolutely essential.

Analysis of the neutral level is a kind of crib, or mnemonic, uncovering a unity that might be overlooked by purely poietic or purely esthesic analysis. We may in certain situations, in this regard, speak of its propadeutic character.

Analysis of the neutral level is perpetually subverted; it is remolded and transformed each time new information leads to introduction of new descriptive variables, to the reorganization of previous analytical parsings-out into new configurations.

---

[31] In her article, the direction of the arrows is symptomatic: the author's approach conforms to the classic schema for communication, as reproduced here, p. 17.

Analysis of the neutral level is only one element of analysis: it does not include all the information necessary to a poietic and esthesic approach, but only a portion of that information. Analysis never stops engineering a dialectical oscillation among the three dimensions of the object.

Analysis of the neutral level is dynamic; it displaces itself constantly, as the analysis takes place: hence its paradoxical character. Given that an analysis is so much more precise than its written form,[32] analysis of the neutral level will always at first take the form of a graphic object, a form of presentation that seems paradoxically "fixed," given the infinite and fleeting character of the interpretants that it attempts to trace. But this "fixed" graphic presentation is necessary precisely because there are interpretants, and an infinite process of referring. The problem addressed by semiology is the nature of symbolic functioning itself.

In short: analysis of the neutral level is *descriptive*. I shall, in the next volume, attempt to show that poietic and esthesic analyses are by nature *explicative*.

6. "Silent Semiology" and the Specificity of the Symbol

Is Molino's theory, which we have attempted to summarize here, an isolated vision of semiology? Yes—if we consider that it has little to do with the semiologies that have recently held, or used to hold, a preeminent position: those of Barthes, Kristeva, or Greimas, to mention only three. The defining characteristic of Molino's theory is recognition of a specific entity, the symbolic phenomenon—with its own level of organization, a level that must be accounted for—as distinct from three other systems into which the global social system divides: the bio-social, the ecological-economical, and the socio-political (Molino 1978: 20–21).

Is Molino's theory the only one to recognize the existence of the purely symbolic? Not at all. The philosophy of science expounded by Locke, Condillac, and Leibniz, long ago distinguished a specific level of symbolic usage within the languages of science. An epistemological tradition that reflects on symbolic systems, and considers them of paramount importance, has flourished continuously, from the "Vienna Circle" to Granger, Gardin, and Régnier (to name only the French scholars). No mode of psychoanalysis—whether Freudian or Jung-

---

[32] Deliège (1974: 33) properly emphasizes the "oral character" of analysis.

ian—could exist without symbols. Various psychological endeavors have accorded a large role to the symbol, especially in recognizing the symbolic function in children (Piaget), and researching the role of the symbol in psychological function (Bates, Bonnet, and the "Project Zero" group at MIT). Anthropologists, for their part, have become interested in the role of the symbol in society (White, Geertz, Durand). Cassirer, and later Susanne Langer, viewed the study of myth, language, and art as a study of symbolic forms, as did Dumézil. Even demography recognizes the role of "symbolic factors" in the evolution of populations.

Not only the human sciences, however, recognize the presence of the symbolic. Leroi-Gourhan suggests a paleontology of symbols (1965: Chapter 10); there is even a move among neurologists toward a "neuro-semiology" (Perron, ed. 1981; Changeux 1983). Duhem, a French physicist better known today in the anglophone world than in France, opined that the laws of physics are nothing more than symbolic constructions, that "theoretical physics does not touch upon the reality of things; it is confined to representation of perceived appearance by means of signs and symbols" (1906: 170). An economist, Guillaume (cf. Guillaume 1975) has more recently shown the decisive part played by symbolic factors in the phenomena he has examined.

One might speak of an "invisible college" to describe scientific fields that are not attached to particular institutions; in the same way, we might say that there has for quite some time been a "silent semiology" that recognizes the presence of the symbolic as paramount. By "silent" I do not mean to suggest some secret or clandestine "school," but, rather, the fact that many writers have developed a more or less heterogenous current of thought, though they do not possess a systematic methodology—a *"silent* semiology" despite the fact that several of its adherents (Granger, Gardin, Bates, Bonnet, Geertz, Guillaume) do in fact use the word "semiology." Molino's perspective is (so far as I know) the only one explicitly to suggest a rough outline for an organized semiology of symbolic phenomena. My undertaking here is an exploration—doubtless still maladroit—of the articulation of three aspects of symbolic objects in the field of music; that is, to advance knowledge of music, within the framework of Molino's theory.

Semiology does not exist. By this, I mean that there is no "general semiology" (in the same sense as a "general linguistics")—that is, no collection of concepts, methods, and rules that permit analysis of the symbolic, in whatever domain it may exist. Only specific explorations, such as mine and perhaps others that deal in other domains, might (if undertaken on the basis of identical theoretical principles) break paths toward a more global methodology—given that such a thing can exist.

The larger characteristics of the symbolic form, and the methodological consequences of its investigation, can nonetheless be summarily sketched. Molino (1978, 1982) suggests the following outline:

(1) The symbolic is a constructive and dynamic phenomenon, characterized first and foremost by the process of referring; in this regard, it is *distanced* from reality, even as it is an element of the real. Meanings transported by the symbolic are not immediately decipherable in the structures of the *trace* that bears these meanings. To read meaning, we must distinguish the three forms of analysis, each relatively autonomous (analysis of the neutral level, of poietic processes, of esthesic processes).

(2) The symbolic is an *autonomous* domain within the totality of social facts.[33] It has its own existence. We must either analyze it and describe it *in itself*, in all its complexity, before situating it in relation to other areas (social, psychological, economic), or to seek to explain it in terms other than its own.

(3) The symbolic is a *thing*: "it maintains itself, it endures" (Molino 1981c: 74), it evolves (ibid.: 75), it has effects. When a formerly unknown trace comes into the realm of lived experience, this new trace will modify the space of forms, as well as the space of meaning. The symbolic defines a potential horizon of new symbolic organizations. The symbolic is a *tool*; "a word operates no more mysteriously than the hammer; it simply operates differently" (1978: 23). By means of the word-tool, mankind modifies and influences his environment.

(4) The symbolic *exists*: "it is as much material as mental . . . the symbolic is not a mental thing—if one understands by 'mental' a closed world, some interior fortress, within whose walls all conspiracies of imagination take up arms; the symbolic is an activity which does not recognize the separate jurisdictions of 'public' and 'private' . . . the symbolic is thus also a prayer, a rite, a greeting, as much as an interior monologue—a smile or a cry, as much as the subtle stratagems that interest us. Culture is not mental, it is a configuration of symbolic behaviors" (1978: 25). The symbolic, as a symbolic construction, is just as real as the "imaginary."

My semiology of music is intended to demonstrate the existence of music as a "symbolic form."

[33] Translator's note: here Molino and Nattiez are evoking Marcel Mauss's notion of the "total social fact"; for this reason *fait musical total* has always been translated as "total musical fact." "Fact" should, however, be understood in its dynamic sense, encompassing the activity associated with the making and perception of music.

7. The Concept of the Symbol

To use the expression "symbolic form" is a formidable decision, even if we have crept toward its definition by offering successive and complementary approximations over the course of this chapter. A favorite pastime of semiologists is proposing definitions of different sorts of signs. The polysemiousness of the words "symbol" (and "symbolic") demands that (after having explored the specifics of Molino's conception of it) we situate it relative to other accepted meanings of the term, even if we believe that foundation of a particular semiology on a typology of signs is neither possible nor useful.[34]

(1) The symbolic function is generally spoken of as a "capacity to represent that which is absent" (Paulus 1969: 21). Mounin suggests a particularly lucid definition: "all acts of mental substitution, that is, the tendency, associated naturally or conventionally with a given object or situation, to use all other objects of perception as susceptible to substitution for that object or situation, whenever that object or situation is difficult or impossible to grasp directly" (1970: 70). To establish the tenets of a symbolic aesthetics of art, Gilson writes, we need only "to include under the rubric of symbol *all signs*, whatever their nature: words, lines, forms, colors, even sounds" (1963: 99). With this, we draw near again to the extended meaning assigned to *symbolic forms* by Cassirer, as "a general function of mediation, by means of which the spirit, consciousness, constructs its entire perceptual and discursive universe" (cited in Ricoeur 1965: 19). *Molino's theory is in this sense a general theory of symbolic facts.* We find the same sense of "symbolic" in the case of "symbolic logic," which has recourse to a special form of language in which signs—defined univocally—express completely unambiguous relations. The same term—"symbol," "symbolic"—will nonetheless always, by virtue of its generality, allude also to the *polysemiousness* of any expression, and to an infinite *exegesis* that carves out that expression's meanings.

(2) A second accepted sense of the word "symbol" takes symbol as an autonomous form, "symbol" as an object of exegesis. According to Ricoeur, hermeneutics as a philosophical activity grounds itself in symbols and the symbolic: "the symbol is a linguistic expression with a double meaning, demanding interpretation; interpretaton is a work of understanding that aims at decoding symbols . . . there is no symbol without interpretation; as soon as one man dreams, prophetizes, writes poetry, another will rise up and interpret it; interpretation is

---

[34] See, for instance, Nattiez 1978, and the reworking in Nattiez 1987.

35

an organic part of symbolic thought, and of its double meaning"
(1965: 15, 26).

(3) But Ricoeur is careful to remind us (ibid.: 25) that the word
"symbol" may have other meanings that do not intersect with his.
Saussure's *symbol* is a particular type of sign, characterized by an analogical connection between the "symbolizer" and the symbolized (as
opposed to the usual "arbitrary" sign). Onomatopoeias in language
and the cross on the road sign for "cross-roads" are both examples of
Saussurian symbols. In Peirce's theory, the word *icon* is used for this
sort of symbol, while Peirce used *symbol* to designate what Saussure
called an *arbitrary sign*. (Given this confusion, it is not hard to understand why scholars—particularly English and French-speaking scholars—sometimes have difficulty understanding one another.)

But is Saussure's notion of the "analogical connection" itself unequivocal? There have been interminable debates concerning the "arbitrary" nature of the sign; these will not be recapitulated here. A few
terminological guides should, however, be provided. Symbol might
be understood as any concrete sign that evokes—by means of a *natural* affinity—something absent or impossible to perceive. But *natural*
does not necessarily mean *analogical*, just as *arbitrary* is not synonymous with *conventional*. The various signals dictated by the traffic
laws, whether "arbitrary" (flashing red means stop and then proceed)
or "analogical" (pointing your arm to the left means left turn), are all
accepted by *convention*. On the other hand, the connection between
the "symbolizer" and the symbolized can *appear* natural, yet depend
on custom, not ("natural") analogy. We know that snakes entwined
around a staff, should they appear in a store window or on a car,
symbolize "pharmacist" or "ambulance." We *may* remember that the
snakes symbolize judiciousness, but do we still know *why*? When mo-
tivation is no longer apparent, we have departed from the symbol in
the Saussurian sense (what Peirce would call an "icon") and return to
Ricoeur's sense of a "linguistic expression with a double meaning, demanding interpretation."

(4) These ambiguities probably impelled Paulus to his own particular definition of the connection between the "symbolizer" and the
symbolized: "what joins them, what determines that one evokes the
other, is the common pool of affective reactions that they provoke, a
common pool which may derive from innate psychism, from cultural
customs, or finally from individual experiences and associations"
(1969: 14). The notion of *analogy* is, nonetheless, present: "the symbol can be degraded, or be refined, into a *sign*, as soon as the affective
component which engendered it is obliterated. The symbol then remains only as a *pure substitute*, stripped of all resemblance—whether

perceptive or affective—to the object. When ancient Achean or Germanic warriors raise their visors as a plea for mercy, we have a gesture whose symbolism is obvious. This ancient practice has a distant descendent: that we take off our hats in front of our superiors. The original, transparent symbol has become opaque, in mutating into a *sign* of respect" (1969: 15).

This "affective" definition of the symbol is critical to music, since the expressive or sentimental component of an artwork justifies appeals to the concept of the symbol, especially in the work of musical aestheticians. But this entire lexicological exegesis also illustrates the difficulty involved in discussing musical symbolism *from the standpoint* of a semiological concept of the symbol. When musical symbolism is at issue, all the variables nicely sorted out in the preceding are vague and jumbled up once again. Musical symbolism is *polysemic*, because when we listen to music, the meanings it takes on, the emotions that it evokes, are multiple, varied, and confused. These meanings, these emotions, are the object of an interpretation that is thus always *hazardous*. Given the looseness of the associations between music and what it evokes, we can no longer say with certainty what constitutes the expressive, the natural, the conventional, the analogical, the arbitrary association.

For this reason, the expression "symbolic form"—which recurs throughout this book—must be taken in its most general sense, *as designating music's capacity (with all other symbolic forms) to give rise to a complex and infinite web of interpretants*. Within the framework of the particular theoretical stance adopted here, my specific goal is to illustrate how these interpretants are divided into neutral, poietic, and esthesic. The four chapters of Part I present the elements of a "general musicology" as approached from a semiological angle. Chapters 2 and 3 investigate definitions of concepts as basic as "music," "the work," and serve as occasion for applying the tripartition to notional analyses. Chapter 4 is a similar consideration of the "sonorous object" in electronic music. Chapter 5 is intended to clear away the jungle surrounding the enigma of musical meaning (an eminently "semiological" question, but one that also marks out the boundaries for all reflections upon musical aesthetics).

Part II, in effect a lengthy preamble to my subsequent volume on musical analysis, draws upon the tripartition to investigate the question of "writing about music." The concluding Chapter 9 is a discussion of the concepts explored in Part II in the context of a specific analytical example, harmonic analysis as it is practiced in current music-theoretical writings (both textbooks and articles), and interpretations of the Tristan Chord.

I

The Semiology of
the Musical Fact

2

The Concept of Music

1. Defining Music: A Semiological Problem[1]

I F MUSICAL SEMIOLOGY has an object, then that object is *music*. But do we really know what music is? Is the concept self-evident? We can start out by applying principles of semiology to a definition of music, the central object of our research. Thus a sonorous fact of any kind is recognized as music when we make the distinction between music and nonmusic; that is, when we associate interpretants conveyed by the concept "music" or "the musical" with that sonorous fact. Clearly, from the outset we must situate the problem of defining music within a larger anthropological perspective, and ask the following questions:

(1) Do we have a stable definition of music, and the musical, available to us?

(2) Is it legitimate to speak of "music" with respect to cultures that do not have such a concept, that do not distinguish between music and nonmusic? And in this case, do we have the right to project our western categories of thought and analysis upon what *we* believe to be music?

For the moment, let us remain within a western, North American-European context. By assembling various different definitions of music, Molino was able to show that the contours of the western concept of music will vary depending whether poietic, immanent, or esthesic variables are included in that concept:

"Is music the art of combining sounds according to certain rules (which vary according to place and time) for organizing a durational unit [une durée] by means of sonorous elements?" (Petit-

[1] The first section of this chapter retains and develops pages 107–109 of the *Fondements*.

41

Robert). Here, music is defined according to the conditions of its production (it is an art) and by its materials: sounds. For another writer, "the study of sound is a matter of physics. But choosing sounds that are pleasing to the ear is a matter of musical aesthetics" (Bourgeois 1946: 1). Definition according to conditions of production has ceded to definition according to effect produced in the "receiver": sounds, to be music, must be pleasant. For others, music is almost always identified with acoustics, a particular branch of physics: "certainly the study of acoustics and the properties of sound in some sense goes beyond the domain of the properly musical, but these 'divergences' are much less important and numerous than is generally thought" (Matras 1948: 5). (Molino 1975a: 37)

There is no limit to the number or the genre of variables that might intervene in a definition of the musical. For Molino, adapting Marcel Mauss's expression, music is a *total social fact* [fait social total], whose definition varies according to era and culture. Music's characteristic traits, considered in the context of all phenomena associated with the musical fact (from the conductor's body language to the physical space of the concert hall), are divided among the poles of the tripartition.

At the heart of *our* culture, then, the concept of music is far from homogeneous. Ruwet (alluding to the model of "paradigmatic" analysis which will be taken up in Volume 2) freely acknowledged that "it does not bother me when a poetic theory in which parallelism plays a central role excludes certain types of modern 'poetry'—no more than it would bother me to have a general theory of music that could account for Mozart, Debussy, Gesualdo, Schoenberg, Gagaku, and Gregorian chant, but that excluded, for example, John Cage's *Radio Music* as nonmusic. I would see in this capacity for exclusion a *corroboration* of the theory. We must remind ourselves that—for historical reasons that are not my part to discuss—we live in an age in which it has become possible (without undue risk) for anyone to baptise anything as 'music,' 'poetry,' or 'painting' " (Ruwet 1975b: 349).

In fact, it often happens that a single feature of the "total musical fact" becomes privileged, and even shoulders aside all others. As Molino wrote, "any element belonging to the total musical fact can be isolated, or taken as a strategic variable of musical production" (1975a: 43). This is what literally takes place, for example, in the performance art of the "Zaj" group of Madrid: on the stage, a piano is shifted around, and three musicians gesture, without speaking, singing, or playing instruments. One is also reminded of Kagel's *Con Voce*, in which three silent, masked performers mime the gestures of instrumental players without producing any sound. In these two cases, the feature that has been isolated is the sheer physical activity connected with music-making. An analogous case is Dieter Schnebel's *Musik zum Lesen* [*Music to Read*], which sets in motion an entirely interior and silent "listening." If such phenomena are considered "musical" by a given social group, this is unobjectionable—at least from a strictly cultural standpoint.

What happens, in fact, is that at a given time and in a given society (though principally in the west), there is never a single, culturally dominant conception of music; rather, we see a whole spectrum of conceptions, from those of the entire society to those of a single individual. We speak of "music" in connection with the three anomalous cases described above because they take certain features of the total musical fact—features that we understand as aspects of "music"—and realize them. The features in question are thus interpreted *with respect to what we otherwise know about "music,"* at least in our culture.

One might expect that any concept of music would (at the very least) always include *sound* as a variable. This is what Cage plays upon in his *4'33"* . . . a silent work in which the pianist places his fingers on the keys and removes them again, repeatedly, without ever sounding a note. Music, Cage tells us, is the noise made by the audience. Legend has it that at the world première, the singing of birds was heard from the forest outside, through the open windows of the hall.

In the West, the general context of the musical fact assures that such special cases (Cage, Schnebel, and the like) are quickly marginalized. Moreover, their creators now perceive them (even if they do not say so publicly) as a way of "speaking" in music about music, in the second degree as it were, to expose or denounce the institutional aspect of music's functioning.

What these special cases show—paradoxically—is that we would not know how to speak of *music* without referring to sonority, *even when the reference is only implied*. We can, then, allow (without too much soul-searching) that sound is a minimal condition of the musical fact.

We can see nonetheless that we cannot restrict music to the merely acoustic dimension of sound: can we think of words recorded on tape as constituting a musical work? In order for something like this to enter the cultural domain of *music*, other variables must be introduced. For example, if the recording had been made by somebody known as a composer, that might be sufficient. Our knowledge of a poietic dimension intervenes, and causes what is on the tape to become "music."

43

On the other hand (to cite a less marginal instance) there is an entire series of nonsonorous phenomena that are quite rightly considered musical, by musicians themselves. One might be a bit surprised to read the following account by pianist Marie-Françoise Bucquet (reported by François Delalande): "certain pianists have the impression that they give 'depth' to a chord by allowing the fingers to slide toward the interior of the piano after they have depressed the keys" (1982: 166)—this account comes from the poietic side, and indicates that a kinesthesic and tactile sensation can intervene in the interpretants that the performer associates with the music produced. But one is no less surprised to learn from Alfred Brendel's memoirs that Brendel recognizes a similar phenomenon—from the esthesic side—in his performance: "the sound of sustained notes on the piano can be modified . . . with the help of certain movements which make the pianist's *conception* of *cantabile* actually visible to the audience" (1976: 31); "there are many examples of pieces where [suggesting things with physical gestures] is necessary. Things like the end of Liszt's *B minor Sonata*, where before the three *pianissimo* B major chords there is a crescendo on one chord that one has to convey bodily, with a gesture. It is the only possibility" (ibid.: 214). Brendel is counting on gestures to make the listener associate certain interpretants—of undeniably musical character—with the sheer physical sound.

Separating the musical from the visual and the kinesthetic is indeed difficult. Dance and opera aside, do we not feel that we are missing something *of the music* when recordings deprive us of live performance's multiple dimensions? Orchestral conductors know that contrasting the styles of hand movements helps the listener/spectator to grasp the structure of a work. For this reason proponents of electroacoustic music, broadcast in concert by loudspeakers, regularly question the very whys and hows of the concert. Certainly records and tape recorders have contributed to reinforcing Hanslickian musical aesthetics, since they helped to reduce our cultural conception of "music" to a single dimension, sheer sound. Yet we cannot fool ourselves: part of the malaise felt by the public at concerts of "tape music" derives from the fact that there is nothing to look at. Is this secret longing for the visual one of the motivations behind the blossoming of "multi-media" events (of which electronic and computer-music composers have grown so fond)? The advent of mechanical means of reproduction in the early twentieth century corresponds in some sense to the nineteenth century's foundation of the concept of "pure music." Recordings produce a schism between sound and source, between sound and environment—yet this schism demonstrates (by means of a sort of *in vivo* experiment) that it is not so easy to do without all those "impurities."

Immediately before writing the preceding paragraph, I was *watching* the Bach *Concerto for Two Violins* on television. I would not have wanted to miss the smile exchanged by the soloists before each of their shared reprises.

2. *Noise as a Semiological Phenomenon*[2]

Let us return to the sonorous per se. Is every sound appropriate for music? Pierre Schaeffer, the founder of electro-acoustic music, asked this central question in his *Traité des objets musicaux* (1966). All twentieth-century music is in effect characterized by a displacement of the boundary between "music" and "noise," and Schaeffer's question should be examined more closely.

We might assume that it is possible to distinguish between musical sound and noise in acoustic terms: musical sound results from regular, periodic vibrations; noise results from nonperiodic vibrations. In France there is even an official physical definition of noise: "an erratic, intermittent or statistically random vibration." The distinction is based on the opposition between "pure and simple sounds" on one hand and "complex sounds" on the other.

These definitions, however, can quickly be called into question; all acousticians agree that what we call "noise," is in effect "any sound that we consider as having a disagreable affective character, something unacceptable, no matter what this character may also be . . . the notion of noise is first and foremost a *subjective notion*" (Chocholle 1973: 38). From the *perceptive* point of view, the criteria that cause a sound to be qualified as noise are numerous and varied. They include too-high volume, absence of defined pitch, lack of organization (complexity, cacaphony, and the like). (Chocholle 1973: 39–40; Gribenski 1975: 24) It is worth noting that these "criteria" are always defined in relation to a threshold of acceptability encompassing bearable volume, the existence of fixed pitches, and a notion of order—which are only *arbitrarily* defined as norms.

Finally, if we venture to compare physical descriptions of noise with the *praxis* of classical musicians—that is, if we postulate the equation sound/noise = music/nonmusic—we quickly discover that most "musical" sounds (that is, sounds used in, say, a classical orchestra),

---

[2] Sections 2 and 3 of Chapter 2 recapitulate two paragraphs from the article "Suono/Rumore" (Nattiez 1981), which appeared originally in Italian; they are reprinted here with the permission of Einaudi Editions Turin.

belong to a category of complex sounds whose spectrum is not harmonious—and, moreover, that sounds our ears spontaneously perceive as "noise" may well have the same acoustic structure as "musical" sounds. Schaeffer himself endeavored to show that the sound of classical music "has decays; it is granular; it has attacks; it fluctuates, swollen with impurities—and all this creates a musicality that comes before any 'cultural' musicality" (Schaeffer 1968: 284). We should not, however, forget that "noises" do not predominate in classical musical sound.

In attempting to define "musical" sound, we have, then, situated ourselves successively within the purview of *acoustic* definitions, *perceptive* approach, and *compositional* attitude. In this, we have returned to the tripartition. The distinction between sound and noise has no stable, physical basis, and the way we employ these two terms is culturally conditioned from the outset. The situations described in the preceding paragraphs might be diagrammed as shown in Figure 2.1.

poietic level (choice of the composer)	neutral level (physical definition)	esthesic level (perceptive judgment)
musical sound	sound of the harmonic spectrum	agreeable sound
noise (nonmusical)	noise (complex sound)	disagreeable noise

Figure 2.1

This figure illustrates a case—by far the most frequent case—in which certain sounds accepted as "musical" by the composer are classified as "unpleasant" by the listener. In the course of a conference on electro-acoustic music,[3] Luciano Berio pointed out that the Tristan Chord, at the time of its creation (1859), was nothing but "noise," in the sense that it was a sonorous configuration that could not be countenanced by contemporary harmonic conventions. Cacophony is anything that is disturbing. The following remarks represent an especially ethnocentric example of a definition of "noise," penned by a German musicologist:

[3] Conference at Metz, February 27, 1976.

Music is a play of tones, that is, of fixed, clearly defined quantities. Other sounds, glissandos, cries, noises, may occur as inserts; if they are numerous the result is partly musical; if they predominate, it is no longer music in the proper sense of the word . . . discussion about the nature of the new art of sounds, those part musical and those totally untonal, is beclouded by the fact that it is called concrete or electronic "music"[4] although it has in fact transgressed the boundaries of *musical* art. (Wiora 1963: 191–92; English trans. 1965: 181, 182)

In definitions of noise, one is always brought back to such notions of fixity, purity, and order.

It is hardly surprising that, at any given time, composers who have adopted sounds that others consider "noise" would either like to be considered revolutionaries, or have come to be regarded as such by others (these are two situations that should be kept distinct from one another). Wagner represents the latter; his essays and correspondence, when set against his musical works, show clearly that he did not write the Tristan Chord to revolutionize musical language or shock the bourgeoisie, but instead because chromaticism was for him one means to express an image of amorous desire as filtered through a lens of Brahmin mysticism. The activities of the Italian *bruitistes,* to the contrary, were situated within the perspective of a much broader, deliberate aesthetic and social subversiveness. The futurists did not scruple to bash—*manu militari*—those members of the audience who disrupted their concerts; in 1919, the central committee of the Dadaists had demanded the "requisitioning of churches for bruitist performances" (Giovanni Lista, cited in Russolo 1975: 22). The French economist Jacques Attali generated his book *Bruits* (*Noises*) (1977)—a work of "musical sociology" that made a big noise wholly out of proportion to its merit—on the basis of contradictory connotations of the word "noise." Its thesis amounted to this: noise—that is, disturbing music—is the harbinger of a new social order. (From now on, it seems, specialists in econometrics need no longer analyze their graphs—they need only listen to a given era's musical heartbeat to predict political upheavals.) The whole question—should one want to make something useful of this Pythian sociology—is to evaluate what is considered "musical disorder" in any given era, and this is a problem in fact not even approached by Attali.

My own position can be summarized in the following terms: *just as music is whatever people choose to recognize as such, noise is whatever is rec-*

---

[4] In this, Wiora is throwing Schoenberg, Orff, Cage, Schaeffer, and Stockhausen into the same bag.

ognized as disturbing, unpleasant, or both. The border between music and noise is always culturally defined—which implies that, even within a single society, this border does not always pass through the same place; in short, there is rarely a consensus.

3. *Composers' Stances Toward Noise*

It would be no exaggeration to say that the extension of the concept "music" (that is, what has been accepted for consideration as "musical" over the course of the centuries, at least in the West) is paralleled by an *acceptance* of sound phenomena that were previously considered "noises." Olivier Alain was able to show that the history of music is not only a tale of transformed forms and structures but, at the same time, also of the integration of new sonorous material (see his interesting table in Alain 1965a: 363–65). Lully had included whistles and anvils in some of his works long before Verdi in *Trovatore* (1853) or Wagner in *Rheingold* (1854). It is, however, worth noting that *Das Rheingold*, in which (in the interludes between scenes 2 and 3, and 3 and 4) the sound of anvils is gradually uncovered, is also a work whose Prelude (perhaps even more clearly) symbolizes a gradual conquest of sonorous space, from the original pitch with its harmonics, through the successive transformations, to the complete saturation of the octave. We are not far from the pitch cluster, or from white noise (that is, a sound that occupies the entire spectrum of frequencies).

This music-historical progression can be diagrammed by placing a tripartite representation of sound phenomena on a diachronic axis, as in Figure 2.2.

In extending the sphere of the "musical," composers generally take the initiative. The line that separates sound and noise—representing the listener's changed perception—sinks lower, but only somewhat later. In this section, we will look at the stances of certain twentieth-century composers—those who, it seems to me, have contributed the most to shifting the border between music and noise: Russolo, Varèse, Schaeffer, Cage, and Murray Schafer. Symbolic phenomena are so complex that examining the poietic stance of these composers will always and inevitably multiply itself anew in terms of the tripartition. Any composer, when confronted with sound, will take either a predominantly poietic or a predominantly esthesic stance. Thus Russolo, Varèse, and Schaeffer, while they manifest considerable differences from one another, have one thing in common: their integration of the noise world into the musical world has not meant abandoning compositional responsibility. We shall see that Cage's choices essen-

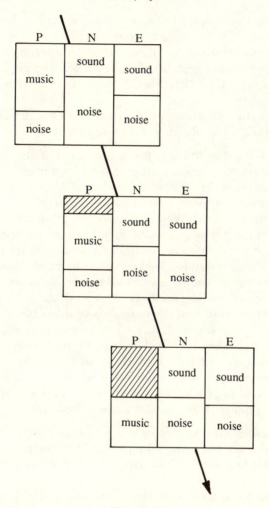

Figure 2.2

tially exist within a *perceptive* (esthesic) stance, and that Murray Schafer's orientation represents a synthesis of the two extremes.

In Figure 2.2, the shaded sections represent a zone of "previous"
music now abandoned by contemporary musicians. In the case of the
Futurists, this music is utterly abandoned; physically defined "noise"
alone now has the *right* to occupy the musical domain: "Beethoven
and Wagner for many years wrung our hearts. But now we are sated
with them and derive much greater pleasure from ideally combining
the noise of streetcars, internal-combustion engines, automobiles,
and bust crowds than from rehearing, for example, the 'Eroica' or

the 'Pastorale' . . . away! let us be gone, since we shall not much longer succeed in restraining a desire to create a new musical realism by a generous distribution of sonorous blows and slaps, leaping numbly over violins, pianofortes, contrabasses, and groaning organs. Away!" (Russolo 1954: 27; English trans. in Taruskin-Weiss 1984, 444).

How does Russolo go about his work? Acoustic definitions, based on Helmholtz's work, are his point of departure:

> *Sound* is defined as the result of a succession of regular and pe-riodic vibrations. *Noise* is instead caused by motions that are ir-regular, as much in time as in intensity. "A musical sensation," says Helmholtz "appears to the ear as a perfectly stable, uniform, and invariable sound." But the quality of continuity that sound has with respect to noise, which seems instead fragmentary and irregular, is not an element sufficient to make a sharp distinction between sound and noise. We know that the production of sound requires not only that a body vibrate regularly but also that these vibrations persist in the auditory nerve until the following vibra-tion has arrived, so that the periodic vibrations blend to form a continuous musical sound. At least sixteen vibrations per second are needed for this. Now, if I succeed in producing a *noise* with this speed, I will get a *sound* made up of the totality of so many noises—or better, noise whose successive repetitions will be suf-ficiently rapid to give a sensation of continuity like that of *sound*." (Russolo; English trans. Barclay Brown 1986: 37)

Russolo pursues this analysis by examining problems of timbre; we must linger a bit over his writings, for they include (in different terms) certain key concepts that Pierre Schaeffer was to develop forty years later.

With Russolo, as with Schaeffer, there is a certain sense of awe in contemplating the vast possibilities cast forth by their discoveries. As Russolo put it, "with the introduction of plentifulness and variety of noises in music, it has ended the limitations on sound as quality or timbre . . . with the introduction of noises in fractions of a tone smaller than the semitone, that is, with introduction of the enhar-monic system, even the limitation of sound in its quantity has been removed" (English trans. 1986: 64). For both Russolo and Schaeffer, this sense of awe makes them particularly sensitive to what is gener-ally called timbre; they privilege it as the locus of maximum possibil-ities for extension of the musical. As Russolo stated, "the *real* and *fundamental* difference between sound and noise can be reduced to this alone: *noise is generally much richer in harmonics than sound . . . this* is the reason for the great variety in the timbres of noise in comparison to the more limited ones of sounds" (ibid.: 38–39). This extension of possibilities is due principally to a more attentive *hearing* of sounds; "a variety of timbre can be found within a single timbre. In some noises with rhythmic beats, like the tick-tock of a clock . . . we can often hear a difference from beat to beat" (47). Russolo thus practices what Schaeffer thematizes under the name *écoute réduite* (concentrated hearing, analogous to what phenomenology calls eidetics). For Russolo, this "concentrated hearing" is effected through the same principles defined by Schaeffer. For Russolo, this happens through repeated hearing of the same sound; for Schaeffer, through experiencing what he calls a *sillon fermé*, the effect caused by a skipping phonograph needle. Russolo described it as follows, "after the fourth or fifth [recurrence], *having developed the ear* and grown accustomed to the pitched and variable noises produced by the noise instruments, [the performers in noise concerts] told me that they took great pleasure in following the noises of trams, automobiles, and so on, in the traffic outside. And they verified with amazement the variety of pitch they encountered in these noises" (48). Russolo manifests the same normative attitude that leads Schaeffer to separate sounds whose origin is too easily identifiable from the *art* of noise—and this is not the least striking of the parallels with Schaeffer. Russolo writes, "it is necessary that these noise timbres become *abstract materials* for works of art to be formed from them. *As it comes to us from life*, in fact, noise immediately reminds us of life itself, making us think of the things that produce the noises that we are hearing" (86). Noise, to be art, must lose all traces of being a *result* or an *effect* connected to causes that produce it. (cf. 86–87) In Schaeffer's terms, "concentrated hearing" must also be *acousmatic*.

The words "art" and "works of art" recur quite frequently in Russolo's writing; one must organize *concerts*, with instruments (his "noise instruments") specially conceived for certain effects: the drone-machines, the crash-machines, the whistle machines, the din-machines, the shrilling machines, and the snort-machines. We do not, unfortunately, know much about these *works*, because Russolo's instruments were destroyed, the scores were not preserved, and (so far as I know) there are only two recordings of Russolo's works, *Serenade* and *Corale*, reissued by RCA. It is therefore difficult to know what these works were like as *compositions*. But Varèse, with his characteristic vigor, reproached them for introducing the noise of the streets—without discernment—into the concert hall: "why, Italian Futurists, did you slavishly reproduce all the agitation of life in the form of noise, which is merely life's most superficial and bothersome element?" (1968: 42).

51

For Varèse, the compositional aspect remains predominant. In an interview he stated, concerning a performance of *Ionization* (which, we should not forget, was the first piece ever written for percussion alone), that "people call them instruments for making noise. I call them instruments for making sounds" (1937). The journalist who reported his words added (with a prescience unusual for the time): "as he employs them in his work, they make more than sound, they make music" (ibid.). Even if Varèse set out to "open the entire universe of sound for music . . . to make music with all possible sounds" (1970: 83), in the last analysis it is still the *composer* who *decided* what he wishes to retain in his work.

Schaeffer, who frequently acknowledged his debt to Varèse, theorized about this issue by making a distinction between the sonorous and the musical the crux of his *Traité des objets musicaux* (1966). The composer of "concrete" music must restrict himself to "the realm of available objects, those which we instinctively feel are appropriate to the musical" (1967b: 83.4). To characterize these objects, Schaeffer combines (a) three criteria having to do with the sound's *articulation* (impulsion, held sound, and iteration) and (b) three criteria having to do with its sound mass (tonic character, complex aggregates, and varied aggregates), to which he adds a criterion of temporal balance. Schaeffer's undertaking became *normative* description, but the composers of the *Groupe de Recherches Musicales* did not take long to extend musical sound beyond the borders established by Schaeffer. Any "instinctive feeling" that a given sound is appropriate for music, after all, remains profoundly subjective, changing with the user and the context of the sound. Schaeffer's typology of sounds has, indeed, created an explosion in recent compositional practice, suggesting that the "musical" is nothing more than those sonorities accepted as "music" by an individual, group, or culture.

John Cage, like Russolo, Varèse, and Schaeffer, has for some time had in mind "an exploration of all the instrumental possibilities not yet in the repertory, the infinity of possible sonorous sources in an empty landscape or a garbage dump, a kitchen or a living room" (1976: 68). Cage's stance, however, differs radically from that of his colleagues: where they undertake an act of *creation* in choosing and organizing sound, Cage defines a new stance toward *hearing*: "The more you realize that the sounds of the external world are *musical*, the more music there is" (84). What, for Cage, is "musical"? He says, "all noise seems to me to have the potential to become musical, simply by being allowed to appear in a musical work. But this is not what Schoenberg taught, not what Varèse's research might tell us" (69). We could say that Cage is practicing a radical nominalism that (as we have seen) has to do with silence as well as sonority; "chess match, I baptize you concerto" he might well have said, just as Duchamp transformed a urinal into a piece of sculpture. Cage makes "ready-made" music, in which anything is acceptable in the quest for absolute freedom. One must "create an entirely new situation, in which any sound whatsoever can go with any other" (71). His penchant for simultaneous performance of his works comes from this attitude, as does his concerto for twenty turntables, and his hope someday to hear all the fugues in the *Well-Tempered Clavier* played at the same time. The pitch cluster was the logical extension of the Tristan Chord, and Cage merely pushed the principle of polytonality a bit further. "Could we not imagine that noise . . . is itself nothing more than the sum of a multitude of different sounds which are being heard simultaneously?" Cage did not ask that question; Rousseau did, in the *Dictionnaire de Musique* of 1767. Rousseau, with his prophetic vision, announced the advent of an era in which one can no longer say whether noise has been admitted into the realm of music, or music has been absorbed by noise, in which there is no longer a schism between music and the experienced world. According to Alan Watts (Cage reports), "it does not do to take the uproar of a big city and transplant it to the concert hall. For him, the separation of sounds from their environment is disastrous. Well, I have never said that it was anything else! My deepest wish is that we would at last listen to sounds in their proper framework. In their natural space" (1976: 102).

Here, Cage's stance is radically opposed to Schaeffer's, for whom "concentrated hearing" must compel us to forget the natural origin of sound. For Cage, we must quaff our music from its source in the city itself, by refusing to fall into what Canadian composer Murray Schafer nicely dubbed *schizophonia* (that is, splitting sound from its source). But can a contemporary composer be *prevented* from hearing sounds for themselves; can he continue to renounce his compositional responsibilities?

In this regard, Murray Schafer's stance represents an interesting synthesis of Cage's viewpoint on one hand, and Russolo's, Varèse's, and Schaeffer's on the other. Embracing the romantic tradition—the tradition of a Kleist who hears concerts in the sound of the west wind—Murray Schafer set himself to *hear* Vancouver. With a team of investigators, he went in search of "musically interesting" noises; he suggested an *acoustic stroll* through a section of the city. The musical ear, if attentive to the symphony played by the world, will select certain sounds, and little by little the composer will again take the upper hand in the process. Murray Schafer conceives of a new discipline, acoustic design, which will, perhaps, someday be imposed by ecological concerns. In his writings, he imagines a "soundscape" (1977: Chapter 19). From now on, it is up to composers to fashion the musical landscape of tomorrow's city, taking a selective study of the sonorous environment as their point of departure.

4. *Musics and Cultures*

The problem of the schism between music and noise in the twentieth century clearly illustrates the *mobility* of interpretants that separate "musical" from "nonmusical." This problem grows more complicated when we move from an exclusively western context to the nonwestern musics of the oral tradition.

Within a given cultural context, music will be allied to associated cultural practices, in ways defined by certain articulations. But these articulations are not necessarily the same as those made by the great majority of westerners. As ethnomusicologist Gilbert Rouget put it, "we are too rarely interested in specifying what defines the concept 'music' in the spirit of indigenous peoples. We would be hard put to say (for whatever population or group we might choose) where music begins for them, where it ends, what borders mark the transition between speaking and singing" (1968: 344). This situation has recently begun to change, due in part to the influence of cognitive anthropology upon ethnomusicology.

We can examine a few exemplary cases.

(1) Examining the borders between music and other symbolic forms along a given continuum reveals that the semantic surface of the concept "music" is displaced from one culture to another. This is particularly clear in societies for which the word "music" does not exist. Persian distinguishes between *musiqi*, the science or art of music, and *muzik*, musical sound or performance. Lorraine Sakata (1983), however, was able to demonstrate that calling something *musiqi* depends on context and the culture's particular evaluation of the musical: songs on religious texts are *musiqi*, but calls to prayer and prayer formulas are not. One could extend this kind of research to other levels: historically, the ancient Greek *mousikê* designates *grosso modo* what we would call "lyric poetry." The history of the word "music" in various languages needs to be written, as does an account of its usage among individuals: what is music for my barber, or for Glenn Gould?

(2) More and more frequently, ethnomusicological literature stresses that "other cultures do not in general have a term for music as a global phenomenon. Instead they often have words that desig-

nate individual musical activities or artifacts, those who sing or play, songs, secular and religious, dance, and other more obscure categories" (Sakata 1983: 19; cf. also Gourlay 1984: 28). Thus the Mapuche of Argentina, studied by Carol Robertson, do not have a word for "music," yet they distinguish between instrumental and improvisational forms (*kantun*), European music and music of nonMapuche tribes (*kantun winka*), ceremonial songs (*öl*), and a separate genre, *tayil* (Robertson 1976: 39). What is *tayil*?

> Understanding, and eventually defining *tayil* demands a delineation of its relationships to other phenomena in the Mapuche world. As a basis for departure we may say that *tayil* is the life-force that an individual shares with all living or deceased members of his/her patrilineage. The shared soul of a patrilineage is termed *kimpen*; the essence of a *kimpen* can be verbalized or activated only through the performance of its respective *tayil*.
>
> The performance of *tayil* is restricted to women termed *eltun*. The verb denotes the act of pulling as associated with extracting teeth, the drawing of water from a well, and the uprooting of a plant. The Mapuche explain *eltun* as "pulling or extracting by force," or "removing something from its source." The performance of *tayil* "pulls" the compounded patrilineal soul out of an individual through a specific combination of melodic contour and iconographic text. (Robertson 1976: 40)

For this reason, Robertson suggests (ibid.: 51) that we temporarily suspend our rationalizations about what is and is not music. If we keep to indigenous descriptions, *tayil* is not music in the western sense of the term. It is clear nonetheless that in *tayil* we can recognize (by analogy with our own categories) pitches, rhythms, and melodic contours that in all respects are compatible with *our* concept of music.

What is interesting in Robertson's theoretical perspective is that she invites us *not* to insist stubbornly upon the music/nonmusic opposition, but to respect the "cultural articulations" of various phenomena. By all accounts, there is no *single* and *intercultural* universal concept defining what music might be. The Mapuche associate different interpretants with their different musical genres—and, in the case of *tayil*, these interpretants are *exclusively extramusical*. Does this mean that we must exclude *tayil* from the field of ethnomusicology? No; since we have the right to be interested in the musical substance of *tayil*, a substance that can be described with the help of our western categories, in the same way one could speak of intonation as a musical dimension of language, or rhythm as a musical dimension of poetry—on the condition, of course, that we always remember that *tayil* exists within a cultural context. Robertson was able to show that a musical analysis of *tayil* uncovers sound characteristics that are unique to this genre, as distinct from *kantun* (for instance, articulation into four phrases, a glissando at the end of each phrase, melodic progressions by whole step, lack of metric reference, and the like). Her discussion shows how analysis of the neutral level is not only legitimate (even when the native peoples describe the genre in nonmusical terms), but also indispensible in making a technical differentiation of genres that the indigenous culture distinguishes by other means.

(3) In the case of *tayil*, we had a genre conceptualized by the Mapuche in entirely nonmusical terms. I would like at this point to give an example in which the distinction between music and nonmusic can be inferred less from explicit conceptualizations than from *behaviors*. These examples will be drawn from music of the Inuit (Eskimos), studied by a Montreal research team under my direction.[5] In the Inuit language, there is no *word* that means what we understand by music, and ethnographic investigation seems to suggest that the *concept* of music as such is also absent from their culture. The word *nipi*, which includes the things that we would designate by the term "music," is much more general than our "music," since it encompasses noise as well as the sound of the spoken voice. We would judge two Inuit practices to be "musical" a priori: dance songs accompanied by drum, and (in a more limited region within the Inuit cultural zone) the *katajjaq*, which is *today* referred to as "throat-*game*." *Katajjaq* as music? Certainly from the western vantage point it *is* music, since the team made a record of it (which was even awarded a prize, by a rather well known Academy). But within Inuit social practice, this complex symbolic form has one *predominant* characteristic: it is a *game*. The principle behind performing *katajjaq* is as follows: it is played by two women; they repeat a brief motif at staggered intervals, until one of the women is forced to stop, having either run out of breath or tripped over her own tongue. There is a winner and a loser.

In the case of *katajjaq*, studying the context of the performance and the stances of the women vis-à-vis *katajjaq* (not some nonexistent conceptual distinction) led our research team (influenced notably by Nicole Beaudry; see Beaudry 1978) to consider the genre principally a game. Despite this, however, we were wholly justified in studying the sound component of *katajjaq* as a musical fact, especially since the Inuit were themselves quite conscious of what linguists call well-formedness in certain sound-parameters of the genre. Studying the begin-

[5] A detailed analysis of this music will be given in a future volume 2.

ners' lessons in *katajjaq* makes this clear. The old woman who teaches the children corrects sloppy intonation of contours, poorly meshed phase displacements, and vague rhythms exactly like a Western vocal coach.

Here again, the analysis of the neutral level is indispensible in describing *katajjaq*'s unique sonorous organization. In short, we started by immersing the genre in its social and cultural contexts, particularly with respect to associated poietic and esthesic dimensions: how is it produced? how is it perceived? This in turn led to *interpreting* repetition and variation as they function within the genre, in terms unlike those one would use, say, for a canon or a piece by Steve Reich. *Katajjaq*, which is at once a ludic and a musical genre, is *culturally* first and foremost a game. But then again, nothing stops us from discerning a "ludic" dimension in canon, in the *Music for Eighteen Musicians* or in the polyphonic chansons of sixteenth-century France.[6] In our culture, the sheerly sonorous dimension has remained the dominant one, yet this did not prevent François Delalande (who in this particular case leans essentially toward a poietic aspect of the musical fact) from approaching music pedagogically as a game (1984). The components of symbolic forms are divided among the poietic, the immanent, and the esthesic. Their culture gives each a specific weight; the anthropological aspect of the semiological approach enables us to acknowledge this "weighting."

(4) There is one situation in which analysis of the neutral level is the only possible analysis, since we can never communicate with the "musician." *Zoomusicology* recognizes this. French composer François-Bernard Mâche has, with great finesse and patience, recently undertaken a work of "ornitho-musicology." (1983) Employing a technique of paradigmatic segmentation analysis developed by Ruwet (1972), Mâche shows that birdsongs are organized according to a repetition-transformation principle. Thus he dares to ask whether birds possess an organized music. In other words, he considers the repetition/transformation relationship a universal characteristic of all musics, to the extent that we can apply it to nonhuman production.

It is equally legitimate to ask this question: to what extent is music *human*? When ethnomusicologist George Herzog asked in 1941, "do animals have music?" he was utterly serious. For Xenakis, rain is as musical as violin glissandi. But in the last analysis, it is a human being

[6] This point was made by Jean-Yves Hameline, during a radio broadcast by France-Culture in 1976, produced by François Delalande, entitled "Les Fonctions de la musique."

who decides what is and is not musical, even when the sound is not of human origin. If we acknowledge that sound is not organized and conceptualized (that is, made to form music) merely by its producer, but by the mind that perceives it, then music is uniquely human.

(5) A final example is that of "intermediary forms" between language and music, which George List undertook to describe as they appear in various cultures (1963). These include the droning of the public auctioneer, proclamations, ritual chant, *Sprechgesang*, and so forth. In western culture, these forms only appear "intermediary" because we so polarize spoken language and singing voice (hence our perpetual astonishment at that alien entity, the half-sung half-spoken voice in *Pierrot Lunaire*). What is interesting in List's analysis is that it proposes a flexible cartography, in which each specific form is inscribed on a *continuum*, by using the concept of "intermediary" states of intonation and fixity of pitch. This is, of course, classification with a universalist bent, but it can serve as referent for the projection of each culture's semantic segmentations: the Hopi Indian language/ song/proclamation division, or the Maori language/ritual song/song/ *haka* division.

The idea of the continuum, as explored by List, could be extended to other collections of symbolic forms. My studies of Inuit music led me to suggest a segmentation along the word/music/game/dance[7] continuum, but a segmentation quite different from what might be implied by western notions of the four terms, and one that takes account of the peculiarity of *katajjaq* with respect to the Inuit language, and their songs and their dances. For instance: Inuit descriptions of drum dances and song contests include the notion of endurance (along with other characteristics). This same notion recurs in *katajjaq*; the performers are supposed to stay in phase as long as possible. So *endurance* establishes a link between categories like song, dance, and game, which in our culture are separate from one another, or conjoined in different ways.

The continuum can, moreover, be further extended with respect to the ways in which one attempts to outline the contours of music: noise/music/language/game/dance/social action.

(a) In ethnomusicology, a tendency to avoid using the word "music" has arisen for cases where the indigenous peoples do not have a term that corresponds exactly. Thus the title of Steven Feld's book on the Kaluli is significant: *Sound and Sentiment.* (1982) The word "mu-

---

[7] Judith Lynne Hanna has assembled certain elements in light of a comparison of music and dance (1979: 86–89; see also 1982). I will not be taking up the problems of the semiology of dance (which does not mean that I have overlooked the work of Adrien Kaeppler, Anya Royce, and Drid Williams).

sic" appears nowhere in the book or in the index. Along these lines, we should also consider Kenneth Gourlay's remarks:

> Writing of her own Igbo music, the Nigerian musicologist Chinyere Nwachukwu maintains that the "concept of music *nkwa* combines singing, playing musical instruments, and dancing into one act" (1981: 59). Whatever concept of "music" is held by members of western society, it is highly improbable that, apart from forward-looking scholars and composers, it will contain all three elements. *Nkwa* in fact is not "music" but a wider affective channel that is closer to the karimojong mode of expression than to western practice. The point of interest here is that Nwachukwu feels constrained to use the erroneous term "music": not because she is producing a "musical dissertation," but because the "one act" which the Igbos perform has no equivalent in the English language. By forcing the Igbo concept into the Procrustean bed of western conceptualization, she is in effect surrendering to the dominance of western ideas—or at least to the dominance of the English language! How different things would have been if the Igbo tongue had attained the same "universality" as English! (1984: 35)

From this, Gourlay postulates the "nonuniversality of music and the universality of nonmusic." But how can we be sure?

Gourlay's position appears strangely nominalist, because it is not only in terms of the existence or nonexistence of the *concept* of music within a culture that one can define the object and the methodologies of musical research. But how can Gourlay speak of the "universality of nonmusic"? Beyond (a) the absence of the concept "music," (b) interpretants different from ours that are associated with the concept "music" in such a culture, and (c) specific cultural connections between organized sound and other symbolic forms within the culture, there is a common core in all the cultures of the world: "humanly organized sound" (to adopt Blacking's expression), which *we* call "music" when we are talking within our own culture. That this core exists, that *we* recognize it, is ethnomusicology's justification; "ethnomusicology as western culture knows it is actually a western phenomenon," as Nettl prudently remarked. (1983: 25)

It is *we*—ethnomusicologists and musicologists—who by means of the concept "music" bind together facts that other cultures keep separate. Moreover, the absence of the word "music" in Inuit culture does not mean that these diverse activities are not bound together at all—they can be bound together through other articulations, specific to that culture. Merriam has emphasized (making a distinction that has since become famous) that there are three components always present in a musical activity: concept, behavior, and sound (1964: 32–33), and the combination of these three givens imparts to music as social fact its unique lineaments within a particular culture.

Any musicologist realizes that music is probably a universal fact (it appears that there is no civilization without music), and realizes that the "faculty of music" is written into the genetic destiny of humanity, like "faculty of language." The moment this is realized, however, the musicologist must be able to relativize the concept of music, and acknowledge that western musicology is itself merely a form of culturally conditioned knowledge.

(b) There is not a music, but many musics—and, one could even say, many musical phenomena. The transition from the noun "music" to the adjective "musical" seems to me both fundamental and telling: that transition allows us to escape a totality wrongly conceived as unique, and to recognize the "musical" aspects of a whole range of sound phenomena. Even within western cultures, the "musical" is not restricted only to music. This is evident in the case of rhythm, whose importance to daily work, dance, and drawing was demonstrated by Fraisse (1974), and in the case of melody, which (with other sorts of intonation) is present in spoken language, to the extent that whole treatises have been dedicated to the "musical elements of language" (for instance, Faure 1962).

There is no reason to reject the analytical tools that have been developed as part of western cultural knowledge. We should moreover acknowledge that musicologists might be interested in musical phenomena that do not belong to "music," or that are encountered in sound productions that are not considered "music" within the culture to which they belong.

(c) Any scientific field establishes categories that are as culturally determined as the categories of the "foreign" societies that we study. Nevertheless, *we cannot dispense with our own descriptive tools, in integrating the conceptualizations of indigenous peoples into our analyses.* We must realize that musical phenomena are necessarily approached simultaneously from an anthropological point of view, and with recourse to *analysis of the neutral level* (in order to describe the morphological properties of the symbolic phenomena we examine). Musicology has the capacity to describe the sonorous particulars of *tayil* or *katajjaq*, because it recognizes their intriguing musical characteristics. At the same time, however, musicology would ideally also take account of the functions (respectively genealogical and ludic) of *tayil* or *katajjaq*, so that their cultural uniqueness might be understood. In other words, *we must relate cultural articulations* (which only ethnographic in-

quiry can disentangle) *to the analysis of the neutral level* (analysis of immanent sonorous configurations). This is why Gourlay's conclusion
seems to me far too restrictive: " 'music' (in the sense of particular
sound configurations) is inseparable from the occasion and purpose
for which it is produced" (1984: 35). We can agree, on the condition
that ethnomusicology is not *limited* to the study of these objectives and
these circumstances, as is becoming increasingly common in the current culturalist climate.[8] " 'Music' (in the same sense) is inseparable
from a broader affective channel and, consequently, the proper subject matter for investigation is this channel itself" (ibid.). I disagree:
the "affective channel" is *one* of music's dimensions as a total social
fact and as a symbolic fact, along with musical organization in itself,
whose importance must not be minimized. One does ethnomusicology because men and women have created sounds whose configuration must be described as well as their context; the tripartition seems
to me a framework adequate to both tasks.

To explain the situation, I should here introduce a conceptual dichotomy that will be encountered many times in the course of this
work, the distinction between an "etic" approach (that is, an analysis
accomplished only by means of the methodological tools and categories of the researcher) and an "emic" approach, an analysis that reflects the viewpoint of the native informants. We will have frequent
occasion to return to this important distinction, and the problems it
involves.[9] For the present, the distinction can serve to underline one
point: if ideally one should adhere to an "emic" approach to the concept of music, we cannot in reality analyze the world's musics entirely
without recourse to *our* conceptual tools. Even if we eschew the
merely "etic" approach, there is no longer any purely "emic" approach; we are "condemned" (as Geertz puts it) to a *dialogue* between
the foreign culture,[10] and the culture of the investigator (Geertz
1973: 13, 24).

(d) As soon as we go off in quest of the universals of music, we
encounter a similar difficulty. *We* recognize the worldwide existence
of music, but all those things that we acknowledge as musical facts are
not necessarily thus categorized by everybody. The investigator's dilemma when confronted by this paradox is inherent not only in the

---

[8] Here I am referring to ethnomusicology's current tricky situation; clarifying the
connections between musical analysis and the ethnographic data is paramount. This
issue will be taken up in Volume 2.

[9] This will be taken up in Volume 2, in the discussions of ethnomusicology.

[10] This foreign culture might as well be that of my next-door neighbor as of the
Pygmies, if we agree with the current "Culture and Personality" school that cultural
specificity recognizes all the intermediate states between the individual and the group.

question of universals. This dilemma is, in effect, the dilemma of any *comparative* study. Any comparison will always be shaped by the comparer's point of view. In this sense, research on universals is invariably, necessarily *etic*. This is true even when the inquiry deals with phenomena that have been initially emically defined (though the degree of emicness or eticness will have to be qualified).

In every case, however, one thing is certain. As soon as we accept the validity of a tripartitional conception of music, we can no longer investigate universals just in terms of sheer sonorous material. We must also look at them in terms of the poietic and esthesic strategies that are associated with that material. In the following section, we will look at the kinds of strategies that exist.

5. The Universals of Music[11]

In speaking of universals, we must begin by discussing immanent structures, because at one time everyone was tempted to situate the "universals" of music within the realm of sheer sound (in some ways, this temptation still exists; see Nettl 1983: 39–40). A strategy of this sort will always encounter difficulties, and I would like to examine these.

(a) For a given trait to be universal, we must prove that it is effectively encountered everywhere, or that there are no counterexamples. So long as this demonstration has not been made, certain traits must be considered only hypothetically universal, with a greater or lesser likelihood that they *are* universal. In some sense, any trait that appears universal is always hypothetically universal, since our knowledge of the musical civilizations of the world is always open to revision. Mantle Hood takes another tack, grounding a trait's universality in high probablities (just as a child is very likely to be born with two arms and two legs, so it is very likely, in his view, that this or that trait is universal) (1977: 66). But musical production is not a biological object, and as soon proposes certain universal traits—for instance, the fact that "music is directed primarily at the emotions, rather than the intellect" (65)—a whole set of counterexamples from Bach to Boulez come to mind, and one asks whether universality can be grounded in any sort of probability.

Research into universals in fact assumes an enormous familiarity with many musics, knowledge both broad (of all cultures) and pro-

---

[11] This section is a revised version of my article "A quelles conditions peut-on parler d'universaux de la musique?" (1977a).

found (of any single culture in detail). But one consequence of the dialectic of universal and relative (and this is another paradox in the quest for universals) is that the more information we accumulate, the smaller our chances become of discovering common characteristics. As Leonard Meyer has written, "because of the variables and the complexity of their interaction, the data assembled by descriptive musicology yield relatively few observable regularities" (1960: 270–71).

As well, the identification of immanent universals raises a delicate question: what is the status of generalizations based on specific observations? The conclusions' validity depends on the intellectual operation that governed the grouping of specific observations into common characteristics (characteristics general enough to be "universal").

McAllester has written, for instance, that "*almost*[12] everywhere there is some sense of the tonic, some kind of tonal center in music" (1971: 379). But he immediately adds, "almost everywhere music establishes a tendency . . . even in aleatoric music there is a tendency in seeking a nontendency" (1971: 380). Here, we are approaching mere word-games.

(b) Even Blacking, who (as we shall see) studies the universals of behaviors rather than those of structures, is able to write that "there seem to be universal structural principles in music, such as the use of mirror forms, theme and variation, repetition and binary form" (1973: 112). The expression "structural *principles*" might suggest that in Blacking's view *processes* in fact engender structures, particularly in the case of repetition and transformation. But this is not the case: binary form, or mirror forms are (whatever their configuration) immanent manifestations pure and simple, and can be found in the sonorous material. Now, perceiving, say, a mirror structure is strongly dependent on criteria whereby we move from observing sounds to assigning them a metalinguistic characterization. Pentatonicism seems universally present, but are we always, in each culture, dealing with the *same* pentatonicism? (Tran van Khe 1977: 83). By means of omissions or distortions, can we not begin to *construct* elegant binary or mirror structures, whatever the material in question? In 1922, Werker could thus "discover" a mirror structure, two halves symmetric around the center, in the E♭ fugue of *The Well-Tempered Clavier*, Book I. Any characterization of something as "universal" will thus depend heavily on which of the object's traits are *selected* in a given analysis, and only subsequently on the comparison of many analyses.

[12] I freely acknowledge that McAllester is always speaking of "quasi-universals," but either a trait is universal or it is not. To me, it seems difficult to accept the "statistical solution" proposed by Nettl (1983: 41–43)—who, moreover, is not looking for universals of strategy.

Difficulties involved in postulating "universal immanent features" may thus be explained in terms of both the object (music), and of musicological discourse itself, *both* of which are symbolic facts, and both of which are exposed as "symbolic" by a semiological approach.

Any trait that aspires to universal status must be verified within all musical cultures; the researcher needs to have confidence in the work of colleagues. Yet in reading ethnomusicologists as diverse as Kolinski, Nettl, Merriam, or McLeod (or even just reading the proceedings of the famous symposium on transcription held in 1964, at a meeting of the Society for Ethnomusicology [cf. England 1964]), what becomes quite clear is how greatly the types of interpretants chosen by each researcher can vary from one to the next, depending on the researcher's theoretical methodology, academic training, and the questions asked. Will musical analysis ever be sufficiently united in its methodology for its results to furnish the information demanded by a quest for universals?

(c) Finally, the elements that the musicologist inventories in studying sound material—elements that he or she may regard as identical—do not necessarily possess the same meaning for each of the native informants involved. "Concepts such as tonality, meter, and specific kinds of form," Nettl has written, "should be used with care, so that they will facilitate rather than obscure the perception of musical styles in which similar but *genetically unrelated phenomena*[13] are found" (1964: 167). Leonard Meyer takes the same position: "Two cultures may appear to employ very different materials, but the underlying mechanism governing the organization of these materials might be the same for both" (1971: 270). At the end of the *Traité des objets musicaux*, Schaeffer imagines a "generalized musicology," founded on acousmatic and perceptive criteria. Though the idea was not developed within the Groupe de Recherches Musicales, it was taken up by certain ethnomusicologists in their teaching strategies. Certainly, it is fascinating to discover analogies between a work by Messiaen and a Tibetan piece (from the perceptual standpoint), but we should always realize that such comparisons—which could lead, after all, to "universals"—always retain their fundamentally etic character.

Do intercultural comparisons in fact make any sense? Blacking asks the following question at the end of *How Musical is Man*: "I seem to suggest that there are no grounds for comparing different musical systems; there is no possibility of any universal theory of musical be-

[13] Emphasis is mine.

havior, and no hope of cross-cultural communication. But if we consider our own experiences, we must realize that this in not in fact so . . . some Venda songs that must have been composed hundreds of years ago still excite the Venda, and they also excite me . . . our own experience suggests that there are some possibilities of cross-cultural communication. I am convinced that the explanation is to be found in the fact that at the level of deep structures in music there are elements that are common to the human psyche, although they may not appear in the surface structures" (1973: 108–9). A decisive step is about to be taken. Since etically similar phenomena can be emically dissimilar, and etically distinct phenomena may result from the same emic categories, *universals can no longer be sought at the level of immanent structures, but in more profound realities.* But what do we mean by this?

Whatever reservations we may have about the term "deep structure" in the following passage, Blacking's emphasis on *processes* is of positive value; "there are other aspects of the Venda musical tradition which are forever changing, and which cannot be learned, except by total participation in Venda society, and by unconscious assimilation of the social and cognitive *processes*[14] on which the culture is founded. These are the deep structures of Venda music . . . they are structures in a dynamic sense, in that they include the potential for growth and development, and so might better be described as *processes* . . . they are the source of creativity in Venda music" (1971: 95).

Blacking thus appears to be concerned essentially with the processes of creation (or "production"), even if his expressed hope for "intercultural communication" takes it as a given that certain deep psychological structures will indeed be universal—that is, identical from the standpoint of production and of reception. "We cannot answer the question 'how musical is man?' until we know what features of human *behavior*, if any, are particular to music" (1973: 7). He could not have expressed it more clearly: the universals of music must be sought not in immanent structures, but in the *behaviors* associated with sound phenomena, particularly in poietic strategies. "It is well known," Boilès has written, "that little can be described as universal when comparing the Ravi Shankar Troupe performing the *Raga Mulkuans* and the Beaux-Arts Trio performing Brahms's *Piano Trio in C Major, Op. 87.* What the two groups have in common is the intent to behave musically" (1984: 52).

In all this, Blacking espouses a position that had been programmatically but firmly stated by Leonard Meyer as early as 1960, and

---

[14] In the following citations from Blacking, all italics are mine.

reiterated since then: "what we should ask about, when considering the problem of universals, is not whether there are scientific laws on the basis of particular physical events. What we should ask is whether, beneath the profusion of diverse and divergent particulars, there are any universal *principles of functioning*" (1971: 271).

Meyer believes that universal principles of functioning can be found in psychological processes associated with music, more exactly, in connotations and values: "the question is whether the processes of association are the same in different cultures; whether similar musical processes and structure give rise to similar or analogous connotations in different cultures. A modest sampling of the evidence indicates these processes are cross-cultural" (1971: 273). Here, as we see, Meyer shifts the inquiry from strategies of poietics to esthesics.

Psychologist Dane Harwood has in this context suggested how the notion of musical universals might be developed: "We must ask whether a cross-cultural musical universal is to be found in the music itself (either its structure or its function) or the way in which music is made. By 'music-making,' I intend not only actual performance but also how music is heard, understood, even learned" (Harwood 1976: 522). What needs to be emphasized here is Harwood's orientation toward process, an orientation that is radical indeed: "the *process* of understanding and engaging in musical behavior may be more universal than the *content* of musical knowledge or action" (ibid.: 523). Harwood cites a series of perceptive behaviors that he considers universal: perception of pitches, generalization of the octave, differentiation between different scales, dividing melody into component units, and grasping melodic contours. (525–27) He subsequently examines how universals of perception are integrated into "universal" types of situations. Music is engendered (1) according to expectations of performers and audience, (2) according to standards of judgment proper to the culture, (3) in terms of the context proper to a particular performance, and (4) in terms of analogies with the listener's way of perceiving the world in general (529–30).

More recently, Lerdahl and Jackendoff set their "generative theory of tonal music" to work at bringing perceptive universals to light. Their contributions are sufficiently important to warrant detailed examination—which can, however, only be done within the context of exploring their theory as a whole.[15]

The following conclusions may be drawn from the discussion above:
(1) The universals of music must now be sought in what Molino

[15] This will be undertaken in Volume 2.

would call "universals of strategy"[16] (whether we term this "deep structures" or "information processing")—and not in immanent data.

(2) We must not forget that we are dealing not with strategies in isolation, but always with strategies associated with phenomena that are (whether etically or emically) considered "musical."

(3) There are at least two large families of "universals of strategy"; accordingly, we can speak of strategies of production, or stategies of perception. This distinction has, practically speaking, never been explicitly thematicized by musicology, though it has been realized de facto and unconsciously, when musicologists view musical phenomena exclusively from one or the other vantage point. We might hypothesize that the poietic and the esthesic strategies are identical. But there is no reason whatsoever to suppose that the cognitive behaviors of a trained composer are completely analogous to those of an uninitiated listener. Only when tabulations of the universals of poietic or esthesic strategies become available can we begin to decide what they have in common.

For this reason, working through the tripartition is paramount if we are to attain a clear understanding of the problems posed by research into music's "universals." The tripartition allows us to classify data before making hasty generalizations.

We can draw the following conclusions from the above remarks:

(1) Sound is an irreducible given of music. Even in the marginal cases in which it is absent, it is nonetheless present by allusion.

(2) The "musical" is any sonorous fact constructed, organized, or thought by a culture.

(3) There are no a priori limits on the numbers of different interpretants that producers or interpreters might associate with a given sound complex.

(4) No semiology of music is possible without taking account of the cultural environment of the phenomenon being studied (in this, I am adopting a point reiterated by Boilès; see 1973a: 40; 1982: 26); this is not merely true of musics of nonwestern oral traditions.

(5) A semiological analysis ensues from combining categories and articulations proper to the culture, with description of the immanent characteristics (analysis of the neutral level) in the sound phenomena under consideration.

(6) If music appears to be a universal activity, universals of music doubtless do exist, but they must be sought in the realm of poietic and esthesic strategies more than at the level of immanent structures.

[16] Personal communication with the author.

This entire debate is by no means academic; it lies at the heart of a question that will recur throughout any musico-semiological inquiry: *if* something we could call "musical" exists everywhere, defined and organized in terms of modalities appropriate to each culture, *if* there are universals of strategy—then are there universal analytical methods?

3

The Concept of the Musical Work

1. The Musical Work: Physical
and Ontological Mode of Existence

W E ARE now in a position to understand more clearly how music *in general* might be approached from the standpoint of semiology. But what about *the work*, an essential category in western music?

From the beginning, we must distinguish between a musical work's physical mode of existence and its mode of being. We are already familiar with the problems associated with music's physical mode of existence: as stated in Chapter 2, music's irreducible dimension is *sound*. The musical work *manifests itself*, in its *material* reality, in the form of sound waves.

However, the moment we ask ourselves about the work's mode of *being* (as did philosopher and aesthetician Roman Ingarden, in Ingarden 1962), the problem becomes more difficult. What defines the identity of a particular musical work? Ingarden shows that this being cannot be reduced to any of the following: a given performance (since the score determines different potential performances); the here-and-now perception of a work (since each listener hears it differently); the acoustic reality (since the work's temporal profile and formal configuration are not, strictly speaking, sonorous elements); or the score (since the work will always and everywhere transcend that score). For Ingarden, the work is a purely intentional object, immutable and permanent, whose heteronomous *existence* is no more than a reflection of its *being*: the existence of the work finds its source in the "creative act" of the performer, and its foundation in the score (English trans. Meyer-Goldthwait 1989: 90). The score constitutes the work's "schema," which guarantees its identity over the course of history, even though numerous elements not fixed by the score "play an essential role for the aesthetic Gestalt of the work" (ibid.: 106), and even though the "schema" allows an enormous number of possibilities for the work's realization. "It is concomitant of this pure intentionality of the musical work that it has, so to speak, different foundations of its being and of its appearing" (117). In other words, there is a poietic process that results in the schema written out as the score, as well as multiple interpretations engendered by various esthesic strategies. Ingarden's ontology of the work is critical to my analytic arguments, since it shows unequivocally that every analysis of a particular work will by necessity stop somewhat short of that work's being proper. First and foremost, however, this ontology suggests that, in order to take account of the work's existential manifestations, we cannot remain content with a unidimensional approach. If—as I believe to be the case—there is no analysis except that which is *written*, that which has a material presence (Granger 1967), we can state, with Molino, that "the work exists at the horizon of all its possible rewritings."[1] But can one speak of an intangible, immutable essence of the work, one located beyond all its concrete manifestations? Carl Dahlhaus states that fixing a musical work through notation is not sufficient for constructing the notion of a work (1982: 94). He defines the musical work as a text, located beyond either its notated form or any acoustic rendering, guaranteed by an explicit or implicit "intentional element." He stresses that, as a text, the work cannot exist independently of the hermeneutic process by which we attempt to understand its meaning (ibid.: 95).

Dahlhaus appeals explicitly to Ingarden's concept of intentionality, but he does not approach the ontological stakes involved in the same terms, because he is on the whole preoccupied with making the work an object for interpretation (interpretation in the sense of exegesis, not performance). Nonetheless, can one espouse Ingarden's position, and situate the work outside any existential manifestation? Semiology's own bias demands that we make an ontology of the work, but I should prefer to locate the work's being in its dispersal between three spheres, in the *interaction* between its symbolic components, as a total musical fact; as poietic strategies, a resultant trace, and esthesic strategies unleashed by that trace.

[1] Personal communication with the author (1975). Discussions I have had with Molino and Delalande on this subject have also informed one of Delalande's interesting essays (see Delalande 1977).

2. Semiology, The Score, and Transcription[2]

Ingarden's position is interesting, especially because it assigns an appropriate status to notation—precisely that status that current fashion would reject, as does Siohan: "the musical sign, which is a graphic element, is neither music, nor its reflection, but a solely mnemonic device. There is no music except in the state of sonorous manifestation" (Siohan 1962: 22). In the western tradition, the thing that ensues from the composer's creative act is the score; the score is the thing that renders the work performable and recognizable as an entity, and enables the work to pass through the centuries.

For this reason, we should linger over two points that Ingarden does not broach.

To me, the score seems to represent something more than mere schema for the work. In his *Ontology of the Work of Art*, Ingarden all but ignores the music of the oral tradition. Now that oral music is (at least, by means of recordings) part of a familiar musical universe, recognizing the *constructive* role of the score in generating *styles of written music* (a process unknown in so-called "ethnic" musics) is paramount. From an anthropological perspective (similar to that adopted by Goody [1977]), we need to stress the fact that writing facilitates manipulation of elementary musical units, in a way not permitted by mere memory. By saying this, I am by no means claiming that musics of the oral tradition are "more primitive" than occidental music. Simha Arom, for instance, has been able to show that Banda-Linda pieces for horn ensemble are based not just on material shared among five instruments, but that the complete polyphonic ensemble of the instruments is controlled by a subtextual melody present in the minds of the performers—a melody that is, however, never realized: this is hardly "primitive" (1985: 501–707). In researching the field of Ainu music (of Japan), I was struck by the genre *upopo*. The second contrapuntal voice had to imitate the musical formula in the first contrapuntal voice (not heard until that moment), at an interval much shorter than that in our western canons, since the second voice attacks the preceding musical formula before the first voice has finished it.[3] Such a performance requires quite sophisticated feats of memory. In order to go farther than this, however, writing must intervene. We cannot overlook the fact that the existence of writing al-

[2] Sections 2, 4, and 5 of this chapter recapitulate (with certain changes and additions) Sections 2 and 3 of Part I, Chapter 6 of the *Fondements*.

[3] Performances of *upopo* have been recorded by the author on Philips 6586045, "Songs of the Ainu," side 1, bands 1, 2, and 5.

lowed polyphony and counterpoint to attain the degree of complexity we know in the works of Gesualdo or Sebastian Bach.

Ingarden's reflections on the score lead us to a further question: since music is an art of "interpretation," where does the poietic process end and the esthesic process begin?

If we conceive of the work as an entity comprised of relations that are fixed by the score, the graphic sign (the score) *is* the work, and the esthesic process begins at the instant the performer *interprets* the work, in both senses of the word: (a) the performer performs the work, (b) the performer makes a personal selection of interpretants, from the moment of the first reading of the work (i.e., he or she gives the work a meaning). The word "interpret" is ambiguous: when used of music, as Adorno pointed out, it can mean play, *or* interpret in a critical sense. This ambiguity illustrates the degree to which a performer is also a "hermeneuticist" in Gadamer's sense (1976:12).

If on the other hand we believe that the work is not wholly "produced" *unless* it has been played, the poietic process extends until the performance is complete. Performance shows itself in this case to be the last stage of the poietic, as well as the first stage of the esthesic. In musics without a score, this border is displaced, since the producer and the performer find themselves intermingled.

The essential difference between the score and the acoustic trace left by any given performance is that the score is an invariable physical reality, while there will be as many acoustic realizations as there are performances. But no matter where the border between the poietic and esthesic processes may lie, we must take account of the *interpretants* that insinuate themselves between the score and its performance. For this reason, I would be inclined (in the context of western music) to apply analysis of the neutral level to the graphic sign alone, because that sign *precedes* interpretation. The performer does not strictly speaking create the work, but instead gives it access to a sonorous existence.

This much, then, is certain: multifaceted analysis of a work—to which musical semiology aspires—cannot be realized without the intermediary of notation, or (expressed more precisely) of *transcription*; music analysis must have the capacity to apply itself to a *symbolic substitute* for the sonorous fact.

Musical semiology is in effect rendered possible by musical notation. As Granger insisted, "writing down ordinary languages is . . . in most cases, nothing more than a transcription, a secondary code . . . writing down scientific equations is no longer a code: writing is the very fabric of the language" (1967: 43). For the musicologist, musical notation functions in two ways. In the first, notation is indeed the trace that renders the work's identity possible. In this case we need to realize that, from the analytical standpoint, notation is an image—imperfect but indispensable—of that notation's sonorous equivalent; this is *prescriptive* notation in Seeger's sense (1958). But notation may well be absent or incapable of guaranteeing a particular sonorous result, and then we must *transcribe* musical sounds; this transcription will be indispensable, since we must be able to identify the reality that this transcription "speaks" (this is Seeger's *descriptive* notation).[4] These two situations are analogous to similar situations encountered in linguistics. One (*descriptive* notation) is expressed as follows:

$$\text{Speaker} \longrightarrow \text{Sonorous Flux} \longrightarrow \text{Writing}$$

When a phonologist analyzes a language, he or she represents the linguistic flux, after the fact, by a phonetic or phonologic transcription.[5] *Writing* is descriptive here, and functions as a substitute. Ex post facto transcription is, similarly, generated by the traditional oral musics and by certain experimental music. This schema also designates the position of the performer in relation to the "work": in musics of the oral tradition, the musical product is merged with the act of performing, and there is no longer a material prototype for the "work":

$$\text{Poietic process} \longrightarrow \text{Musical Result} \longleftarrow \text{Esthesic Process}$$

But with western art music there is, so to speak, an extra step:

$$\text{Poietic process} \longrightarrow \text{Score} \xrightarrow{\uparrow} \text{Musical Result} \longleftarrow \text{Esthesic Process}$$
$$\text{Interpretation}$$
$$\text{(performance)}$$

In comparison to the situation diagrammed above (with a Speaker, a Sonorous Flux, and an ex post facto act of transcription), the positions of "what is written" and the "sonorous flux" are inverted:

$$\text{Composer} \longrightarrow \text{Score} \longrightarrow \text{Analysis}$$
$$\text{Performance}$$

---

[4] Seeger's distinction between prescriptive and descriptive notation parallels in some sense the opposition between poietic and esthesic.

[5] Musicological applications of phonology will be taken up in Volume 2.

The score fixes those distinctive features that permit us to recognize, say, "The Fifth Symphony." All in all, then, the score is like a phonological transcription inside out.

A work of western art music thus belongs to what Goodman calls "allographic art"—art in which (by contrast with painting, an "autographic art") any "execution" that creates an acceptable correspondence between graphic source and performance may be considered an "authentic execution" (Goodman 1968: 113). In this sense, Goodman is perfectly justified in claiming that "all copies of scores define the same class of performances" (129). But correct as this position might be, it leaves open the question of the performer's *fidelity* to the work. On this point, Ingarden adopts a relativist attitude that I share, and to which I shall presently return in some detail: "one cannot even directly imitate the musical work, for all that can serve as a model is either the incomplete set of instructions for performance given by the score, or a certain form of the work which the work assumes in a performance, and which can be more or less a distortion of the work, but which must always be one-sided [univocal] because it cannot exhaust all the possibilities the score leaves open" (110). "For we must always take into consideration the fact, which we know from history, that the individual works are performed in different epochs in a way imposed on them by the important artists of the epochs in question, but at the same time also determined by the taste of the public" (108). "Every epoch of musical life (which epochs are, of course, part of the general atmosphere of cultural life and are conditioned in their attitudes by this atmosphere) has the inclination to seek and find that form in the individual performances, in the (properly speaking, false) opinion that this form is the only 'Correct' or 'authentic' form of the work, and thus is actually the work itself . . . if this fact is taken as the basis for consideration, then it is easy to arrive at the idea that the work itself changes in historical time" (116–17).

3. The Semiology of Interpretation[6]

I had arrived at a similarly "relativist" notion of performance (before reading Ingarden) in the course of examining the controversial 1976 Bayreuth *Ring* production conducted by Pierre Boulez and directed

---

[6] This section recapitulates certain theoretical conclusions drawn from my book about the (already "historic") 1976 Bayreuth *Ring*, *Tétralogies* (1983a: 250–53), in which questions of fidelity in performance were taken up at length.

by Patrice Chéreau, which was in repertory from 1976–1980 (see Nattiez 1983a). At this point in my argument, I want to emphasize that interpretation (as performance *and* reading) involves not one but many symbolic forms. Doubtless, interpretations made by the director and the conductor constitute a privileged form of *perceiving* Wagner's text, but these theatrical and musical realizations are, in turn, themselves symbolic forms, produced by a human activity, and thus also subject to semiological analysis. It is possible (as I have suggested elsewhere) to offer an *immanent description* (i.e., an analysis of the neutral level) of Chéreau's scenographic style and Boulez's conducting, by classifying their individual characteristics (Nattiez 1983a: 122–77, 208–46). But a *poietic* inquiry deals with the origins of Chéreau's understanding of the *Ring* myths, of his particular staging (72–80; 174), and of this or that in Boulez's reading of the score (234–41). Finally, these two symbolic forms—scenic and musical realization—are themselves the object of an *esthesic* interpretation on the part of spectators and critics.

If we want to understand public reaction to the production, however, we cannot stop there. The libretto and the score of the *Ring* have their own *poietic* factors (29–62, 181–207). To interpret the work's meaning we must return to Feuerbach and Schopenhauer. Obviously, *Thoughts on Death and Immortality* and *The World as Will and Representation* are also symbolic forms: Wagner, occupying an esthesic position in relation to them, read them in a certain fashion; we, in turn, understand the two texts according to our own personal bias, and furthermore we can suggest an interpretation of both informed by *Wagner's* understanding of their works. Finally, the spectator judges Chéreau's and Boulez's work relative to his or her knowledge of Wagner and the *Ring, and relative to the idea that he or she has formed of both.*

We can represent the symbolic forms being considered, the tripartitions to which they give rise, and the chains of interpretants brought into play, by Figure 3.1. Wagner creates a work over the course of a dynamic genetic process (1), moving from a philosophical, literary, and musical background (2). This poietic process gives rise to a complex trace: the libretto and the score (3). Taken up by the performers (4), who interpret according to their knowledge of Wagner (5) and their personal poietic processes (6), the trace becomes a performance (7). This performance constitutes, in turn, a symbolic form (8). The spectators and the critics occupy an esthesic position, not only in relation to this production (9), but in relation to what they know of

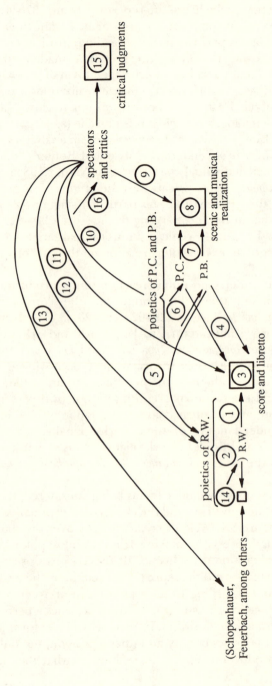

critical judgments

spectators
and critics

scenic and musical
realization

poietics of P.C. and P.B.

P.C.

P.B.

score and libretto

poietics of R.W.

R.W.

(Schopenhauer,
Feuerbach, among others

Figure 3.1

Boulez and Chéreau (10), Wagner's text (11), the creative process of the composer (12), and indeed, what they know of the artists who influenced Wagner (13)—for all of which we can, of course, advance to a tripartite semiological analysis (14), and so on ad infinitum. The public produces either less or more elaborate verdicts: applause and hisses, comments expressing pleasure or indignation, intermission analyses, critical evaluations, journalistic reviews, analytic articles, entire books (15). These traces left behind by members of the public may in turn be explained not only in terms of what they have retained of (9), (10), (11), (12), (13), or (14), and in terms of the interpretations they made of this material, but also in terms of each person's personal poietic process (16): for instance, it is obvious that Jean-Jacques Nattiez's approach to Chéreau and Boulez has been conditioned by the theoretical, semiological perspectives described in this work.

Is it really necessary to bring such a sophisticated model to bear upon the problem? Yes. Beyond what I believe to be this model's inherent interest for developing semiological thought, it allows us to understand why the question of Boulez's or Chéreau's fidelity to Wagner cannot be solved in five minutes' time (and to understand why the same holds true, in a general way, for the controversial issue of "authentic" performances, especially of early music). What, in effect, is a *judgment* about the fidelity of this or that performance? It is the juxtaposition of one *interpretation* (the spectator-listener's interpretation of the musical performance and mise-en-scène) with another *interpretation* (that same spectator-listener's suppositions about "the true" Wagner, or "the essence of" the *Ring*).

This little semiology of performance leads us to the threshold of an important issue: if *judgments* about an interpretation (interpretation in the broadest sense, performance *and* "reading") ensue from this juxtaposition of symbolic forms, is it possible to speak of *truth* or *authenticity* in interpretation, as Leibowitz put it (1971b)? This question will be considered in detail below, in the course of a more general consideration of the epistemological problem of *truth in analysis*,[7] inasmuch as a theatrical or musical interpretation/performance is an act of exegesis (just as analysis is an act of exegesis), for if truth exists, then truth in analysis and truth in interpretation (performance) are interconnected. For the moment, however, we must establish the problem's semiological foundation.

[7] This is a crucial question discussed in Volume 2, but an initial stance toward the question of truth in analysis is taken in Chapter 9.

4. Notation, Composition, and Analysis

Whatever the written trace may be (in the western tradition), performance takes this trace as its point of departure. What status should we assign to the score in semiological analysis?

In prescriptive notation, the analyst can take the score as a kind of preformalization, since in making the score there was a selection of certain variables from the universe of sonorous facts, a selection indispensable to the permanence and transmission of the work. The entire history of musical notation is the story of a dynamic process, in which variables necessary to guarantee the "eternal" status of music are transferred into graphic representation. The difficulty, of course, is that using a given notation is only possible within the context of specific acquired practical skills, and the moment a given practice falls out of use, the notation falls silent.

This is what has happened for music up to the Baroque era. Harnoncourt writes unequivocally that he is "quite sceptical; I ask myself whether we can, today, still understand this music in any complete way. We must always bear in mind that all the treatises were written for the benefit of the author's contemporaries (in the seventeenth or eighteenth centuries), and that the author could assume the existence of important reserves of knowledge, self-evident knowledge that no one needed to speak of . . . the unwritten, the assumed, would undoubtedly be far more important than what is written . . . we must not overestimate the degree to which we can understand historical music . . . for there is no uninterrupted tradition of performance" (1984: 40, 42). Notation—as a semiographic instrument for transmitting musical thought—must be itself the object of a semiological examination. *Mutatis mutandis*, the epistemological operation is no different from that engendered by the question "what did Wagner want to say?"

As soon as a score is deemed an adequate reflection of the class of its possible sonorous realizations, then the musicologist can build upon it. In this situation, the classical score plays the same role for the musicologist as a descriptive transcription might for the ethnomusicologist, but with the difference that the choices translated by the score are not the musicologist's, and he or she has no control over them, no opportunity to correct them.

The historical development of notational systems may be conceptualized as resulting from an operation that retains, out of all substantive musical facts, only those that are absolutely necessary, relevant either to preserving coherence in the system of reference (the tonal system, for example), or to transmitting the essence of the work. Notation once established in turn becomes a factor in musical creativity, and never stops impelling that system of reference toward further evolution. When composers invent music that the semiographic system can no longer represent, a period of crisis ensues, in which composers cannot free themselves totally from the old system, yet they seek to represent their intentions by means of new notational signs, which—because new—are often without universal meaning. This situation will give rise to different attitudes toward the score: from searching for optimally precise notations, or tentatively inventing new universal symbols, to rejecting the score, or making an ironic mockery of it. In this last case, the deviation between formal score and sonorous result is so great that the notation can no longer be thought of as a valid image of the work (the Cordiform Chanson is one instance of this phenomenon). Today we are experiencing a crisis of notation comparable to the one that inspired the shift from mensural neumes to the modern notational system as we know it. Once all this is accepted, we must (in the modern context) differentiate between two situations: that of the composer and that of the musicologist.

For the composer, the question is this: how does one know whether the score actually functions as an intermediary, something that would guarantee the work's permanence, or, to the contrary, whether the score is merely a simulation or pretext? We know that the score may respond to extramusical or ideological pressures: here I am thinking of the experiments in musical iconicization discussed by Gillo Dorflès (1973), evinced in a book such as Cage's *Notations* (1969). To know whether aleatory music and improvisation are (among other factors, of course) a *cause* or an *effect* of the current semiographic crisis, we would have to make a strictly empirical study of both. If, however, the composer does not want to command a system of universally comprehensible notation, I do not see why we should enforce one: the ensuing problem with regard to "reading" the works will be the musicologist's problem, not the composer's. If it is a matter of guaranteeing consistent performance results, however, we might well imagine that nothing less than an international conference, staged by composers willing to negotiate, could put an end to the current notational crisis. Still, the international symposium on problems of musical graphics, held in Rome in 1972 (the proceedings were published in 1974), could do no more than confirm the impossibility of establishing such a consensus.

In reality, however, the difficulties are due less to the diversity of graphic signs than to the present state of musical language itself. Duchez, in her study of the historical development of musical nota-

79

tions (1983), has emphasized the link maintained between the graphic sign and the theory of reference: "the note is not a sign of sound *unless* music and concrete sound remain within the context of the theory supporting the notation; the system of notational signs corresponds to the system of sounds described by the theory" (1983: 48). It seems fairly obvious that modern music does *not* ground itself in a universal theory, as *was* (for example) the case with tonal music. It is hardly surprising, then, that there was no consensus about the semiography to be used for its notation.

We need only turn to *analyses* of contemporary music to recognize the difficulties inherent in the situation. Schaeffer's morphology of sound-objects (in the *Traité des objets musicaux*) is founded on a descriptive inventory of their characteristics. What Schaeffer lacks is the sort of thing we have in linguistics: explicit criteria for segmentation and denomination of objects, and notation precise enough that a given class of sounds (which have been verbally described) will invariably and unambiguously correspond to a given symbol. In short, music should have a means of symbolic description, one that would also help us to show how different sound-elements combine within a work. Significantly, Delalande's 1972 analysis of Schaeffer's *Étude aux objets* had to employ both a verbal description of various sound-objects and a diagrammatic representation that clarified their superimposition and succession (that is, their syntax). Confronted with *Carré* or the *Variations pour une porte et un soupir*, we find ourselves in the same situation as an ethnomusicologist confronted with an indigenous music: before analyzing, a descriptive transcription will be necessary.

The prospects for analyzing these musics, indeed, is dependent on advances in the graphic representation of sound. These advances can be defined in terms of our own increased capacity for segmenting an object that, when subjected to analytic scrutiny, naturally resists such discretization (such is the case with electro-acoustic music). I am, of course, by no means suggesting that we limit ourselves to considering works that lend themselves to analysis because they are easily notated in a certain way. (Science, after all, cannot always do what it wishes to do, or what it should do.) I am, however, suggesting that (from the standpoint of rigorous musical analysis) articulating music into discrete units, and this alone, allows us to define *the musical facts or musical units under consideration* in an unambiguous way, rendering possible a permanent critical debate and a progressive accumulation of knowledge. The written note is, after all, a graphic sign for a given sound-material. The written note articulates, within an exterior continuum, units that have a beginning and an end. It captures a certain number of that sound's salient characteristics—those that are essential to preserving certain systems (in classical music, first and foremost, pitch and duration; to a lesser degree, intensity, timbre, and tempo). When we analyze music by articulating a musical continuum into segments (whether we are working with a "reliable" score or with a transcription), we are operating on material already composed of discrete units, and we go on to define units larger than the single note, larger units that are also in some sense "discrete." Analysis of the neutral level is only possible if one has at one's disposal this general discretization process.[8]

When the analyst is compelled to make his or her own transcription (as with "ethnic" musics and certain contemporary works), we may well think that we forego any possibility for "analysis of the *neutral* level," since, by definition, such transcriptions are only made after the experience of hearing the piece, and as such, will always be mediated by the analysts' interpretations. We might cite the example of the "Hörpartitur" or "score for listening" made for Ligeti's *Artikulation* by Rainer Wehinger (1970). In making the score, Wehinger categorized different families of sonorous effects, and assigned each family a specific graphic symbol; his categorization, of course, was made in terms of his own personal *esthesic* criteria.[9] But as soon as that "Hörpartitur"

---

[8] If this is the case, then the written note and the linguists' phoneme have the same epistemological status. Saussure reminds us twice in the *Cours de linguistique générale* that linguistic units are not "naturally" given: "Other sciences work with objects that are given in advance and that can be considered from different viewpoints; but not linguistics . . . far from it being the object that antedates the viewpoint, it would seem that it is the viewpoint that creates the object" (1922: 23; English trans. 8). "Language is characterized as a system based entirely on the opposition of its concrete units. We can neither dispense with becoming acquainted with them nor take a single step without coming back to them; and still, delimiting them is such a delicate problem that we may wonder at first whether they really exist" (1922: 143; English trans. 107).

Phoneme and note are, then, "discretized" units rather than discrete units. This notion of "discretization" explains why analysis of classical music—given that the score is accepted as reliable image of the sound—is facilitated (since the semiography is given, it does not need to be constructed). On the other hand, when we make a transcription, we have a sense that there is a distance between the material reality of the work and the graphic trace. This makes semiological analysis of contemporary works or music of the oral tradition much more difficult.

Analysis is made difficult, but not impossible, since the object to be parsed out is not a conceptual object (as is the case in linguistic semantics or analysis of myths) but a material one: what is needed, then, is to find empirical techniques that are up to delimiting and constructing these units.

[9] The work of the analyst is *de facto* situated on the esthesic side. But this is an esthesic process in the second degree, as can be seen clearly in the schema suggested in Chapter 7 (page 153). The following paragraph, which existed already in the *Fondements*, p. 117, seems to me still to have given (in advance) a sufficient response to the

is established, a distinction between poietic, neutral, and esthesic will reemerge. In Wehinger's case, it would go something like this: the text accompanying the "Hörpartitur" and the recording provide a formal analysis of the piece, one made according to indications supplied by Ligeti himself. This analysis (which is based on the "Hörpartitur") clearly has poietic pertinence. Taking the "Hörpartitur" as a representation of a musical fact, we could suggest an analysis of its neutral level. Using high-level experimental methods, we could conduct an esthesic analysis. Wehinger's transcription constitutes a descriptive tool, serving as a material representation, a starting point for poietic and esthesic analyses. Once we use the "Hörpartitur" as the basis for an analysis, its status is no longer in question, no more so than with the scores of classic tonal works when *they* are taken as a basis for analysis. They all serve as an anchorage, a benchmark, an intermediary in our *designation* of sounds.

5. *The Problem of the Open Work*

The work's physical mode of existence is, then, divided between score and performance. The work's ontological mode of existence is situated in the realm of pure intentionality, beyond the score, yet guaranteed, rendered possible by the score. But is my view of this matter subject to challenge by the "open work"? I do not believe so.

The notion of the open work finds its origins in Mallarmé's *Livre*. He remarked (and this is true, we should emphasize, of all artistic productions), that once given over to readers, his verses took on a different meaning for each one, and that the book had been in some way extended by the reader: "a book neither begins, nor ends: at most, it feigns doing so" (cited in Schérer 1957: sheet 181). On the basis of this insight, Mallarmé envisages transposing his image of perception into a design for the very nature of the work, and "dreams of a universal work, capable of encompassing all the others" (ibid.). He imagines inventing a work of twenty volumes, made up of interchangeable pages, and he calculates how recombining only ten elements will give him 3,628,800 possibilities (ibid.: 86). "The order of reality," comments Schérer, "is not a successive order, and we would under no circumstances think that the Book in which the world must end would be organized successively. The metaphysics of the Book thus entail an explanatory physics of the Book" (ibid.: 24).

It is important to recall that the chief modern theorist of the open

---

question addressed by Delalande (1986) concerning the concept of the neutral level from the perspective of electro-acoustic music.

work, Umberto Eco, adopts exactly the same stance: "the work of art is a fundamentally ambiguous message, a plurality of signifieds that coexist within a single signifier . . . today, this ambiguity is becoming an explicit goal of the work, a value to be realized in preference to all others" (1965: 9).[10] "To acknowledge ambiguity as a value, contemporary artists have often had recourse to the informal, to disorder, to chance, to indeterminacy of results" (ibid.: 66).

This brief quotation, which summarizes perfectly the "poetics" of the open work, suffices to show how the idea of the "open work" is grounded in a confusion of the three semiological levels. As soon as we note a message's ambiguity, we position ourselves deliberately on the esthesic level, the level of perception. "In reacting to the constellation of stimuli, in trying to perceive and understand their interrelationships, each consumer exercises a personal sensibility, a determined culture, tastes, inclinations, prejudices that orient his or her interpretive play within a perspective that is his or her own" (Eco 1965: 17). "This condition is characteristic of all works of art" (65). Contemporary artists and intellectuals go from this universal observation, to normative considerations that are the province of the discipline of "calology," which, according to Deprun (1979), would draw up an empirical and historical inventory of various conceptions of the beautiful across historical eras and cultures.

"Basically," Eco writes, "a form is *aesthetically valuable*[11] only insofar as it can be envisaged and grasped through multiple perceptions, manifesting a variety of aspects without ever ceasing to be itself" (1965: 17). Making a criteria of value out of a multiplicity of interpretations is, of course, already a tautology, since there are no works that dictate one single meaning. As Eco himself acknowledges, "in this primary sense, any work of art, even when it exists in a finished form and is 'closed'—in possessing organizational perfection nicely calibrated—is 'open' in that it can at least be interpreted in different ways without its irreducible uniqueness being thereby altered" (15).

Be this as it may, the goal of the artist, as with Mallarmé, is to transmute this esthesic clash into a normative poietic principle: *normative*, since the openness of the work is perceived as a value that should be realized, and *poietic* because the perceptive indeterminacy is going to be transferred to production. Eco cites the following musical works as realizing openness on the physical level: Stockhausen's *Klavierstück*

[10] Translator's note: because of variations between the French and Italian versions of *L'opera aperta*, I have chosen to translate Nattiez's citations of the French *L'oeuvre ouverte*, rather than cite Anna Cancogni's English translation of the Italian original (Harvard: Harvard University Press, 1989).

[11] Emphasis is mine.

XI (which is certainly the first "open" work in the history of music), Berio's *Sequenza* for solo flute,[12] Pousseur's *Scambi*, and Boulez's *Third Piano Sonata*.

Eco takes ample account of the difficulties provoked by a move from the esthesic to the poietic: "works such as those by Berio or Stockhausen are 'open' in a less metaphorical, more concrete sense [than other works of art]" (1965: 17). He writes further that "we must eliminate one ambiguity right from the start: obviously, the intervention of the interpreter we call the performer . . . cannot be confused with the intervention of that other interpreter we call the consumer" (38, note 1). It seems nonetheless that the move between the esthesic and poietic is grounded here in mere play of words. As a preface to the first sentence quoted, Eco writes, "to enjoy an art-work [on the esthesic level, to be sure] is tantamount to interpreting it, performing it, reanimating it from a novel perspective" (17). In the note cited above, moreover, Eco himself denies the methodological import of a distinction he himself had made between the two meanings of interpretation [i.e., performing and hearing], when he adds the following phrase: "nevertheless, on the level of aesthetic analysis, the two interpretations may be considered different modalities of the same *interpretive* attitude: 'reading,' 'contemplating' a work of art, the 'enjoyment' of a work of art, all represent an individual and tacit form of 'performing.' The notion of an *interpretive activity* encompasses the totality of these behaviors." Constant recourse to quotation marks speaks to the terminological imprecision that underlies the whole of this "poetics."

Perception of openness is paramount; if not, the "open" work does not achieve its goals. "In all music composed with interchangeable elements," Stockhausen states, "one must grasp the interchangeability at first hearing; if not, then the piece has simply been composed badly" (1970–71: 112). To express oneself in these terms is to give expression to doubt: listener reactions will not always be astute. But in the same interview, Stockhausen expresses a belief that the "open" work has certain immanent characteristics that permit identification as "open": "I believe that music whose form is variable is recognizable as such; such music does not develop linearly toward a goal . . . when I play *Klavierstück XI*, a sense of interchangeability is communicated. A certain indifference about connections between disparate musical moments hovers over the piece. The piece involves neither deviation, nor a final, linear process" (ibid.).

Stockhausen's positive statement—that *Klavierstück XI* "communi-

---

[12] Although I do not see in what sense the *Sequenza I* is "open."

cates" a sense of the interchangeability of its parts—cannot be verified except by inquiry among informant-listeners. I tried the experiment with semiology students (nonmusicians) at the Faculté des lettres in Aix-en-Provence. Stockhausen's *Klavierstück XI*—played as one in a group of other piano pieces—is *not* recognizable as open, unless one describes what constitutes "openness" (a succession of formants not connected to one another) as a preamble to the audition. In the case of Pousseur's *Ephémérides*, chance intervenes at certain points, but these are not perceptible, unless one knows *in advance* that a group of four notes is going to serve as a signal for them.

"In music," writes Daniel Charles, "the difficulty is in some way ensuring that the process of change is perceptible" (1967: 192). Naturally—but for there to be perception of change, we would need a basis for comparison.

To be sure, the composer of an open work has the option of mentally comparing the score to any one of its performances. Ultimately, the listener could realize that the work is "open" when many versions of the "same work" were offered on the same recording, or during the same concert. In principle—and this remains to be proven—the listener would have to discern some family resemblance between two "versions." But even then, the intellectual and perceptive process will not be unlike that involved in, say, hearing two Haydn piano sonatas. In Pousseur's and Butor's *Votre Faust*, one of the work's sections can be presented in two different fashions, but Version 2 is a tape "reflection" of Version 1, taking the form of shattered fragments of 1. If we should want to perceive the relation between 1 and 2, we must *first* have heard Version 1—but it is stated explicitly that only one *or* the other version is to be played. This kind of "openness" is totally unlike that of a Calder mobile (an object that Eco assigns to the same category as works of aleatoric music). Sculpture and music have different *physical modes of existence*, and this difference comes into play in determining their "openness." Sculpture—even mobile sculpture—is offered globally to our perceptive faculties; if it moves, the variations inscribe themselves within a perceptive field that would be the same if it had remained immobile. In music, on the other hand, a variation does not exist except in relation to a musical given engendered (as a consequence of music's linear temporality) before or after, but never during the variation itself.

I once took advantage of Henri Pousseur's visit to Montreal to ask if he thought that listeners really noticed the "openness" of *Votre Faust*. He replied that the *impossibility* of noticing remained a merely theoretical claim. His affirmation is, however, called into question by a quite specific fact: in *Votre Faust*, one of the characters—the theater director—*explains* its aleatoric nature to the spectators. Now, Pousseur is in the habit of doing this: in his piece *Répons*, a text by Butor "metaphorically illustrates the individual or collective activity of the musicians and permits the public to sense the aleatoric nature of the work's global form, i.e., the aspect that depends upon the musicians' choices during the performance" (Charles 1970–71: 83).

If, in order to be understood, the *poietic* phenomenon of "openness" must be explained before or during the performance, then this "openness" is not perceptible on the *esthesic* level.

The advent of "open works," thus, has not altered the status of the "work" in general. When we recognize "*Pastoral Symphony*," we do not make a connection to a thing in itself, but to a certain number of relevant constants that recur from one performance to another. In the *Klavierstück XI* we do not find these relevant constants, because in each performance we hear a unique exemplar of a work that only recording is able to fix. All production of sounds, because it results from an *activity*, gains (even when broadcast) a certain empiricism, one that can be frozen *a posteriori* by recordings or scores.

Scrutinized more closely, what I would dare to call the *failure* of the "open work's" attempt to deny "the work" is not something new. It strongly resembles surrealism's failure in this regard. Sartre wrote that "it is always by *creating*, that is, by adding paintings to already existent paintings, books to already published books that [surrealism] destroys. . . . in the end, [surrealism] did a lot of painting and writing, but never actually destroyed anything" (Sartre 1964: 225–26; English trans. 136). The work resists all too well: perhaps this explains why some have attempted to take refuge either in action designed to annihilate it, or in silence.

All misunderstandings of the "open work" are in the end grounded in a conception of "the work" that remains fundamentally romantic, even among the modernists. But if beyond the *x* versions of *Klavierstück XI* we still speak of *one* work, this work cannot exist except in the realm of intention, as Stockhausen's own project. One cannot simply turn up one's nose at musical results that are different at every performance, perceived each time as a new reality; if the "arts of the Beautiful" (to use an expression employed by Gilson) are poietic arts, then it is critical to avoid reducing the work to one of its three levels— poietic, material, or esthesic. In each era (as with defining the concept of music), the accent is placed on one or the other of these poles, or upon two among them. Musical semiology cannot normatively choose which of the three is proper to defining a work. Semiology can, though, recognize that the work—culturally speaking—has been reduced (for its theorists) to one of the poles. Global semiological analysis, nonetheless, is obligated to take account of all three.[13] In the case of an open work, the work demands that we examine its poietic matrix, the many diverse results engendered, and how the listener reacts when confronted with a result, or various results.

The open work, as much as "normal" works, does not *exist* on only one of these three levels. But the criterion of identity has quite simply been transferred to the compositional side of things, perhaps ultimately to the composer alone.

6. Process and Improvisation

We need to go even farther in problematizing the notion of the work. Is that notion still adequate if we take up the music of the oral tradition? Romanian ethnomusicologist Constantin Brailoiu has insisted (he was probably the first) that in fact there is no single standard version for a given popular song (identified by its title), since every time a new performance is recorded, we notice significant differences in comparison to previous versions (modifications in melody, rhythm, and text; additions, omissions, interpolations, and so forth). Brailoiu, following Bartók, called this the *impulse toward variation* (*Variationstrieb*) (1931: 55), and it was greatly to Brailoiu's credit that he proposed a method for studying this impulse. The method involves superimposing different versions of the same melody, recopying only those elements that are new.[14]

We can only regret that Brailoiu (whose extensive work, incidentally, is some of the most remarkable in all ethnomusicology) wrote no study taking advantage of his systematic recordings of variables within a given piece. Such a study would doubtless have shown how it is possible to proceed from an inductive analysis of the neutral

[13] For this reason, I believe that Vanasse subjects me to a false trial in his critical examination of my concept of the open work. He writes, "we must not forget that from the composer's point of view, *Glossolalie* (by Dieter Schnebel) corresponds to a unique process of production, even if more than one totally different musical realities, executed according to this sonorous plan, boast the same title. The composer for himself wrote only one *Glossolalie*" (1983: 116); in so writing, Vanasse displaces the criterion of identity for the work, for its text, to the poietic pole. What we have, again, is a reductive approach of the sort that I explicitly wish to avoid.

[14] Brailoiu becomes, by virtue of this technique, one of the undeniable precursors of the sort of paradigmatic analysis that will be considered in the next volumes.

level—since each performed version will have its own structure—to a poietic analysis.[15]

In this context we may hesitate to speak of the work. But should we bring up the word "improvisation"? Undoubtedly so, as long as we see improvisation as the simultaneous performing and inventing of a new musical fact with respect to a previous performance. Even in improvisation, however, the song remains recognizable, can still be identified despite the depredations of memory, which cause forgetfulness, intervention, and modification. There is a continuum of possible cases, running from strict reproduction (but does that ever exist?) to completely free improvisation (does that, also, ever exist?). Most scholars agree that in any improvisation some sort of *model* can be discerned, and that we can examine various types of improvisation in terms of (a) the nature of the model (mode, thematic material, melodic-rhythmic formula, abstract formal schema), (b) the nature of the distance between realization and model, and (c) whether the musician is or is not conscious of the model (Lortat-Jacob 1987). In the case of *bocet* (the form studied by Brailoiu), memory of previous performance serves as a model for the new performance. In *bocet*, however, we are (despite appearances) not far removed from a score-model for performance, since the performer *reproduces* a song that has already been heard. In the Inuit *katajjaq*, the singers draw motifs, shaped according to certain rules, from a stock furnished by memory; these rules are not (so far as I know) explicitly defined within the culture, though they can be reconstructed inductively by analysis, based on observing the singers' practices. Can we speak of improvisation only when it is a matter of the explicit intention of playing upon a well-defined model, a model of which the performer(s) is(are) conscious?[16] This is what happens in the so-called art-musics of Asia and the Middle East (Indian *raga*, Arab *maqām*, Iranian *radif*), yet also in the music of the Sardinian *launeddas*. But whatever possible cases, whatever thrilling typologies one could propose,[17] we should focus on

[15] On the inductive move from analysis of the neutral level to the poietic, see Chapter 6, Section 2.

[16] Lortat-Jacob rightly observes, "in most cases (and this is the mark of an active tradition), the improvised musical construction goes through a precise act of will; improvisation brings into play a certain level of consciousness that may emerge as explicit, indeed, as verbal" (1987: 46).

[17] The reader is referred to the collected volume *L'improvisation dans les musiques de tradition orale* (Lortat-Jacob, ed. 1987), which bears witness to the intensity of European research directed toward the subject of improvisation during the past ten years.

the fact that, in all musico-symbolic forms, *process* coexists with stabler aspects.

As before, we cannot, in approaching improvisation, simply remain content with a single dimension. Symbolic forms give rise to interventions by poietic and esthesic processes, whether one is talking about the most frozen work (in which the performer is excluded, as in the case of music for tape), or the most free improvisation. But in open works, in minimalist music (Reich, Glass), and in music of the oral tradition, symbolic forms also create a dimension of *"process"* that is *consubstantial with their existential modality.*

Is this to say that such acts of musical production—for which the term "work" appears inadequate—must lead us to reject analysis of the neutral level? Doubtless this is what Lortat-Jacob has in mind when he writes, "research on improvisation invites the musicologist to go beyond conducting simple formal operations upon a body of music, because these operations, no matter what their breadth, constitute only the tip of the iceberg" (1987: 46). In reality, the music in question does indeed have a surface *style*; what we *hear* is not the process but the *result* of a process. Neutral analysis of improvised music, while necessary as a prelude to esthesic analysis, is also legitimate in its own right.

Lortat-Jacob adds, "confronted with the problem of improvisation, analysis has a duty to 'unglue' simple inventories, to disengage itself from transcriptions (to the extent that transcriptions themselves risk being superceded by an unpublished improvised variant), in order to go beyond the field of given realities, to consider virtualities" (ibid.). Of course, but—as the majority of essays that he has edited themselves prove—one is most often able to arrive at poietic characteristics by superimposing empirical documents (the transcriptions) upon models of reference that can in turn be inductively derived from those transcriptions, and that (implicitly or explicitly) are the starting point for the improvisations. As for the rest, Lortat-Jacob himself acknowledges that "research on improvisation . . . inventories actual materials and relationships (*in this, such research resembles study of any and all musical systems*);[18] above all, research on improvisation establishes principles that enable us to explain heretofore unknown relationships" (ibid.). Analysis of processes requires, in short, an alternation between analysis of the neutral level, which is relatively static, and poietic analysis, which is unquestionably dynamic.

Open works and improvisations, then, reinforce my claim that tri-

[18] Emphasis is mine.

partitional semiology must be adopted if we are to account for different kinds of symbolic forms. This remains true even though the unique nature of such processes demands that poietic models be assigned a dominant position. The tripartitional model, universal though it claims to be, remains valid only so long as it can be adapted to the natural articulations of the phenomena it studies, and can embrace the respective hierarchic weights of each phenomenon's component parts.

4

The Status of the Sound-Object

THERE is one musical domain that obviates the need to distinguish among the poietic, the neutral level, and the esthesic in defining a musical work—or so we might imagine. This is the domain of electro-acoustic music, also called in French "acousmatic music" (*musique acousmatique*; the name evokes Pythagoras's curtain, with its function of veiling sound from its source). The composer attempts to present a work as it is heard in the process of creation, without mediation by an intermediary. Pierre Schaeffer's theoretical work, *Traité des objets musicaux* (1966), is a piece of contemporary musicography that merits detailed examination, since it seems to challenge the usefulness of the tripartition.[1]

1. *The* Traité des objets musicaux *and Musical Semiology*

Upon initial examination, Schaeffer's *Traité* seems in fact to establish a distinction between poietic and esthesic similar to the one I have suggested, since Book I is entitled "To Make Music," and Book II "To Hear." In Book I, Schaeffer evokes primarily the existence of the studio, the machinery, and the procedures; he dwells on the fact that, during an audition, tape allows *not knowing* the technical or anecdotal origin of the sound that is heard. He makes a pregnant comparison between tape and Pythagoras's curtain, which separated the Master from his disciples and forced them to concentrate on the content of the discourse rather than on the gesticulations (or identity) of the producer. Thus Schaeffer introduces the notion of the acousmatic,

---

[1] This chapter recapitulates (with few changes) my article of the same title (Nattiez 1976), but omits the original introduction and conclusion.

and of "concentrated hearing" (*écoute réduite*), an idea further developed in Book II. The acousmatic dictates that a sound be described less in terms of its origin than in terms of its heard morphological qualities (form, mass, profile, and so forth).

If musical semiology's sole contribution were replacing what everybody calls "composition" and "perception" with barbarous neologisms like "poietic" and "esthesic," then semiology would entail risibly small profits. There is, of course, more to it than that. By "poietic" I understand describing the *link* among the composer's intentions, his creative procedures, his mental schemas, and the *result* of this collection of strategies; that is, the components that go into the work's material embodiment. Poietic description thus also deals with a quite special form of hearing (Varèse called it "the interior ear"): what the composer hears while imagining the work's sonorous result, or while experimenting at the piano, or with tape. By "esthesic" I understand not merely the artificially attentive hearing of a musicologist,[2] but the description of perceptive behaviors within a given population of listeners; that is, how this or that aspect of sonorous reality is captured by their perceptive strategies. In both cases, obviously, the entire enterprise assumes us to be capable of *giving a name to sound material*, so that relevant poietic or esthesic components might be identified and integrated into a model. The stakes offered by semiology are these: that recognizing, elaborating, and articulating the three relatively autonomous levels (poietic, neutral, and esthesic) facilitates knowledge of all processes unleashed by the musical work, from the moment of the work's conception, passing through its "writing down," to its performance. In short, semiology makes knowledge possible of the phenomenon we know under the name music, in its totality.

If this is indeed the case, does the *Traité des objets musicaux* provide us with tools for a semiological approach to electro-acoustic music? The treatise affirms throughout Book III that what we hear does not necessarily correspond to what is described by purely acoustic analyses; this would seem to be an excellent semiological tool. Schaeffer thereby recuperates the spirit of the distinction between acoustic phonetics and auditory phonetics, between acoustics and psycho-acoustics. Even though (as I see it) we cannot bring analysis of the neutral level down to merely acoustic analysis, the distinction suggested by Schaeffer reaffirms the difference between neutral and esthesic

---

[2] If not, one could declare that all musical analysis is perceptive—which is a tautology, since one always accesses sonorous reality through auditory perception. In Chapter 7, Section 1, I lay considerable stress on this.

levels. But before we can accept his distinctions as analytical tools, we need to explore his arguments in some detail.

Book I, "To Make Music," takes up a certain number of facts relevant to the *poietic* pole of description. Book I, however, like the later discussion of the so-called "descriptive memo [*fiche signalétique*] for the object" (Schaeffer 1966: 595), in fact gives us what amounts to a first, elementary recipe-book for composition. Several remarks by composers involved in the Groupe de Recherches Musicales are eloquent testimonials to this: the *Traité* never describes the link between the sound qualities of the musical object on one hand, and the mental operations of creation on the other. The question of this link has been broached by Schaeffer's disciples; according to Reibel, we must think about studio operations and the musical material that results from them; according to Dürr, we must thematicize the question of "access to the instrument" (by which he means the connection between making sound and creating music). The concept of musical "writing," so paradoxical when formulated in the context of electro-acoustic music, has been circulating within the group for some time: creating a work of electro-acoustic music depends on an agenda that is both technical and intellectual. To compose, one must dirty one's hands in the studio; to "write" a coherent work, one must have certain mental schemas of composition.

Does Book II provide material for an esthesics, in the sense that I have defined the esthesic? In working his way toward an inventory of different ways of hearing (in Chapter 6), in bearing in mind that the same sound may be heard various ways by different people, Schaeffer puts his finger on the basic difficulty in research on auditory perception: in any live hearing of a work, various separate esthesic behaviors will become hopelessly intermingled. Normal hearing, writes Schaeffer, is "by far the most complicated" (151). "One only hears what one wants to hear" (140). But the perceptual phenomenon that Schaeffer investigates is not the average listener's ordinary and habituated hearing. Instead, he discusses a very special form of hearing, a "concentrated hearing" that entails observing and lingering over a single sound-object, discerning all its facets (this principle is allied as much with cubist aesthetics as with phenomenology's *eidetics*). "With each repetition of a recorded sound, I hear the same object, even though I never hear it the same way, even though the unfamiliar becomes familiar, even though I would successively perceive different aspects of it, such that it would never be the same, still I always identify it as *this* quite securely determined object" (115). By means of this "concentrated hearing," the morpho-typology of Book V becomes possible.

Paradoxically, given Schaeffer's own subtitle "To Hear," this special perceptual phenomenon is not at all the same as those perceptual strategies of listeners as studied by *esthesics*. This is because Schaeffer has a conscious, idiosyncratic prejudice—the *Traité des objets musicaux* deals only with isolated sound-objects contemplated for their own sake, and not with sound-objects integrated into a musical work. "Discovery of sound-objects was primordial; it was necessary at first to create a great many of them, to determine their categories and families, even before knowing how they might evolve, how they might be sorted out and combined among themselves" (Schaeffer 1967: 27). Faced with the choice between investigating the material and investigating the work, Schaeffer chooses "the material alone" (1966: 38). Inspired by linguistics, he distinguishes three levels in musical works, comparable to the phoneme, word (or morpheme), and sentence; these are (a) the components that go into the sound-object, (b) the sound-object as a unit, and (c) integration of the sound-object into a structure, giving it meaning (1967: 36–37).

By staying on levels one and two, Schaeffer avoids consideration of larger structures in which sound-objects are included. But such an exclusion naturally raises an important question: how is this central poietic element—integration of sound-objects into larger structures—perceived? Ordinary perception of a sound-object within a work, of course, never operates independently of what precedes and follows that element. But Schaeffer's "lesson" of the skipping needle (*sillon fermé*), by isolating a sound-object from its context, creates a kind of perceptual "blockage": "the phonograph needle doubles back in the groove, causes us to hear an object that does not evolve, that congeals within time" (Schaeffer 1968: 286). "I arrived at an itinerary leading to sound . . . through experiencing a skipping needle (without that skipping needle, my method would doubtless never have seen the light of day)" (1966: 390). It is as if Schaeffer's theoretical thinking were unable to go beyond his experience of a scratched record. "Ordinary" hearing, on the other hand, owes its characteristics to the *temporal* nature of music—"music is motion in time," as Felix Salzer phrased it (1965 I: 30)—and to the successive perception of events, whose "being understood" is continually called into question by new musical events that subsequently appear. The difficulty of grasping "ordinary" hearing can be traced back to this fact.

If the methodological proposals in the *Traité des objets musicaux* correspond neither to the poietic nor the esthesic, why are they relevant? The *Traité*, as noted above, passes over one important poietical question entirely: the question of *access*—that is, of the *link* between studio and the sound-creation that results. But the poietic issue is not limited to this link alone. I believe that Schaeffer's "concentrated hearing" is, contrary to his own implicit claim, essentially poietical in that it is in fact hearing *as experienced by a composer, who hears sounds with extreme attentiveness before integrating them into a work.* Thus the morpho-typological descriptions of sound-objects are *primarily poietically* relevant. They do not emanate from the perspective of habituated, ordinary hearing, which Schaeffer himself favors as very different from "*specialized* hearing, the result of coaching or special competences, [which] loses the characteristic virtues of ordinary hearing, its universality and global intuition" (Schaeffer 1966: 121).

I have shifted Schaeffer's "concentrated hearing" to the poietic side with great care, and this shift may seem a bit academic. Delalande, for instance, prefers to speak of perceptual phenomena as a whole, distinguishing among them the perceptive behaviors of composers and those of listeners. There is nothing wrong with this as a working perspective; I will even grant that Delalande's inventory of the perceptual behaviors of listeners is useful in untangling the prickly issue of auditory perception. Yet this perspective also seems to me too restrictive, especially by comparison with musical semiology. Semiology, after all, seeks to grasp the phenomena associated with the musical fact *in relation to* the materiality of musical works. It seeks to investigate all phenomena involved in a musical fact—in which not everything is by nature and necessarily merely perceptive. (For instance, the poietic schemas for the work's construction may be abstract; the real question is, certainly, how many of them remain accessible to perception—but to know this, we need first to have identified those schemas from the side of compositional intentions.)

Schaeffer's morpho-typological descriptions may in fact become quite useful when we describe the listener's perception of a *sequence* of objects through time; that is, of the musical works themselves. This, in my view, is the only proper sphere for esthesics. If, while listening to a piece, one perceives links between various sound-objects, the nature of these links cannot be described unless an inventory of the constituent parts of each object is available. When different perceptive behaviors have been identified, when we know the principles that determine how and in what circumstances *this* behavior imposes itself on, or combines with, another behavior, then we shall need a descriptive inventory of the objects' traits (such as Schaeffer's) in order to identify those that are esthesically relevant.

Concentrated hearing thus has both an immediate poietic relevance and a more long-term esthesic relevance. What do we mean by this? Concentrated hearing is essentially a form of *arrested* perception, that of the composer in choosing materials for the work, and that of

95

the musicologist in describing them. But is this to say that *all* the sound-object's components are poietically relevant, or that *all* will be esthesically relevant? By no means. The level of description at which Schaeffer arrives is *neutral* (in my sense) precisely because not all identifiable traits within the object's material presence are necessarily relevant either to the poietic on one hand, or the esthesic on the other. Traits can be heard without having been intended, and they can be intended without being heard.

Description of the neutral level has either a poietic or an esthesic relevance, depending in large part on the type of work or music under consideration. Between the poietic and esthesic poles of musical "communication," the neutral level is *in motion*. In the case of the electro-acoustic music of the Groupe de Recherches Musicales, compositional strategies have been invaded by iterative perception of sound-objects to the extent that concentrated hearing is a priori poietically relevant. In studying the "throat games" of the Inuit, on the other hand, we are able to recognize a superimposition of two sound-objects (which therefore constitute what Schaeffer calls a "composite object"). One sound-object is low, one shrill, but each of these sounds is produced alternately by each of the two women, by means of an extremely complex procedure. In this instance, concentrated hearing is esthesically relevant, helping us to hear the configurations of a sound trace.[3]

In order to establish clearly the poietic relevance of neutral description, we need to know the composer's reasons for a given disposition of his objects. Neutral description's esthesic relevance will only be defined later, when we have a greater appreciation of those perceptive strategies that a musical work, in being unwound, brings into play. When Delalande says, "one might imagine that the listener, quite spontaneously, practices all these types of hearing,"[4] he collapses or confuses the neutral and the esthesic, by hypothesizing that ordinary perception is identical to "arrested" perception. "The analytical point of view," he has written, "must be the listener's point of view" (1974: 54). Yes, but on condition that the musicologist does not set him- or herself up as a "collective consciousness" of all possible listeners—that is, that a distinction can be made between what is

---

[3] Given the present state of research, we must be more exact, "relevant to a white listener's perception," since the indigenous peoples know how the games are produced, even if they do not themselves execute them, and they do not necessarily perceive them as we do.

[4] A statement he made in a truly remarkable broadcast on Berio's *Omaggio à Joyce*, produced by France-Culture in 1975.

"heard" in the silence of the study, and what happens during live listening, in real time.[5]

2. *The Communication Utopia*

In going a bit farther into Schaeffer's treatise, we realize why the status of concentrated hearing is ambiguous: we do not always know if Schaeffer's book is an academic research project or a treatise on composition. The *Traité des objets musicaux*, taken from the standpoint of its descriptive contents (its morpho-typologies), has an essentially *normative* air that precipitates us backwards into that old, nasty, normative rut of traditional musicology.

Music is made to be heard (so we read in the first pages of the book). Well and good, but there are two ways of understanding the import of "made to be heard": "it is music's nature to be heard" (which is self-evident) or "music must be conceived according to what will be heard." This is an entirely different kettle of fish. This latter statement (and not incompatible personalities) constitutes the real grounds for the divorce between the "concrete" and serial composers, between Schaeffer and Boulez as symbols for entrenched positions.[6] For the former, it is axiomatic that one renders unto others' hearing only what one hears oneself; the latter is preoccupied with an un-hearable system of thought that forms the basis for creating a work. Despite the fact that this concrete-serial issue involves musicians, neither side "listens" to the other at this point: it is a nondialogue of the deaf.

Schaeffer, however, has gone much farther. "Never separating *hearing* from *making*" (1966: 37) is no longer enough. We read (on the

---

[5] Obviously, one can well understand why the phenomena examined by Schaeffer and Delalande are qualified as perceptive: for Schaeffer, the "concrete" composer forbids himself from giving out, for others' hearing, anything that he himself does not hear. As for Delalande, the absence of a score gives him the impression that he is on the direct line to the perceived sonorous material. In reality, the situation of the musicologist who is de-composing a *written* work is no different from Delalande's: any paradigmatic analogy between two units is based, of course, on a perceptive judgment of their equivalence, but this analogy is not to be confused with properly esthesic research, that establishes how these units, identified in isolation, are then perceived in real time.

[6] See, for instance, Boulez's famous article on *musique concrète* in the *Encyclopédie Fasquelle* (reprinted in Boulez 1966: 285–86). During his lecture at Metz on 28 February 1976, I asked Boulez if his position had changed since I.R.C.A.M. opened an electronic and computer music division. Boulez: "only imbeciles don't change their minds, and in this case, I am an imbecile."

record jacket that accompanies the reissue of his *Études concrètes*)[7] that "the work is no longer an object that will respond to any and all questions; the relationship between subject and object is already inscribed within it. The work expects the listener to accept this relationship. If he or she moves outside, directs his or her attention to sound qualities other than those the composer has dealt with as values, the structure will escape; only chaos will be perceived." In other words, the listener *must* discover what the composer wants him or her to hear. Schaeffer is, in short, a man obsessed by communication. In his comparison between music and language (1966: Book IV), he does arrive at an idea of different levels (compositional, perceptual) in music. It appears, however, that he also hopes that linguistics will supply the secrets of human communication (in which language plays an exemplary and central role).[8] Knowing that music is not a language, he nonetheless hopes in the end that it might turn out to be one—if by "being a language" we understand his idea that compositional intentions can be transparent to the listener, thus "*compelling*[9] these new structures to complete a communication between those that cause them to be, and those who perceive them" (1957: xi).

This helps to explain his dismissive attitude toward "a priori *musics*," the music of early Stockhausen, of Babbitt or Boulez: "we are witnessing a divorce between what they want to write and what we know is heard" (1966: 614). But his condemnation of "a priori *musics*" is not consistent: in his *Que sais-je?* (on *musique concrète*), he proposes making an acousmatic description, by means of concentrated hearing, of works by Webern and Boulez (1967a: 51). These descriptions are *esthesically* relevent. (The poietic aspect of such music would have to be investigated in terms of the row, or of relatively abstract structures). If such analyses are possible, this demonstrates that "a priori *musics*" are, indeed, *audible*, in the sense that they can be listened to and interpreted. We do not, of course, hear those elaborate poietic structures. But why should we? Only those who continue to harp upon "communication" will insist that all compositional devices be perceived by all listeners. Boulez, a man who employs all his wits to shuffle the cards of his compositional schemas, has certainly never demanded that we unearth these carefully buried structures. Apart

---

[7] Philips 6521021, in the series "Prospective 21st Century."

[8] Nonetheless, if this was indeed Schaeffer's intention in 1966 (since I am, here, interpreting somewhat), he has largely been disabused of the illusion since. As he rightly says, "linguistics is not a science of communication, it is a science of the thing we call language" (response to the session "Pourquoi? Comment?" held on 25 February 1976 at Paris conference on the "Symbolics of Acousmatic Music").

[9] Emphasis is mine.

from all questions of compositional intentions, serial works at times command interest for their genuinely musical qualities.

A given type of music should not be condemned because its poietic strategies can never be captured by our perceptive strategies. In fact, a perfect balance between the poietic and the esthesic, in which poietic and esthesic strategies closely correspond, seems to be the rarest of birds in the history of music; perhaps this was realized only in the Classical Era. If we compel the composer to write in terms of what the listener is able to hear, we flirt with the danger of *freezing* the evolution of musical language, whose progressive development comes about through *transgressions* of a given era's perceptual habits. We should not dream of issuing some kind of strict command, of enforcing identity between what is given to be heard, and what is actually heard: that would be (among other things) a gesture that would deny history.

Schaeffer's critique of "a priori *musics*" can in fact rebound against electro-acoustic music itself. Despite all the good will in the world on the part of the "acousmatic" composer, it is quite possible that such works will not actually be heard in the way he or she wished them to be. The *Traité* includes a critical passage bearing on this issue: "in the most scrupulous *Étude aux objets* [here Schaeffer is making a pun on the title of one of his own pieces] perception of structures prevails immediately over perception of objects. So much so that the results we derive are often quite different from what we expect in hearing the object itself. It is frustrating to see the structures enhancing criteria (often unexpected ones), enhancing functions within objects *other* than those functions one had wished to make them assume" (1966: 488). Here, clearly stated, is an acknowledgment that hearing on the level of the object cannot be the same as hearing on the level of the work. In other words: concentrated hearing does not correspond to the esthesic, and compositional intentions to render something hearable do not guarantee a corresponding perception in the listener.

Schaeffer's argument is based on what I will call the communication utopia, since the *normal situation* in musical, linguistic, or human "communication" in general is precisely the *displacement* between compositional intentions and perceptive behaviors. Because perception bears upon an object that *materially* is the same as the one that was created, description of musical "communication"—that is, of the passage from the poietic to the esthesic—must be grounded in knowledge of those elements that make up the sound material. Such knowledge is supplied by analysis of the neutral level, and, in the case of isolated sound-objects, concentrated hearing furnishes such analysis with a great number of necessary tools.

3. *The Concept of the Object and the Thread of Musical Discourse*

Toward 1975, the composers of the Groupe de Recherches Musicales reopened debate on the concept of the sound-object. In my own view, the sound-object is an ambiguous phenomenon, by reason of its semiological essence. It is first and foremost a *poietic* unit (as it is, essentially, in the *Traité*); Schaeffer never conceived electro-acoustic works as anything other than "studies upon objects." In the recordings of *Solfège de l'objet sonore*, Schaeffer declares that his experiments in "training the ear" "from the outset avoid indicating agency"; that is, indicating the *source* of the sounds (1967b).

When it became a question of hearing works, rather than sound-objects, there was an acknowledgment that sound-objects have an esthesic function that had not been forseen in Schaeffer's essentially poietical interpretation. In making this subsequent acknowledgment, the composers of the Groupe de Recherches Musicales stopped conceiving musical works as mere successions of objects. The concept of the sound-object "leads to confusion," wrote Michel Chion, "in this sense: that it evokes this object as if it were a ball that hearing grasps so to speak in the blink of an ear, when actually sound *unscrolls itself*, manifests itself within time, and is a living process, energy in action" (1975: 65). "The value of the musical object defines itself in terms of criteria invested in the work by the object in order to fulfil a given function with what precedes or follows it" (Dürr 1976: 52). Thus the concept of sound-object becomes resolutely *esthesic*. In this, has the notion of a sound-object lost all analytical interest? Only if we believe that the fundamental objective of analysis is reconstructing the intentions of the composer (a traditional musicological assumption). The sound-object is no longer the basis for the Group's compositional practice, but the concept does retain *its descriptive validity on the neutral level*. The sound-object is nothing more than a unit, and we always need units in describing the materials and the organization of pieces. In going from one work to another, from instrumental music to electro-acoustic music, the dimensions of the units, their functions, the hierarchical structures in which they are integrated, the depth of their articulation, may all change. From the analytical standpoint, the main problem will be deciding how we go about making segmentations of these units.

The concept of the sound-object has turned out to be *poietically* limited for composers, because its status as an *arrested* fact is hardly compatible with the temporality of all musical works. One American composer seems nevertheless to have succeeded in reconciling the static character of the object with its insinuation into a linear course: Steve Reich. In Reich's minimalist works, the same pattern is heard to the point of saturation, then a tiny variation is introduced. We need a little time before realizing that we are in a new sequence, because the pregnant quality of the previous sequence acts upon our perception of the following one. In other words, we need simultaneously to grasp characteristics of a single object, and to experience the link established in the *succession* and *enchaining* of object-sequences. It is as if Reich were writing out Schaeffer's avatars of perception. The composer prepared the work by hearing many sound-objects again and again. For the listener to penetrate these objects, the work must be created out of iteration itself.

For many years now the composers of the Groupe de Recherches Musicales appear to have discovered a *sense of musical duration* through other means, in works such as *L'expérience acoustique* by Bayle, or *De natura sonorum* by Parmegiani. Of all these individuals, which one is creating what Molino (referring to literary narrative) called the thread of the discourse in modern music; whose is the dominant creative voice?[10] Let us return for a moment to Stockhausen's *Gesang der Jünglinge*, or to Berio's *Omaggio à Joyce*, or hear Boulez's *Répons*: a certain *logic of continuity*, achieved on the basis of relatively sober sound material, explains in great measure the success and (in the end) the value of all these works.

The objectives of semiological analysis of contemporary electro-acoustic music should, then, be clear. On the neutral level, it would be easy enough to identify and describe the sound-objects that make up these works, to describe the laws governing their succession and their integration into various syntactic arrangements, on various levels. We would then, from this *arrested* description of the material, *proceed to extract* those constituent traits that account for a sense of continuity within the succession of isolated moments that make up the work. But this essentially esthesic explanation (we perceive a "sense of continuity") will never be possible unless one first has access to a material description of the work; that is, to an analysis of its neutral level.

[10] "What is a narrative?" (unpublished lecture given at Montreal in March 1975).

5

Musical Meaning: The Symbolic Web

MUSIC as a symbolic fact is characterized by the presence of complex configurations of interpretants. As a symbolic fact, music has the potential to *refer* to something; it has *referential* modalities [modalités de renvois].* In Chapter 1, I gave a general description of meaning as "existing when an object is placed in relationship to a horizon." But what horizons of experience might a musical work evoke?

First of all, these horizons are immense, numerous, and heterogeneous; my object is not to draw up an exhaustive list, but instead to try to inventory the field, to give a sense for the great diversity of possible dimensions of musical meaning. This is a critical issue, since it thus links music to other human facts—biological, social, and cultural—and constitutes music as an essential part of man's anthropological aspect. Blacking saw this clearly when, in a small but very important book, he asked the question, "How Musical is Man?" As in Chapters 2 and 3, however, I will show that anthropological investigation is not far removed from semiological investigation.

If I insist upon underscoring the size and difficulty of the question of musical meaning, this is only by way of attempting to suggest certain guidelines for issues that crop up regularly in reflections about music. Yet I also wish to stress from the beginning that musical semiology (given the current state of research) will not necessarily provide the answers to all the questions it raises.

* Translator's note: *Renvois* has most often been given in the gerund form *referring*, rather than the noun form *reference* (which in English implies both the object and the process of referring to something), in order to retain the active, dynamic sense of the French. In some cases, however, where "referring" was simply too awkward in English, "reference" was used instead.

1. *The Universe of Musical Symbolism*

What sorts of interpretants are associated with music? The objective of this chapter is to propose a first cartography, and I shall take as my point of departure a convenient classification suggested by psychologist Robert Francès (1958: 259–60), whose results (obtained during tests dealing with musical perception) suggest differentiating among four kinds of judgments.

(1) Normative judgments (personal evaluations, judgments of taste).

(2) Objective judgments, or judgments of a technical nature, about the properties of the musical stimulus (timbre, tempo, vibrato), the form of the music (genre, historical style, parts), or the type of writing.

(3) Judgments about meaning, in which the subject attributes to the stimulus a content referring to an extramusical referent. Francès sorts them into three types:

(a) an individual referent: "the meaning relates to some kind of personal experience"; "meaning is accompanied by images, or is not."

(b) concrete meaning: a specific aspect of nature, phenomenon in the outside world, or dramatic situation.

(c) abstract meaning: psychological traits (happiness, playfulness, serenity), or generalized representations (order, disorder, hierarchy).

(4) Affirmations of interior order related to the psychological effect experienced by the subject.

I begin with normative judgments to emphasize, as does Molino (1984b), that the Beautiful is irreducible: there is no musical fact that does not engender an evaluative reaction—I like that, I do not like that. This includes the societies of the oral tradition, to which we shall return.

With the so-called objective judgments, we are plunged into the middle of an issue essential to reflecting about music: is music a pure play of forms; in other words, does it refer to nothing but itself, or does it inspire external associations? We will see below that musical aesthetics is divided down the middle, according to whether music is characterized "in essence" by its capacity for intrinsic or extrinsic *referring* [renvois]. We shall also see that various conceptions of musical semiology are founded principally upon this basic conception—at once ontological and semiological—of music. The fact that Francès includes objective judgments in his list of verbal associations for music is sufficient to remind us at any rate that all observations about musical substance will always be mixed up with semantic judgments. (These latter are designated by his categories 3 and 4.)

For the sake of simplification, and following the familiar convention, we will call *"semantic"* any sort of *extrinsic* association with music, and we will call *musical semantics* the discipline that deals with explicit verbalizations of these associations, associations that (in current experience) most often remain in the state of latent impressions. In so doing, I am adopting for my own purposes one usage of the word "semantic" currently accepted by experimental psychologists. When we attempt to connect these associations to the musical material that has unleashed them, then we return to musical semiology strictly speaking, since semiology seeks to describe the link between a signifier and a signified (though I prefer to say between a sign and its—extrinsic—interpretants).

Generally, verbal associations with music are drawn from an experience of the world unique to each subject, and the manner in which a subject reacts to music is similarly mediated by the listener's *socio-cultural* baggage. But we should also stress the *biological* anchoring of symbolic associations. Molino suggests distinguishing between a *coenesthesic* dimension of musical symbolism and a *kinesthesic* dimension.[1] By coenesthesia, we can understand the impression, or the emotions, that result from nonspecified internal sensations that inhabit our bodies. Taking his lead from Leroi-Gourhan, Molino sees in the coenesthesic the biological anchoring of the *Beautiful*: to say that one likes or does not like a musical work is to symbolize (or verbalize) an organic reaction.

The kinesthesic concerns the impression of movement that one feels in certain portions of the body. If music rouses us (as Combarieu once wrote) it is because "it incites us to be [literally] moved" (cited in Francès 1985: 342).

In the discussion below, there will be no question of opposing Nature and Culture, but rather the contrary—showing that if musical symbolism is at first directly connected to the body, then the biological basis of musical semiosis is a component part of the semiological fact only insofar as there *is* symbolization, and that this symbolization subsequently takes a specific form, and follows the contours dictated by the individual's experience of the world and his or her socio-cultural milieu.

---

[1] Personal communication with the author, July 1982. I would like to thank François Delalande and Jean-Christophe Thomas for making the transcription of these conversations with Molino.

2. *Musical Beauty*

At times (notably in France during the structuralist era) it has been fashionable to sneer at the existence of the Beautiful and at the legitimacy of aesthetic reflection. Little by little we have witnessed the return of the Beautiful, but it crept in through the back door: fashion dictated that we should speak of *pleasure* (Barthes 1973; English trans. 1975) without ever alluding to beauty; that is, we should speak of pleasurable or unpleasurable feelings that an object provokes in us. The thing that distinguishes a purely functional train whistle (as a warning signal before a level crossing, for example) from a train whistle integrated into a work of *musique concrète* is that the latter can be the object of an aesthetic evaluation, even if this is not the composer's wish.

In the past few years, there has been another impediment to acknowledging the Beautiful: the idea that indigenous musics do not have any meaning (for the native person) except in the institutional role they play within the culture (most often in the context of work or religion). This idea is current among ethnomusicologists influenced by narrowly functionalist currents in anthropology. What is at issue in recuperating the Beautiful is not, however, the repudiation of a strong functional dimension in music of the oral tradition. We know that repertories may die out when their function disappears. Nevertheless, the presence of functional aspects does not imply that the aesthetic aspect is squeezed out. Feelings of love appear to be a universal characteristic of human beings; it would be most surprising if some feeling for the Beautiful were not equally widespread. But this universality does not mean that the feeling always manifests itself, translates itself, in an identical way from one era to another, or from one culture to another.

One of the great virtues of ethnomusicology's anthropological orientation (now that it is emerging from its strictly functionalist phase) will, in retrospect, have been a new interest in "ethnotheories," in the conceptions that indigenous peoples form of their own music.[2] We have gradually discovered (by examining the metaphorical language borrowed from the conceptual universe, especially the religious universe, unique to each culture) that the "savage mind" can also operate in the realm of music theory, with a precision that is a bit disturbing for smug western feelings of superiority. This is the import of work

[2] The conclusion of this section recapitulates certain passages from my article "Le beau et le primitif" (Nattiez 1983c). (The editors of the journal—without consulting me—changed my original title, which was "Peut-on dire d'une musique de tradition orale qu'elle est belle?" ["Can we say that music of the oral tradition is beautiful?"]).

done in France by Hugo Zemp,[3] and in the United States by Steven Feld (1982). In the case of the Kaluli, studied by Feld, a leap of an octave is designated by the image of a waterfall, which is metaphorically charged—but then, so are our western concepts of masculine and feminine themes, inherited from the nineteenth century.[4] Feld's book ends with a chapter on "Kaluli aesthetics," in which the aesthetic emotions experienced by the Kaluli are described in terms of qualities associated with birds. Emotions analogous to our own aesthetic reactions are, clearly, experienced by indigenous peoples, but are not expressed in the same way. These different expressive modalities are exactly what a yet embryonic "ethno-aesthetics" (Marshall 1982) will have to identify and categorize.

Fragments of such an "ethno-aesthetics" exist here and there. Herndon and McLeod (1973) were able to show that the popular musicians of Malta employ a detailed hierarchy of surnames to evaluate the quality of execution and the inventiveness of improvising performers. I was able to ascertain that among the Inuit, performers and listeners expressed preferences for this drum-dance song rather than that one, and that these preferences varied from one person to another. This does not necessarily translate into an abstraction like our western concept of the "Beautiful," but it does at least signify the existence of attitudes and tastes, as manifested by the participants.

In fact, even in a western context, the conception of the Beautiful varies according to individuals, groups, and eras; it is combined with other factors. Aesthetics has attempted to define this transcendental object. But aesthetics will also have to try to develop a "calology." In other words, now that metaphysics is dead, we must categorize variable criteria of the Beautiful within our own culture. In other words, we must undertake for the West the same aesthetic anthropology demanded by study of musics of the oral tradition.

These claims, these suggestions, may seem banal. If so, they nonetheless deserve to be stressed, above all when we remember the recent popularity of certain structuralist myths—like the myth of "fixed societies"—which would have us believe that, within a narrowly defined community, everyone shares the same values and thinks in a one-dimensional way. The studies cited above in fact contribute to smashing these simplifying views, and make us realize more and more that, in traditional societies, musical thought—since what we encounter is indeed musical thought—proves to be as complex and

[3] Cf. his film on the "Are" are (produced by the C.N.R.S. in Paris) and articles in *Ethnomusicology* (1978, 1979, 1981).

[4] We shall return to this issue of the metalanguages of indigenous peoples in Chapter 8, Section 2.

heterogeneous as in ours. This is not to say that we do not encounter dominant ideas now and then among certain generations, groups, or eras—*there*, again, as much as *here*. The content, the modalities of these ways of thinking will, however, be different.

3. *Aesthetics and Musical Meaning*[5]

This section is no whirlwind tour of the history of musical aesthetics. In English, the recent anthology *Music in European Thought 1851– 1912* (Bujic 1988) gives an overview of primary sources for the romantic and modern eras. The point of this section is, rather, simply to recall that many great aesthetic doctrines took sides (each in terms of their own problematics) in an oft-argued question: is music a nonsemantic or a semantic art, and, in the case of the latter, how? This area of musical semiology thus broaches problems that have preoccupied humanity for many years.

There are two convenient classifications of musico-aesthetic conceptions—that of Leonard Meyer in *Emotion and Meaning in Music* (1956) and that of Etienne Gilson in *Introduction aux arts du beau* (1963). I shall use these two classifications because they favor the semantic aspect.

For Gilson, the history of aesthetic ideas divides into four large families, each reacting against the previous one—which is not to say that they cannot at certain times coexist. These doctrines are imitation, expressionism, symbolism, and formalism. Aesthetic theories for which music has the capacity to reproduce, express, or symbolize meaning, feelings, or more generally any reality exterior to the work correspond to the first three. For the fourth, musical meaning is conveyed by music itself in an immanent and intrinsic fashion.

Doctrines of imitation are based, naturally, on the principle *ars imitatio rei*. This was not a problem as long as music was primarily vocal, but the appearance of instrumental music on a large scale in the classical era distressed the philosophers: "sonata, what do you want of me?" exclaimed Fontenelle. D'Alembert extricated himself from the dilemma by pirouetting around it: "[music] imitates just as well as any other art, so long as we are considering something that music would be able to imitate." Thus the slide toward expressionism gradually begins, since what music is best able to imitate is emotion: "at issue is knowing if the artist's work is or is not an expression of emotion or feelings, an expression that we like to think is an artistic

[5] This section is a revision and development of pages 129–34 of the *Fondements*.

translation of these feelings" (Gilson 1963: 91–92). But the solution to this problem is not an easy one—hence the idea of "substituting the notion of the symbol for that of expression, since symbol is more flexible and is above all more general" (ibid.: 99). Thus one avoids having to determine where the sentiments are situated: in the consciousness of the artist or in the work itself. Music is an "unconsummated symbol," as Suzanne Langer would say (1941: 189) in a work that figures in the history of musical thought, but that does not lead to an *empirical* analysis of symbolic functioning.

Formalist doctrines may be considered as reactions against various semantic conceptions of music, and they are hardly new. For Descartes, the musical work does not have a unique expressive power: "the same thing that makes some people want to dance, may make others want to cry" (letter to Mersenne of 18 March 1630; cited in Roland-Manuel 1963: 87). Descartes, it should be noted, does not deny the existence of music's semantic effect, but as Boyé would write more than a century later (1779), "to inspire passions, and to express them, are two absolutely different things" (cited in Roland-Manuel 1963: 89). For Chabanon (in his *Observations sur la musique* of 1779), music is moving because it is in motion; this is the analogy that "allows us to call this art imitative when it is imitating very little" (ibid.: 90).

The decisive turn was taken in 1854 with Hanslick's essay *Vom Musikalisch-Schönen*: "the beauty of a musical work is *specifically musical*—i.e., it inheres in the combinations of musical sounds and is independent of all alien, extramusical notions" (English trans. 12). Varèse writes that "I believe my music is not able to express anything other than itself" (1983: 41), and Stravinsky, that "I consider music, by its nature, incapable of expressing anything, whether a feeling, an attitude, a psychological state, a natural phenomenon, etc. Expressiveness has never been an immanent feature of music" (1971: 116). Yet this game with labels is actually not so simple, since Hanslick also referred to "those charming reveries, by means of which music soothes us," and Stravinsky did not deny that in the *Rite of Spring* he had wanted to "express the renewal of the natural world" (cited in Chailley 1963: 408).

This is where the categories proposed by Meyer may be useful. For Meyer, there are on one side *absolutists* who believe that musical meaning is based exclusively on the relationships between the constituent elements of the work itself, and on the other *referentialists* for whom there cannot be meaning in music, except by referring to an extramusical universe of concepts, actions, emotional states, and characters. (1956: 1) But this first dichotomy is mirrored in another that does not exactly correspond to it: the *formalists* who (according to Meyer) do not acknowledge that music can provoke affective responses (it has an intrinsic significance given to it by the play of its forms), and the *expressionists* who acknowledge the existence of feelings. But though formalists are necessarily absolutists, expressionists will be absolutists if (for them) the expression of emotion is contained in music itself, and they will be referentialists if the expression is explained in terms of music's referring to the external world. This can be represented in Figure 5.1.

Meyer, using this classification, writes that "when formalists such as Hanslick or Stravinsky, reacting against what they feel to be an overemphasis upon referential meaning, have denied the possibility of relevance of any emotional response to music, they have adopted an untenable position partly because they have confused expressionism and formalism" (1956: 3).

Now, if there is one thing that the "formalists" admit, it is music's potential for arousing emotions. Stravinsky did not say that music does not provoke associations in us, he said that, from the immanent standpoint, music is not expressive. The same attitude is adopted by Hanslick: music gives birth to feelings within us, but this is only a secondary consequence of the musical fact.

In order to understand Hanslick's position, we need to distinguish what is for him an *empirical* claim: "far be it from us to underrate the deep emotions which music awakens from their slumber" (English trans. 26), and a *normative* position: "if contemplation of something beautiful arouses pleasurable feelings, this effect is distinct from the beautiful as such" (English trans. 18). We should not forget the subtitle of *Vom Musikalisch-Schönen*: "an essay in the *reform* of musical aesthetics" (emphasis is mine).

With the help of the tripartition, we can summarize Hanslick's position according to its two chief dimensions:[6]

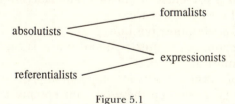

Figure 5.1

---

[6] The following is a summary of a long commentary on Hanslick's aesthetics from a semiological point of view, from the preface of the French translation of *Vom Musikalisch-Schönen*, *Du beau dans la musique* (Nattiez 1986).

The empirical point of view:
(1) from the poietic side, emotion exists in the composer, but does not manifest itself except in a purely musical form;
(2) on the immanent level, music's content is its form;
(3) from the esthesic side, emotion is the result of the form's effect, and its origin must be sought in the music itself.

The normative point of view:
(1) Poietic: one should not write program music, or imitative or sentimental music. In opera, music should occupy the predominant position.
(2) Immanent level: "the Beautiful is nothing more than form" (French 16).
(3) Esthesic: perception is not exempt from emotions, but it must try to elevate itself to pure contemplation of forms.

Hanslick as an exemplary case shows us how risky it might be to place our trust in the more or less clear connotations of a word like "formalist." I had to combine two series of variables—the opposition of the empirical and normative dimensions on one hand, the poles of the tripartition on the other—to nuance the Hanslickian conception into six large propositions.

Once beyond this methodological difficulty, the study of Hanslick's text has considerable merit. It clarifies the following point: knowing to what extent music does (or does not) possess a semantic dimension depends less on empirical observation than on an a priori ontology of the essence of music. But at the same time, since Hanslick's system of thought is also inscribed in history, it invites consideration of this ontological position not as an absolute, but as a way of thinking about music proper to a given era and culture.

The different positions quoted in this section in any case bear witness to one constant: thinking on musical aesthetics oscillates between two extremes (as represented in my diagrammatic summary of Meyer's analysis). These extremes are:

—The formalist-absolutist position: music means itself.

—The expressionist-absolutist position: music is capable of referring to the nonmusical.

The history of musical aesthetics may well impress us as a kind of pendulum, swinging between these two conceptions, across a whole spectrum of intermediary nuances. We should, nevertheless, remember that different conceptions often coexist, as in the Romantic era, when Hanslick was set against his contemporary Richard Wagner. But across the ages, one or the other takes *a dominant position*, as did the formalist position after World War II. The dominance of one or the other position owes a great deal, I believe, to the importance and esthesic success of the musical schools that embody them. Let Boulez be the leading man in the neo-serialist school, and we are ready to acknowledge that "music is a nonsignifying art" (Boulez 1981b: 18), but let Stockhausen sucessfully make music into a vehicle for cosmological visions, and music once more bears meaning.

4. Musical Semiology and Musical Meaning

This polarity crops up again in works by writers who have attempted to define the nature of musical meaning; especially writers who specifically make use of musical semiology. We can divide them into two large families, depending whether they ascribe to music a capacity for referring to something external, and whether the option chosen depends on an empirical claim, or a personal, philosophical, even metaphysical choice.

To me it seems telling, first of all, that all these writers have reached a consensus in acknowledging that music has two *referential* options, though at the same time they invariably put greater weight on one or the other of these options.

Jakobson thus distinguishes between *introversive semiosis* and *extroversive semiosis* of music (1970: 12). This terminology parallels that employed by Bright, who takes up terms first used by Guizzetti, and applies them to a comparison between language and music: he makes a distinction between *endo-* and *exo-*semantics (1963: 28–29). We find the same distinction in Stockmann (1970: 81), who differentiates between "semantisch" and "exosemantisch." But Jakobson makes a choice between introversive and extroversive semiosis: "instead of aiming at some extrinsic object, music appears to be *un langage qui se signifie soi-même* [phrase in French in the original]. Diversely built and ranked parallelisms of structure enable the interpreter of any immediately perceived musical signans to infer and anticipate a further corresponding constituent . . . and the coherent ensemble of these constituents. Precisely this interconnection of parts as well as their integration into a compositional whole acts as the proper musical signatum" (1970: 12). In other words, musical units manifest a semiological peculiarity; they refer first (according to Jakobson) to other musical units either already heard or yet to come: "The code of recognized equivalences between parts and their correlation with the whole is to a great degree a learned, imputed set of parallelisms which are accepted as such in the framework of a given epoch, culture, or musical school" (ibid.: 12).

Jakobson does not deny the existence of "the emotive connotation carried by music" (13), but this semiological dimension is not, as he sees it, primordial: "in poetry and in the bulk of representational visual art the introversive semiosis, always playing a cardinal role, co-exists and coacts with an extraversive semiosis, whereas the referential component is either absent or minimal in musical messages, even in so-called program music" (12). With this he appeals, implicitly, to the basic notion of Prague functionalism, dominance:[7] introversive semiosis is dominant in music. Jakobson offers us a distinct semiological image for music, yet this image, to me, seems tinged with normativism.

The same conception of music, and the same problem of normativism, is encountered in conductor Leonard Bernstein's *The Unanswered Question*: "music has instrinsic meanings of its own, which are not to be confused with specific feelings or moods, and certainly not with pictoral impressions or stories. These intrinsic musical meanings are generated by a constant stream of metaphors, all of which are forms of poetic transformations. This is our thesis" (1976: 131). We will explain below what Bernstein means by "metaphor" and "poetic transformation"; we shall see that these signify the same "code of recognized equivalences" mentioned by Jakobson. We shall also see how the technique of paradigmatic analysis allows us to describe these equivalences. For the moment, however, we can simply stress the fact that Bernstein, in playing Beethoven's Pastoral Symphony for the audience at his Norton Lectures, demanded that they "[rid themselves] of associations," and "[shed] extramusical associations" (1976: 187). In short, what was required was "to hear the music as music only" (189).[8]

For Jakobson, as for Hanslick, Stravinsky, and Bernstein, music is first and foremost a play of forms. Though they do acknowledge a certain esthesic effect of an emotional kind, for them it exists *despite* the purely formal nature of music. The semiological definition of music suggested by Jakobson depends a priori on structuralism: the proper *being* of music and of poetry, according to Jakobson, resides in their structures.[9] This is the same conception of musical meaning

---

[7] Cf. his essay of 1935, "The Dominant."

[8] One could cite many other arguments in the same vein, made both by musicians and musicologists. We should mention here Deliège's recent work on intrinsic meaning in his study of tonality (1984: 26–35; 252–66), which will be discussed in Volume 2, apropos the experimentalist approach.

[9] Milan Kundera (1984) hypothesized a causal link between the emergence of Prague structuralism and the importance of music in the cultural life of Czechoslovakia. Jakobson's ideas in fact go back to the beginning of the century, and were born in Russia,

that is found in Ruwet's work (also quoted, incidentally, in Jakobson 1970).

> Music's meaning cannot manifest itself except in descriptions of music in itself . . . the signified (the "intelligible" or "translatable" aspect of the sign) is, for music, conveyed by the description of the signifier (the palpable aspect). Our only means of access to a study of musical meaning is, indeed, a formal study of musical syntax, and a description of the material aspect of music on all levels where music has a real existence. (Ruwet 1967: 91)

We might think that we can characterize Ruwet's position as "formalist-absolutist." On the level of his deep aesthetic and ontological convictions, this is probably true. Yet it is precisely the extrinsic dimension that he cannot escape. This becomes clear in a passage (which I discussed in my first essay in semiology, Nattiez 1971) that reproaches me for conceiving musical meaning as a purely extrinsic thing:

> Linguists, structuralists, and practitioners of generative grammar have taught us that internal examination of a system is more important than examinations of its psychological or physiological circumstances . . . analysis of a fragment, a work, a collection of works, the style of a given epoch, if sufficiently detailed, would enable us to disentangle those musical structures that are homologous with other structures, those arising from reality or lived experience; it is in this homological correspondence that the "sense" of a musical work is unveiled. Let us take a simple example. Suppose there is a fragment of tonal music made up of two parts, A and A′; A ends with an interrupted cadence, and A′ begins the same way but ends with a perfect cadence. Within the framework of the tonal system, the first part will obviously be interpreted as a movement, directed toward a certain point, but interrupted or suspended; the second as repetition of the same movement, this time continued to its end. We see in this instance that simple description enables us to extricate a certain structure—movement, sketched then suspended, then repeated and continued to its end—that is homologous with an indefinite set of other structures that might be found in reality or lived experience. I would see in this homological correspondence what one can call the (partial) meaning of the fragment in question, and it

---

in the work of the Russian Formalists. But it is not impossible that the cultural milieu of Prague tended to favor the development of structuralism; in any case, the suggestion is intriguing.

is clear that only an internal, formal analysis allows us to extract it. (1972: 13–14)

Thus, when Ruwet affirms that musical meaning situates itself in the homological correspondence between a formal musical structure and an external structure belonging to lived experience, he reintroduces an extrinsic dimension, since he has compared the musical form to an affective or corporeal state. To say that an interrupted cadence is "movement sketched, then interrupted," is to introduce a semantic judgment that derives its data from an extramusical sphere. Only the notion of homology, itself rather problematic, allows him to rescue his fundamentally immanent conception of musical meaning.

The distinction in French between *sens* (sense/meaning) and *signification* (meaning/what is signified) has sometimes been exploited by writers who then choose to speak of "purely musical *sense*": "music is only rarely reduced to the state of conveying a meaning (*signification*); it is sufficient that is has a sense—like the waters of a river, however, not like a syllogism" (Mâche 1969: 287). "When music is at issue, we have avoided the use of the word 'meaning,' which is too directly evocative of a code, or the connection between signifier and signified, something purely arbitrary that would make sound refer to a concept. On the other hand, it seems difficult to deny that music has a sense" (Schaeffer 1966: 377). "One can engender sense with notes, if by sense we understand the expression proper to melody" (Dufrenne 1967: 84–85). I will not enter into a subtle exegesis of this semantic difference, which leads straight to the Tower of Babel once we start bringing in Frege's "Sinn" and "Bedeutung," not to mention "sense" and "meaning" (in English). In French, the word *sens* seems to connote more a meaning proper to structures, and *signification*, as opposed to *sens*, the process of referring to lived experience, to something outside the structure itself. This jockeying for position should at least serve to remind us how Hanslickian aesthetics endures, even today: the sense of music resides in form itself.

Not all these writers, however, inscribe themselves within the same tradition.

One encounters the dichotomy present in Jakobson and Bright in Coker's *Music and Meaning*, in which the author distinguishes between *congeneric* and *extrageneric meanings* (1972: 34). All internal formal relationships correlate with the former: "*congeneric musical meanings* are those resultants of a predominantly iconic situation in which someone interprets one part of a musical work as a sign of another part of that same work or a different musical work ... *extrageneric musical meanings* are those resultants of the iconic sign situation in which someone interprets a musical work or some portion of it as a sign of some nonmusical object, including sounds not then organized as part of a musical work" (61). But Coker accords more or less equal weight to both kinds of referring; he devotes five chapters to the former and three to the latter. In a reversal of the structuralist position, he states that form can indeed serve quite nicely to convey extrinsic meaning, "a fundamental objective of a musical work is, in general, its extrageneric reference to the attitudes and responsive behaviors of listeners and performers, which constitute the basic meaningful interaction of music and listener or performer" (153).

This is similarly the position adopted by Deryck Cooke, whose *The Language of Music* not only affirms that music conveys content, but endeavors to show exactly *which* musical configurations correspond to certain determined contents. "Only a certain type of music to a certain degree can legitimately be regarded as pure, quasi-mathematical form . . . music does in fact express composers' subjective experience" (1959: 10). For Cooke, compositional intention (from the poietic side) aims for the transmission of a message: he admits no doubts. Leonard Meyer's position is only a tiny bit different; he acknowledges the coexistence of "absolute" and "referential meanings" within a single work (1956: xi), but for Meyer, extrinsic meanings, whose existence he freely admits, are of secondary importance: musical meaning exists when a musical event gives rise to expectations for another event, within the framework of a given style (35), and in this (to borrow his own terminology), his position remains that of an expressionist-absolutist.

It is time for me to expose my own position in this debate, since this position will inform the remainder of the book. No one will be surprised to hear (after all that has been said so far) that I consider the concept of the *nature of musical meaning* itself as a semiological phenomenon, to the extent that, in each epoch, culture, or theory, a certain greater or lesser *weight* will be accorded to music's internal or external *referring*. Two facts seem conclusive here:

(1) Intrinsic referring is considered by at least two writers (Jakobson, Coker) to be a matter of *semiosis*. This claim allows an escape from an intenable position that takes (most often only by implication) the meaning of human language as a model for all types of meaning, musical meaning in particular.

This, unfortunately, is a mistake made by more than one semiologist, including the most important. Benveniste, for example, wrote that "musical 'language' consists of combinations and successions of tones, divided up in various ways; the basic unit, the note, is not a sign. Each note is identifiable within the scale of which it is a part; none is endowed with significance.[10] With music, we have a typical example of units that are not signs, that do not designate anything, being merely the steps of a scale whose extent is established arbitrarily. Here, we are following a principle that discriminates (among all systems based on units) between systems with signifying units, and systems with nonsignifying units. In the first category is language, in the second, music" (1969: 128). For Benveniste, then, there cannot be a musical semiology, no more so than for Françoise Escal: "music does not possess signs" (1979: 37). But in order to make this claim (admitting the formalist position to be true), the notion of the sign must be limited to "something that refers to the exterior world." In fact, one cannot develop a semiology for a special domain such as music, except by agreeing to inventory *all possible forms of referring* without limiting oneself to the single example of referential modalities in verbal language. Otherwise we run the risk of overlooking the *symbolic specificity* of music. In the case of music's referring *intrinsically*, we would then distinguish (adopting Coker's theory) between *intramusical* and *intermusical* reference (1972: 62).

(a) Jakobson insisted upon the first of these, *intramusical referring*, in the passage cited above. I shall show (in Volume 2) that the paradigmatic techniques suggested by Ruwet, in the tradition of Lévi-Strauss and Jakobson, allow us indeed to analyze a good number of relationships between musical units. Having reached moment *y* in a musical work, we tend to establish a connection with an *x that has already been heard*. Analysis of the neutral level allows us to categorize *possibilities* for establishing these relationships.[11]

But the technique of paradigmatic analysis (on which I lay a certain emphasis because it is an original method of analysis, developed during a period of contact between linguistics and semiology) is not the only means of describing relationships involving intramusical referring. A given moment in tonal music opens up a whole range of possibilities for that moment's future development. Meyer (influenced both by the Schenkerian concept of prolongation and by information theory) has elaborated upon this important aspect of musical *semiosis*, "one musical event (be it a tone, a phrase, or a whole section) has meaning because it points to and makes us expect another musical event" (1956: 35). In this sense, Meyer's entire oeuvre can be considered by rights a musical semiology. We had to wait for a recent article

[10] By "significance," Benveniste means the capacity to signify.

[11] In this, analysis of the neutral level can constitute a preliminary to esthesic analysis. Cf. below, on the notion of inductive esthesics (cf. p. 141).

by linguist Robert Austerlitz to see this conception of music styled as "semiological" (though Austerlitz apparently was not aware of Meyer's work): "the meaning that is conveyed by a musical text is basically deictic, cataphoric, in the sense that it is *prediction*. The musical text makes reference to the future, in that it challenges the listener to predict the shape of the musical substance to come in the immediately impending future—on the basis of the musical substance perceived in a given moment" (1983: 4). "If anything can be called meaning or *semiosis* in music, then it is the experience required to predict immediately impending musical substance" (ibid.: 6). Once we have recognized the existence of this type of musical meaning, the problem will be to determine the type of analytical tool appropriate to the analysis of musical expectation.

An attempt will be made in Volume 2 to show that these two types of intramusical meaning each demand two genres of analytical methods: taxonomic analysis on one hand, and a (post-Schenkerian) analysis of musical connections on the other, an analysis that would take account of music's dynamism.

(b) What is the process of *intermusical referring*? Essentially, it is that through which we associate a particular music with a larger musical universe, to which it belongs. This is, in effect, style; and in Volume 2, without rehashing the history of stylistic analysis in music, I shall offer an extended reflection on the semiological nature of musical style and our methods for describing it.

(2) The fact that I fully acknowledge the existence of *intrinsic referring* does not mean that I will *reduce* musical *semiosis* merely to the play of forms. We have seen that Ruwet was forced to take extrinsic meaning into consideration. Thus (and this seems to me critical), no one ever denies that there are two types (intrinsic, extrinsic) of music's capacity for referring. Later on, when we have specified the nature of introversive *semiosis*, and possibilities for extroversive *semiosis*, we will attempt to grapple with the difficult matter of the connection between these two *semioses*. We will then be in a position to evaluate the semiological differences between music and language. We can, however, affirm (to the extent that practice and theory in western music convince us of the *relative autonomy* of introversive *semiosis* in comparison to the extroversive) that one of the semiological peculiarities of music is owed to the existence of *two* domains, intrinsic and extramusical referring.

This position implies no ontological prejudice on my part, since I do not claim a priori any preexisting connection between the two kinds of *referring*. Similarly, I would not say that the composer or the listener privileges sometimes one, sometimes the other, since I believe that (on the poietic as much as the esthesic side), the two are inextricably mixed. Only because they are different by nature, and for the sake of analytical clarity, can (must) they be distinguished from one another.

But I would be contradicting my own previous statements if (in bad faith) I should deny the existence of an implicit ontological position on my part. If as prisoner to my own rules of the game I must confess what I profoundly believe *to be the case*, I would say that musicians and musicologists, following the tendencies of their age and their personal convictions, are led to privilege one of the two semiological dimensions to the detriment of the other. These two semiological dimensions are always present in all musics; I believe also that it would be wrong to confuse the variable *representations* that musicologists or musicians make of music (through their arguments or their behaviors) with an assumed intemporal essence of music. If there is an *essential being* of music defined from a semiological vantage point, I would locate that being in the *instability* of the two fundamental modes of musical referring.

5. Referring Extrinsically

Turning to a characterization of music according to its possibilities for extrinsic symbolization, we can establish a division into three large fields: the spatio-temporal, the kinetic, and the affective.

Music is an experiencing of time, in an immediate fashion, because it unrolls linearly, because it is an alternation of sound and silence and (from one period to another) a particular way of filling silence. Imberty, in his second essay on musical semantics (entitled—significantly—*les Écritures du temps*), insisted with some force on this aspect of music.

Francès has recapitulated the general observations of his predecessors,[12] giving them a scientific basis: "almost all our emotions, Goblot established, tend to evoke movements within us" (1901: 69). Francès writes:

> The kinship between rhythmic and melodic pattern in music, and the patterns of gestures that accompany behavior, represents one of the basic elements of music's expressive language . . . the basic psychological states (calm, excitation, tension, relaxation, exaltation, despair) normally translate themselves as ges-

[12] From here on, I have adopted (with revisions) pages 147–57 of the *Fondements*.

tural forms that have a given rhythm, as tendencies and ascents, as modalities for organizing fragmentary forms within global forms (constant repetition, diversity, periodicity, evolution) . . . the transposition of these rhythms, tendencies, and modalities of movement into the sound-structure of music constitutes music's basic expressive language. (Francès 1958: 299)

Or, to cite Imberty's summary of Francès, "a significant connection between a subject's emotional state and physical, corporeal effects has been established. This connection is sufficiently strong that after a subject experienced music as evoking *either* a corporeal pattern, *or* a psychical attitude or state, the connection between the two would re-emerge in the verbal description the subject was asked to make, taking the form of responses that made reference to movement as well as feelings" (1975: 95).

This explains the tremendous richness of music's *representational* capacities: go from low to high, and we create movement. We could cite a number of examples: in *Parsifal*, the descent to earth of the angels bringing the Grail is said to be represented by ever-lower pitches (Goblot 1901: 68). In Scene 3 of *Das Rheingold*, "the pattern of violins and tubas represent the spiraling motion of a monster crossing the stage" (Combarieu 1893: 130). In Mendelssohn's *Spinning Song*, the spinning wheel is evoked by an ascending and descending melodic line (ibid.). Musical movement similarly enables Bizet, in the *Scènes et jeux d'enfants*, to describe a swing, a top, and a shuttlecock in music (ibid.). The same thing happens in *La toupie* by Pierné, and in Debussy's *En bateau* (Goblot 1901: 67). In Mozart's *Don Giovanni*, the play of the swords in Act I is rendered by the rising violin scales. In *Tristan*, the movement of the sailor who sings his song up in the rigging is paralleled by movements in the violin (Horowicz 1946: 199).

Movement, of course, creates a space; to do this musically, one essential procedure involves volume. "In *La damnation de Faust* (Berlioz), the ear has the impression of an object closer or farther away from the characters, depending whether the horns play *f*, *mf*, or *pp*" (Combarieu 1893: 132). In the *Ring*, the volume of the backstage horn tells us Siegfried's location in relation to the scene on stage. Music can also evoke the form of objects; Fafner the Dragon is assigned to the contrabassoons, the elephants in *Carnival of the Animals* to the basses. "In the *Creation*, Haydn uses the lowest notes of a bass voice to tell us of the great oxen who till the soil with heavy step" (Goblot 1901: 75). In *Don Giovanni*, the evocation of the cemetery's horror is assigned to the horns; and the terrors of the commendatore to horns and trombones *ff* (Siohan 1955: 118). High, rapid, or plucked notes are, conversely, used to suggest light things; we think of the storm in the Pastoral Symphony, or the clouds of sparks in the finale of *Die Walküre* (Goblot 1901: 75). The low/high opposition, with all the possible intermediate steps, constitutes the point of departure for *connotative chains* that refer to various orders of reality, even to colors (dark for low sounds, light for high sounds) (Belvianes 1950: 192), doubtless by means of a mental process that makes an identification of depth with darkness, and height with light.

The analogy between music and sensations induced by a psychological state, it seems, must be kept in mind here, in order to explain the semantic mechanism at work in the preceding examples. "A music will be tender, melancholy, calming, depending whether the sensations of hearing that it causes correspond to emotional tenderness, melancholy, or peace" (ibid.). We should, nevertheless, remember the detail added by Francès: "if we have been able to verify experimentally and rigorously the association of height with high notes and lowness with low notes, the association of high notes and low notes with other, visual qualities, like luminosity and other variations in intensity, has only been the object of infrequent, partially controlled experiments, or of isolated individual testimony" (1958: 333).

A psychological and emotive sensation of calm has its origins in a physical given and here we have arrived at a kinetic model: "every melody encloses a kinetic scheme involving certain musico-rhythmic resources . . . that can be projected as space, figured as a contour of bodily movement or bodily repose appropriate for characterizing an attitude, a state, or a feeling" (Francès 1958: 314–15). In melody, in effect, organization of duration (length of the notes, silences) can be interpreted in the sense of a motor or driving force: tonal amplitude suggests amplitude of movement; finally (as we saw), the direction of the melody suggests a movement from high to low or vice versa (ibid.).

This is why music does not merely represent the movement of objects, but also the movement of feelings deriving from the bodily movement that music *provokes*. But this is not automatic—there is not, there cannot be, by virtue of the *specific processes of symbolization*, a one-to-one correspondence among a musical signifier, the movement aroused, and the feelings evoked. The problem, Francès says, is to "know what, in the experience the individual has of his psychological states, of his emotions, of his feelings, tends to enter into the patterns of musical meaning. What is accessible to musical symbolization, what are the rhythmic types of segmentary kinesthesia and the degrees of tension and relaxation" (1958: 339). Further on, Francès writes, "access to meanings does not reside in some rudimentary imitation of expressive contents, an imitation that maintains these meanings in musical form. This access consists solely in the *recognition* (implicit or not) of a familiar structure within an aesthetic construction, whose stylization of that familiar structure may be more or less pronounced, up to the point where nothing remains of the structure but a simple turn or aspect that generally recalls a manner of being" (ibid.: 343). As he explains once more, the biological given (heart rhythm, contractions of smooth muscles, depth of respiration) is a sort of framework, on the basis of which musical symbolization constructs itself: "who would not know to take account of the differences connected to each nuance of a feeling, each meaning of an attitude" (ibid.: 340).

Emphasizing certain degrees of the scale within a melody, or a chord, could provoke a specific psychological state. For Max d'Ollone, the diminished seventh chord expresses a particular feeling of anxious expectation, and for this reason Puccini uses it in *Madame Butterfly* to underscore Cio-Cio-San's vigil, as does Berlioz in *Roméo et Juliette*, and Tchaikovsky in the *Pathétique* (1954 I: 113). The diminished seventh chord is a pivot chord to many keys; it evokes aberration, uncertainty, trouble. If it resolves to a perfect triad (as it frequently does in Liszt, Schumann, or Chopin) it releases a feeling of light, of triumph. On the other hand, the sense of aberration increases if seventh chords follow one another in succession (as in Meyerbeer and Wagner) (see Francès 1958: 369), which explains why Wagner's music seems to be in such a constant state of tension.

All tonal music similarly seems to play semantically with certain fundamental centers of the tonal system. The tonic degree has always given the impression of closure and rest, "just as the resolution of a dissonance into a consonance," Goblot wrote, "is synonymous for us with 'relaxation, reconciliation,' so an uninterrupted sequence of dissonances are equivalent to 'incessant movement, agitation, disorder, a feeling of evolution' " (cited in Francès 1958: 363).

One might think that all these symbols have a natural basis, but we should remember that we never believe so strongly in the naturalness of things as when we have become totally conditioned to them. This is the case, for example, with musical spatialism: the lateral localization of sound sources depending on variations in volume or intensity. The distance seems greater with the lowering of the volume, or with a predominance of low notes. Analogously, the higher a sound, the more "elevated" it seems, as Pratt's tests confirm (1930). According to Rèvesz, "when a sound of a given frequency is heard, the localization of that sound is effected by a sensation of 'resonance' in some area of the body proper: chest, head, abdomen (independent of the question of vocal training)" (cited in Francès 1958: 310).

For a western musician, these perceptions are an "automaticized associative result" that is based, in the end, on a series of connotations of this kind:

high   shrill   clear   happy   joyous   (and so forth)

low   deep   dark   sad   tragic   (and so forth)

But it is by no means certain that these symbols have a natural basis. Francès reminds us that "before getting any musical education, children do not in any way situate high and low sounds in space" (310). In Greek, Arab, and Jewish music these associations are reversed. According to Francès, the spatial associations cannot be strictly biological in origin (high notes are sung in head voice and low notes in chest voice) because women and men do not produce vocal sound in the same way.

Chailley, in an article written after Francès's book, has shown that this apparently natural symbolism is based on *convention*:

Among the liturgical chants for the Ascension, two successive pieces set the text *ascendit Deus*, a phrase that one would suppose eminently suited to an ascending musical direction. Now, only one of the two contains the expected musical representation. The nonrepresentational piece is older, and anterior to the linguistic convention in which a high pitch is called *high* and a low pitch *low*; this convention, in turn, appears to arise at the same time as the adaptation of diastematic notation, which in effect pictures melodic movement on paper. What originally *was* an *association* of external ideas with musical essence, has ended, through a long and constant *praxis*, by being *idenitified (for us) with this essence itself*, in such a way that it would be impossible for us (without repudiating all our instincts), to abandon this convention, which we take (in good faith) to be musical expression itself. (1963: 411)

Chailley gives a striking example: "Debussy, in setting the falling of Mélisande's ring in Act II of *Pelléas*, initially (in the first draft) indicated an ascending harp passage; he corrected it later: the ring falls, the passage descends" (410). Combarieu had noted, "we cannot imagine a musician using tenor instruments to illustrate hell, and bass instruments to illustrate heaven" (1893: 129). He also shows how, in Massenet's song "Sous les branches," it is possible (with variation in registers) to describe real space in music: "in a high register, a series of arpeggiated seventh chords creates a descending motion; and below this pattern of sixteenth notes (whose symbolism would seem self-evident) a single accented note is held through three measures. Suppose this note, instead of being put two octaves below the series of arpeggios, had been put two octaves higher: this musical gesture will translate an entirely different idea; the scene would be located above the branches, and not below them" (131). This single registral example shows that the musical signs that symbolize space can take different forms: in Ravel's *Daphnis et Chloé* (an example given by Francès), timbral effects, a progressive rise in tonal register, and crescendos of volume combine to engender a sense of space (1958: 312–13).

We can, of course, acknowledge that many meanings that we perceive as "natural" are the result of codified systems to which we have become acculturated. The Greek system, the *ethos*, associated moral character with genres, modes, and rhythms. For Ptolemy, the chromatic contracted the soul, while the diatonic fortified and expanded it. In Plato and Aristotle, each mode reflects a state of the soul: the mixolydian reflected an unhappy and serious soul; the dorian evoked for Aristotle a sense of the grandiose, for Heraclitus of the gloomy and energetic. Certain degrees of the scale are determined by the *ethos*: the tonic is active as a final, others are not active in that position, and so forth (Francès 1958: 350). In the Far East, musical scales and their degrees are connected to a cosmology, to the planets or the hours of the day (ibid.: 348). Combarieu (1893) cites a "sidereal" scale, in which the D represents the moon, the C Mercury, the B♭ Venus, the A the sun, the G Mars, the F Jupiter, and the E Saturn.

It is nevertheless impossible to find the smallest natural relationship in these conventional codes between the referents and the musical signifiers. The connection is, in effect "established through the influence of an exterior determinism, social, religious, which is applied to an art at a specific historical moment, and ends by rendering the connection 'naturally' self-evident, as are all long-established associations" (Francès 1958: 361). Only a musical apprenticeship allows access to a convention that praxis institutes a posteriori.

The *ethos* of tonalities has also attracted the interest of classical composers. The question of tonal *ethos*, raised by Plato in *The Republic* (III: 398) and the *Laws* (800c–802b), was taken up again by Zarlino (1558), Mersenne (1627), and Saint-Lambert (1707). A complete table of modal *ethos* can be found in the *Résumé des règles essentielles de la composition et de l'accompagnement* of Marc-Antoine Charpentier, and in Chapter 24 of Rameau's *Traité d'harmonie*. Rousseau also speculated on the question. Schubart devoted considerable thought to it in the chapter of his *Ideen* devoted to tonal symbolism (1806). In the nineteenth century, Hoffmann offered a number of interpretations in *Kreisleriana*. In the early twentieth century, Albert Lavignac established a similar listing in the "Aesthetics" chapter of *la Musique et les musiciens* (1942: 424).

Table 5.1 collates suggested interpretations of tonal symbolism from Charpentier, Rameau, Hoffmann, and Lavignac. If the table seems puzzling, this is because the discrepancies are difficult to account for. Still, could we imagine Rachmaninoff's Prelude in C♯ Minor (which, according to tradition, represents the despairing efforts of someone buried alive to escape his tomb) in C minor or F minor? To what do the various keys owe their expressive differences, since the relationships among notes within all scales follow the same pattern? Did Beethoven choose F major for the Sixth Symphony (the "Pastoral") because F major is (according to Lavignac) a "bucolic, pastoral" key? Or is it not rather that we (with Lavignac) associate a bucolic character with F major because Beethoven picked it for the Pastoral Symphony? The fact that Charpentier and Rameau speak of F major in terms of an "atmosphere of anger and fury," leads us to wonder whether Lavignac was not primarily thinking of Beethoven when he made his table. For Francès, these various tonal attributes have an "institutional" character that works to suppress "the possibility of casting doubts upon them, wondering about them in terms other than the theological—in terms of a 'discursive universe.' The tonal codes are quite numerous in Europe up to the twentieth century, and depend for their essence on a process of mental analogy. To learn music is not merely to learn an arrangement of notes compatible with the tonal system, but also to command all the twists of a signifying code, one that is not always coherent, not always explicit" (1958: 252).

What conclusions can we draw from this panorama? Musical semanticism has biological, psychological, and cultural bases, but we must beware of all reductive or mechanistic explanations. Above all, we must not confuse music's meaning, properly speaking, with *translation* of that meaning, since verbalizing music's meaning is itself a special type of symbolization. Francès has already drawn attention to this difficult question: "musical meaning is not identical to the meaning of the word, or phrase that emerges, because the attitude these words or phrases give rise to is univocal . . . semantic judgment applied to music is only the last link in a process that, if it remains nonverbal for some individuals, is no less real and effective (on this prereflective level). If musical signification is potential, this potentiality is based on a psychological reality that may well remain latent, as a

Table 5.1

Tonalities	M. A. Carpentier	Rameau	Hoffmann	Lavignac
C major	cheerful and warlike	liveliness, rejoicing		simple, naive, free, common
C minor	gloomy and sad	tenderness, lamentation		somber, dramatic, violent
C# minor				brutal, sinister, somber
Db major			alarming color	full of charm placid, suave
D minor	solemn and devout	sweetness, sadness		serious, concentrated
D major	joyous, quarrelsome	liveliness, rejoicing		gay, brilliant, alert
E minor	effeminate, amourous, plaintive	sweetness, tenderness		sad, agitated
E major	quarrelsome, shrill	songs tender, gay or grand, magnificent	firmness, courage, brilliant, glittering	brilliant, warm, joyous sonorous, energetic
Eb major	cruel and hard	?	?	?
Eb minor	horrible and hideous	?	?	?
F major	raging and quick-tempered	storms, rages	passionate dialogue	pastoral, rustic
F minor	gloomy and plaintive	tenderness, lament, dismal		morose, sorrow, energetic
Gb major				soft, calm
G major	sweetly joyous	songs tender and gay		rustic, gay
G minor	severe, magnificent	tenderness, sweetness		melancholy, suspicious

Table 5.1 (*cont.*)

Tonalities	M. A. Carpentier	Rameau	Hoffmann	Lavignac
A♭ major			gracious spirits	soft, caressing, pompous
A♭ minor			country of eternal desire	dismal, anguish, very somber
A minor	tender and plaintive	?	tormented charm	simple, naive, sad, rustic
A major	joyous and pastoral	liveliness, rejoicing		free, sonorous
B♭ major	magnificent and joyous	storm, rages	rustic, springlike	noble, elegant, gracious
B♭ minor	gloomy and terrible	gloomy songs	?	funereal or mysterious
B minor	solitary and melancholy	?	?	savage, somber, energetic
B major	hard and plaintive	?	?	energetic

vague impression, as long as the subject's own prejudices do not dictate that it be made verbally explicit" (1958: 275–76).

Semantic potentiality: on this basis, certainly, we can attempt to outline music's semiological specificity. Music can refer in two different ways—intrinsically and extrinsically. In this, it represents a superimposition of two semiological systems. For users of music, composers, performers, and listeners, all participants in a "total musical fact," musical material will establish connections to their lived experience and to the exterior world. These semantic interpretants will be split between the poietic and esthesic, and semantic analysis of a musical work must be able to verify whether the meaning that a composer invests in the work is perceived and understood by performers and listeners—and if so, how. But musical material's play of forms is itself a semiological system, inasmuch as it functions and develops independently of the extrinsic meanings conveyed (tonality is one good example). In contradistinction to human language, musical discourse does not strive to convey conceptually clear, logically articulated messages.

For this reason, we may well ask whether one can speak of such things as "musical narrativity."[13]

6. *The Narrative Impulse*

Can we say that when we hear a musical work, it is explicitly narrating something? When I read the phrase "the marquise went out at five o'clock," I don't need a *title* to know what has been narrated. When I hear the beginning of *The Sorcerer's Apprentice*, I have to know that I'm dealing with a symphonic poem in order to approach the work with the intention of hearing it as narrative. This is a trivial example, but, if music could, in itself, constitute a narrative as language can constitute a narrative, then music would speak directly to us, and the distinction between music and language would disappear.

Nonetheless, if so many composers have chosen to write works with explicitly literary titles, this must be because they have confidence in music's semantic possibilities (as discussed in section 5). Where, then, does the shoe start pinching?

Musical discourse inscribes itself in time. It is comprised of repetitions, recollections, preparations, expectations, and resolutions—and in the realm of melodic syntax, Meyer has gone farthest in classifying what one could call the techniques of continuity (as we shall see in Volume 2). If we are tempted to speak of musical narrative, we do so because music has this syntactic dimension. Literary narrative also involves expectations: "the marquise . . ."—what did she do? She went out. We have not been told that. When did she go out? "At five o'clock." To do what? We'll find out later. Here there are, in principle, no ambiguities in identifying the actors, or the nature of their actions. Linguistic syntax, as we know, is grounded principally in a subject and a predicate, and the predicate tells us what has been

[13] The following discussion is based on excerpts from a paper presented at the *Royal Music Association* Meeting in 1989. My conclusions were in many cases informed by the far-reaching discussions on this subject at the Stanford-Berkeley conference on musical narrative in May 1988; I would like to thank Karol Berger and Anthony Newcomb for inviting me to participate in the latter. Carolyn Abbate's *Unsung Voices: Opera and Musical Narration in the Nineteenth Century* (Princeton: forthcoming, 1990) is a provocative and disturbing study of the question of musical narrative, one that in some ways parallels my own views on the matter.

stated concerning the former. There is a logical connection between the two.

In music, however, connections are situated within the sonorous discourse, not on the level of a story that this discourse is said to narrate. When I hear a march in Mahler's second symphony, I imagine that it's got something to do with a band of people, but I don't know *which* people. The march may come closer, or fade into the distance; two processions can cross one another (as in Ives's *Three Places in New England*), but I don't know where they are coming from, or where they are going. Hearing *Till Eulenspiegel*, I can (aided by the title) recognize that it deals with the life and death of an individual. I hear how he runs, jumps . . . but what, exactly, is he doing? I cannot know. "Music has no past tense," as Carolyn Abbate rightly observes. It can evoke the past by means of citations or stylistic borrowings, but it cannot narrate, cannot speak what *took place* in time past (1990: Chapter 2). Literary narrative is an invention, a lie. Music cannot lie. The responsibility for joining character-phantoms with action-shadows lies with me, the listener, since it does not lie within *music's* semiological capabilities to join subject and predicate. If the listener, in hearing music, experiences the suasions of what I would like to call the narrative impulse, this is because he or she hears (on the level of strictly musical discourse) recollections, expectations, and resolutions, but does not know what is expected, what resolved. The listener will be seized by a desire to complete, in words, what music does not say, because music is incapable of saying it. Such things are not in music's semiological nature. Music, to cite Adorno's paradoxical comment on Mahler, is "a narrative that narrates nothing" (1976: 117). When I see initials carved into the trunk of a tree, they unleash in me, the onlooker, a *narrative* behavior: John loves Mary, or Mary loves John, or John and Mary are in love, or here on this spot, John met Mary, or John remembers Mary, or Mary remembers John. Interpretive freedom remains immense, since in this case, as with music, the narrative does not exist except as a virtual object. For music to elicit narrative behavior, it need only fulfill two necessary and sufficient conditions: we must be given a minimum of two sounds of any kind, and these two sounds must be inscribed within a linear, temporal dimension, so that a relationship will be established between the two objects.

Why does this happen? Human beings are symbolic animals; confronted with a trace they will seek to interpret it, to give it meaning. We ascribe meaning by grasping the traces we find, artworks that ensue from a creative act. This is exactly what happens with music.

Music is not a narrative, but an incitement to make a narrative, to comment, to analyze. We could never overemphasize the difference between music, and music as the object of metalanguages to which it gives rise. Only thus can we start to outline its symbolic functioning. Since music remains an "unconsummated symbol," to cite once more Langer's happy phrase, the semiological status of discourse about music is a tremendous problem. Musical semiology must attempt to resolve it.

II

The Semiology of
Discourse on Music

6

The Object of Musical Analysis

1. Three Music-Analytical Elements:
Object, Metalanguage, and Method

UP TO THIS POINT, we have dealt with the musical fact as a symbolic fact. But we cannot advance farther in the semiological approach to music without bringing the investigation to bear upon analysis itself. An analysis in effect states itself in the form of a discourse—spoken or written—and it is consequently the product of an action; it leaves a trace and gives rise to readings, interpretations, and criticisms. Although we find the tripartite dimension of all symbolic forms in analysis as well, analysis is nonetheless not merely a semiological fact comparable to others discussed so far. Analysis exists because it deals with another object—the musical fact being analyzed. In other words, discourse about music is a *metalanguage*.[1] Consequently, an epistemological and semiological examination of analysis involves three elements:

(a) *The object.* The object of a science is not an immediate given; all description, all analysis considers its object from a certain standpoint. Characteristic standpoints determine how the object is articulated by the observer; I will call this collection of standpoints the observer's *analytical situation*. There are at least three factors involved in this *situation*: the physical dimension of the corpus being studied, the question of stylistic relevance, and the tripartition. Depending on the standpoint adopted, a certain number of *variables*, of *parameters*, will

[1] Scruton has reproached me for using this term (1978: 174). In response, we might refer to one of the greatest French specialists in empirical logic, Pierre Jacob, who writes, "Tarski's solution rests on a distinction between language and metalanguage: *whatever the object-language being considered* [emphasis is mine], whatever the universe of discourse, the predicate 'true,' applied to phrases in the object-language, is not a predicate of the object-language but of the metalanguage" (1980: 114).

be filtered out of the actual substance of the musical object; the aim of this chapter is to examine the implications of this from a semio-logical angle.

(b) *The metalanguage*. This leaves a trace. What are the *types of discourse* used in musical analysis? The metalanguage has a *poietics*, and I will examine a number of elements that determine an analysis's orientation. The metalanguage is itself the object of *readings*: how is analysis structured, what is the influence of analytical discourse on music itself? Chapter 7 will take up the semiology of musical analysis per se.

(c) *The methodology* of analysis. Analysis is no pure reflection of the object (music). There is, in the analytical process, a transition, controlled by implicit or explicit *procedures*, from the work to the analysis. Chapter 7 will also allude briefly to the methodology of analysis, but Volume 2 will grapple constantly with this question, which is at the heart of a semiological interrogation of music.

One might regroup these three elements of musical analysis as in Figure 6.1. In what follows in Part II, I will elaborate upon certain aspects of this conception.[2]

Why is it so important to inventory all factors that intervene in an analysis? We might consider the reasons to be both epistemological and pedagogical: One cannot help but be struck by the diversity of analytical styles on the market, particularly in the case of divergent analyses of the same piece. As well, these days it is important that we help our students understand the how and why of these different approaches, and their divergences in dealing with the same object. This divergence, troubling as it may be for the novice, should not be thought of as some sort of institutional scandal. *It is, instead, the inevitable result of the symbolic nature of musical and analytical facts*; that is, it results from the fact that we are presented with a very large latitude

---

[2] Influenced by Molino's critical analysis of Barthes (1969), I had proposed an analogous diagrammatic analysis in Nattiez 1972a, classifying the different elements of musical analysis influenced by linguistics. In the diagram here, I have eliminated the aspect of "return to the corpus, by means of validation," in the original diagram, which posed difficult problems (they will be discussed elsewhere). A French archeologist, Jean-Claude Gardin has proposed an analogous approach in his *Une archéologie théorique* (1979: 57, 177, 242), which in essence provides a critical framework for analysis of constructions of the work for the discipline of archeology, but which could apply to all sorts of humanistic disciplines. This is not the place to mount a comparison of the two approaches, but I have added to my original diagram of 1972 (and would add to Gardin's perspective) the symbolic dimension, for which the tripartition can account. The existence of the symbolic (absent from Gardin's considerations) prevents me from endorsing entirely his otherwise brilliant and sensible analyses, notably his critique of J.-P. Roux's analysis of a Konya Stele (Gardin 1979: 184–202).

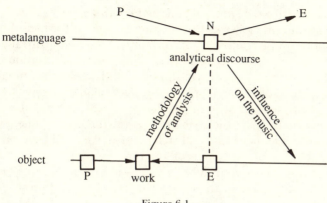

Figure 6.1

of choice between all possible interpretants released by the corpus being studied.

This is why it matters that we *thematicize the objectives* of an analysis, especially when we are reading an already existing analysis. What does the author want to tell us about? This question, if kept in mind, will prevent us from reproaching the author for not having done what he or she did not want to do, or could not do. This is also the case with analyses yet to be written; we can thus avoid idle questions and misunderstandings. A musicologist always takes a stance, locates him- or herself (consciously or not) opposite a corpus in a certain way, in his or her *analytical situation*. In the remainder of this chapter, we will be looking at various aspects of this process of situation.

2. *Analytical Situations*

(a) The first aspect of an analytical situation is this: what is the *physical dimension* of the corpus being examined? Are we analyzing an isolated piece, or does our work bear upon a group of pieces? The question may seem academic, and has seldom been raised (see, however, Nettl 1964: Chapter 5). In fact, this aspect dictates the nature of our analytical approach. It is not the same thing, for instance, to study a work for its own sake, to describe the style instantiated by the work, or to establish stylistic constants within a collection of works.

(b) In all these cases, the initial situation chosen determines the level of *stylistic relevance* that preconditions our view of the object. We might represent levels of relevance in the form of an inverted pyra-

135

mid.[3] At the tip we have traits unique to a given work (which can be deduced from other works in the same group, with which the piece in question can be compared). From there, we ascend through more general levels of relevance: the style characteristic of a certain period in a composer's oeuvre (early, middle, or late Beethoven, for instance), or the style characteristic of a particular instrumental genre by that composer (the style of Beethoven's late quartets); the totality of Beethovenian style; the style of a genre (the concertante style) or of an epoch (Viennese Classical style). Farther up, we have the tonal system (or some other system of reference)—which, as we shall see later on, must also be considered a style—and finally the universals of music. All analysis implicitly or explicitly adopts one of these levels of stylistic relevance; it may even happen that an analysis "navigates" from one level to another. I believe that a rigorous analysis, one conscious of its objectives, must specify exactly the level of stylistic relevance on which it is located.

(c) Besides the physical dimension of the corpus studied and the stylistic relevance, there is another analytical situation that will be chosen (again, explicitly or implicitly) by the musicologist: is he or she describing the work's immanent structures, its relation to history or to compositional processes, or the way in which it is perceived? If many analyses mix up the three poles of the tripartition, there are on the other hand many that exploit one of the three. Musical semiology does not constitute a revolution in musical analysis, and in the following discussion, I will borrow examples of poietic, immanent, and esthesic analysis from the classic musicological repertory.

In an article already cited (Molino 1975a: 50–51), Molino was able

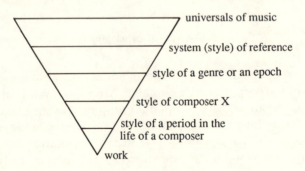

Figure 6.2

---

[3] Obviously, I am not the first to point out the hierarchicization of stylistic phenomena, even if the pyramidic diagram is original; see (for instance) Nettl 1964: 177; or Boretz 1972: 146. Meyer has, independently, proposed the same view.

to show that the history of musical analysis, at the beginning of the eighteenth century, was displaced from the poietic vantage point (how does one produce a work?) toward the esthesic (how is a work perceived?). Attention later shifted to the immanent level, with Hanslick taking the aesthetic tack (as we have seen) and Riemann developing formal technical analysis. This shift to the immanent level occurs even though, in most cases, there is a confusion among levels: with formal analysis, for instance, the expectation is that the analysis will correspond to strategies of production, though this is not guaranteed a priori.

One can try to classify various analytical standpoints in terms of the tripartition, and show that each option (i.e., a poietic, immanent, or esthesic bias), even when it claims to deal with the "essence" of music, will leave aside things that the other options consider analytically relevant. I borrow my first, exclusively poietic definition of analysis, from Jacques Chailley, who taught an entire generation of musicologists at the Sorbonne, "since analysis consists of 'putting oneself in the composer's shoes,' and explaining what he was experiencing as he was writing, it is obvious that we should not think of studying a work in terms of criteria foreign to the author's own preoccupations, no more in tonal analysis than in harmonic analysis" (Chailley 1951: 104). The question is, obviously, how these compositional preoccupations might be identified. It seems natural a priori to *explain* a work from the composer's point of view, or (enlarging the perspective) from the vantage point of an epoch or culture to which that work belongs.

But there are other musicologists who put forth an equally legitimate point of view: "analytic discussions of music are often concerned with processes that are not immediately perceivable. It may be that the analyst is concerned merely with applying a collection of rules concerning practice, or with the description of the compositional process. But whatever his aims, he often fails—most notably in twentieth-century music—to illuminate our immediate musical experience" (Fay 1971: 112). "True analysis works through and for the ear. The greatest analysts are those with the keenest ears; their insights reveal how a piece of music should be heard, which in turn implies how it should be played. An analysis is a direction for performance" (Cone 1960: 36). Or, still again, "it seems only reasonable to believe that a healthy analytical point of view is that which is so nearly isomorphic with the perceptual act" (Thomson 1970: 196). How can we deny such claims? Is music not made to be heard?

A type of analysis that could be styled immanent *did*, of course, develop; it proposed to engage the properties of a work independently of that work's genesis. Boulez is typical; he wrote concerning

137

his famous analysis of the *Rite of Spring*: "must I repeat here that I have not pretended to discover a creative process, but concern myself with the result, whose only tangibles are mathematical relationships? If I have been able to find all these structural characteristics, it is because they are there, and I don't care whether they were put there consciously or unconsciously, or with what degree of acuteness they informed [the composer's] understanding of [his] conception; I care very little for all such interaction between the work and 'genius'" (1966: 142). We could trace historically the emergence of a structural approach to music—one independent of "structuralism" properly speaking, which created a furor in the humanities in the 1960s—beginning with the organic conception of the musical work whose cultural roots can be traced back as far as Goethe's *Metamorphosis of Plants* (1790), later blossoming in the work of Adler and Schenker (to cite only the two most famous names). Boulez's standpoint inscribes itself, strictly speaking, in the line of *ontological* structuralism: the *being* of the work resides in its immanent configurations—an idea that one can trace back to Hanslick's formalism (1854).[4]

Each of these three standpoints—that we analyze music in terms of compositional conceptions, immanent structures, or how it is heard—is legitimate. Each one, however, conventionally asserts itself at the expense of the others. This is difficult to accept. What I am suggesting that we call poietic analysis, analysis of the neutral level, and esthesic analysis, thus do correspond to three autonomous tendencies already present in the history of musical analysis. But the musical-semiological project for analysis has two special features of its own. One is its examination of how the three dimensions can be brought together in analysis of a single piece. (This exceedingly delicate issue is not being avoided, but rather deferred to Section 3, below, where it is an integral part of my argument.) The second is the semiological project's insistence upon the *methodological* necessity of analyzing the neutral level.

We can give two reasons to justify this necessity:

(a) Poietical and perceptive approaches are (in comparison to the work's actual unfolding) necessarily *partial* approaches: we do not

---

[4] In Boulez's writings one finds a distinction made between the poietic and neutral levels and the neutral and esthesic levels (though it is not thematicized as a method). As an example of the first, we read that "we need not be preoccupied with the mechanism that has the work as its goal, but rather with the work itself, which, once written—by the very fact that it has been realized—sets all that initial research rocking in the night [fait basculer dans la nuit]." As an example of the second, we read, concerning a particular analytic stance, that "it appears that perception of the work has been confused with the work itself" (1966: 189, 191).

know all compositional strategies; do we know exactly how perceptive strategies work? A wish to account for a work in its *totality* is actually a perfectly legitimate desire (a desire shared by partisans of structuralism as well as those of *Gestalttheorie*). To understand a work as a whole, immanent analysis takes as its objective an examination of the work from its beginning to its end.[5]

(b) Second, if the objective of semiology is to show how poietic and esthesic interpretants are linked with the work's material presence, we must first have a *description* of that material's constituents. Analysis of the neutral level provides us with the tools necessary to make this description.

Whatever counterarguments might be offered, it seems to me crucial to distinguish among three levels of analysis applicable to the work. The proper challenge of semiology is determining how these various analyses of a single object will be interrelated.

3. *Articulating Three Families of Analysis: A First Approximation*

We may be tempted to consider the three poles of the tripartition as radically autonomous entities. If so, we should realize from the beginning that it is possible for a musicologist to offer reflections of a poietic or esthesic character that take as their point of departure an analysis of the neutral level. The musicologist him- or herself possesses knowledge or intuitions about the poietic process of the composer, or about perceptive processes in general; this knowledge enables the analysis to take on its poietic or esthesic coloration.

A series of six schemas conveys some preliminary idea of the connections among poietic phenomena, esthesic phenomena, and the trace. I have, throughout this book, been suggesting such "locally refined" schemas, which are intended to encircle, little by little, the rich complexity of the symbolic.[6] In what follows here, it is important to note that the order of my presentation does not necessarily suggest a chronological order for adopting one approach before some other. To state it more elegantly, the order of explanation does not correspond to the order of knowledge. The objectives of the analysis, the documents we have at our disposal, may well demand that we begin

[5] I do not say "a total analysis of the work," because an analysis is never exhaustive: it chooses a limited number of characteristics and parameters. Musical analysis (like Freudian analysis) is interminable!

[6] These replace the particularly complex and labored schema in the *Fondements*, page 60.

with something other than an analysis of the neutral level. But any analytical undertaking that wishes to command the totality of the musical phenomenon it examines cannot, from one moment to the next, avoid passing through such an analysis.

If we envisage the possible relationships between (a) the trace and (b) two groups of processes (poietic and esthesic), we come up with six *analytical situations*:

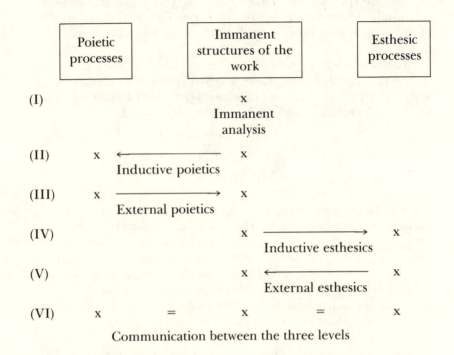

Let us examine these six situations in greater detail

(I) Immanent analysis. This is a type of analysis that, working with an implicit or explicit methodology, tackles only the immanent configurations of the work. Boulez's analysis (cited previously) in effect "neutralizes" the poietic. The structural configurations exposed by Boulez would not have to be considered esthesically relevant a priori—in any case, not completely relevant. Allen Forte's set theory (to give another example) constitutes an analysis of the neutral level of atonal music.

(II) One can proceed from an analysis of the neutral level to drawing conclusions about the poietic. For this particular instance I suggest the term *inductive poietics*. This, it seems to me, is one of the most frequently encountered situations in musical analysis. We observe so many recurrent procedures within a work or body of works that we find it hard to believe that "the composer had not thought of them." This is the case in Réti's analysis of Debussy's *la Cathédrale engloutie* (1951: 194–206), which reveals the fundamental importance of fifths, fourths, and thirds within the thematic germ of the piece, and views them as basic motifs for the entire work.

In many cases, the musicologist's decision is confirmed or helped along by what he or she knows of the epoch's characteristic style, or of other works by the same composer. In Volume 2, we shall see that the inductive ascent from the neutral to the poietic is not easily made unless the work is placed within a series of other stylistically related works. This is what is called a "seriation process," and a more elaborate example of such seriation in music analysis will be given in Chapter 9.

(III) In the third case, the situation is reversed. The musicologist takes a poietic document—letters, plans, sketches—as his or her point of departure, and analyzes the work in the light of this information. We might cite the example of Paul Mies's stylistic analysis of Beethoven in terms of the sketches (1929). The term *deductive poietics* would be inadequate here; I propose instead *external poietics*.

Mutatis mutandis, we find the same two cases on the esthesic side.

(IV) *Inductive esthesics* constitutes the most common case, primarily because most analyses wish to style themselves perceptively relevant, and most musicologists set themselves up as the collective conscious-

Example 6.1 Bach: *Fugue in C Minor, BWV 847*

ness of listeners, and decree "that this is what one hears." This sort of analysis grounds itself in perceptive introspection, or in a certain number of general ideas concerning musical perception. In a discussion of the following passage from the C minor fugue in Book I of the *Well-Tempered Clavier*, Meyer states that the sequence through the circle of fifths is developed from measure 9 to measure 11; at that moment (measure 11), the listener discovers that this motif is the head of the fugue subject (Meyer 1956: 48): Here, a musicologist bases his or her statement on an analysis of the work, then describes what he or she thinks is the listener's perception of the passage.

(V) One can, on the other hand, begin with information collected from listeners, to attempt to understand how the work has been perceived. This is, obviously, how experimental psychologists would work.

(VI) To these five analytical situations, we need to add a sixth, one that appears simple, but is in reality extremely complex. This is the case in which an immanent analysis is equally relevant to the poietic as to the esthesic. Schenker's theory is a good example, since Schenker claimed to take Beethoven's sketches as a point of departure, yet considered that his own analyses showed how the works *must* be played and *must* be perceived. This particular case is complex because it necessitates pinning down the exact nature of the connection between the neutral and the poietic, and the neutral and the esthesic, in order to devise a detailed classification of analyses belonging to this family. To do this for Schenker, one could go back to the analytical situations (III) and (IV) as described previously. In Schenker's case, the appeal to the poietic is *external*, but his esthesics is *inductive*. Beyond this, however, we would also need to distinguish between the descriptive and the normative. All evidence points to Schenker's esthesics as normative.

As noted above, this rapid summary of what I believe to be the six major *situations of musical analysis* from the tripartitional point of view refers to examples derived not from semiotically inspired analyses, but from current musicological literature. Musical semiology is able to propose a *critical* framework for existing musical analyses. In one sense, one could view these six schemas as the skeleton of a "systematic musicology" in the German sense.[7] Above all, however, they

[7] This is indeed what Stefani indicated in his "project for a systematic musicology" (1974), which is based on the distinction between "production," "text," and "perception." Supičic has established a filiation leading from Stefani to . . . Molino and Nattiez

sketch what might be called a *geography* of analysis—one that allows us to define the real import of a given analysis, or a potential analysis, among the totality of musical processes.

We can see that, despite the holistic ambitions of the tripartition, it serves above all to delineate *limitations* of musical analysis. We could state it more positively, and say that this framework of six *families* of analysis allows us to determine what the *relevance* of a given analysis may be. This determination must be made, because circumstances—absence of information, knowledge, or the appropriate methodological tools—sometimes prevent us from undertaking the type of analysis that reason might command. (Contrary to Marx's dictate, mankind does not ask itself questions that it cannot resolve.) We will need to examine this definition of *analytic relevance* thoroughly when we take up presently the methods characteristic of each wing of the tripartition.

4. *The Autonomization of Variables*

Analysis does not just inscribe itself within a given analytical situation. It also proceeds from the musicologist's *selection of variables* from the musical fact—variables he or she considers worthy of being retained in analysis. In Chapter 2 I spoke of music in a Maussian way as a "total musical fact" but I need to differentiate between variables that are *extrinsic* in comparison to the musical text *stricto sensu*, and intrinsic variables. We saw, in Chapter 2, that contemporary examples of "music for reading" or "music without music" play with peripheral variables, things (like performers' gestures) that are "peripheral" in comparison to the element of sound, yet are nonethelesss part of the total musical fact. "All aspects of musical practice," Molino writes, "may be disengaged, and privileged, in order to give birth to new forms of variation: variations on the relationships between the composer and the performer, between the conductor and the performer, between the performers, between the performer and the listener, variations upon gestures, variations on silence that end in a mute music that is still music because it preserves still something of the musical totality of the tradition . . . *all elements belonging to the total musical fact may be separated and taken as a strategic variable of musical production.* This autonomization serves as true musical experimentation: little by

---

(1975: 198). (Render unto Caesar?) Perhaps Stefani's text gives rise to some ambiguity. . . .

little, the individual variables that make up a total musical fact are brought to light. Any particular music then appears as one that has made a choice among these variables, and that has privileged a certain number of them. Under these conditions, musical analysis would have to begin by recognizing the strategic variables characteristic of a given musical system: musical invention and musical analysis lend each other mutual aid" (Molino 1975a: 42–43).

This long passage from Molino has been recapitulated here because it seems to me to describe an autonomization that is not only applicable to poietic processes, but that is also characteristic of symbolic forms in general. Four ideas derived from his text and its implications should be kept in mind.

(a) Musical poietic processes are based on an autonomization and particularization of certain variables.

(b) Musical analysis must identify these privileged variables, and, in a diachronic perspective, describe the transition from one collection of variables to another.

(c) What Molino says about variables that are, on the whole, extrinsic, is applicable to intrinsic variables as well, those characteristic of a particular musical style.

(d) Development and particularization of certain variables constitutes no more than a particular case of a more general property of any symbolic collection. Academic disciplines, for example, also separate themselves out and autonomize themselves after a certain stage of development (cf. for instance the birth and development of ethnomusicology in comparison to musicology); the same is true for learned societies and institutions (cf. the birth of the Society for Music Theory out of the American Musicological Society).

Molino's theory of autonomization of variables may have been suggested to him by Meyer's extraordinary consideration of stylistic metamorphosis in *Music, the Arts, and Ideas* (1967: Chapter 7). Meyer proposes in effect a true *description of style's symbolic functioning*: "a style tends to change or develop in its own way, according to its own internal and inherent dynamic process" (114).[8] "It is partly because famil-

---

[8] In Volume 2 I will take up Meyer's conception of style in some detail. Suffice it to say here that he immediately refines the "internal-dynamic hypothesis": this principle in fact depends on other, cultural, conditions; socio-cultural forces (extrastylistic forces) play their role in the development of a style's potentialities (1967: 115; cf. also 132). This latter aspect of his thinking—emphasizing external factors—plays in his most recent work *Music and Style* (1989) a greater role than does his earlier notion of style's autonomy. Meyer's insistence upon intrinsic properties of style, his anti-reductionism (as in *Music, the Arts, and Ideas*), remain nonetheless quite remarkable.

iar works and accustomed styles become *exhausted* that new compositions are needed and new styles are developed" (53). "A considerable amount of evidence indicates that, once its material, syntactical, and ideological premises have been established, a style, if it is going to change at all, tends to change in its own way and may conceivably do so even at a time when other aspects of the culture are quite stable" (109).

Meyer, then, affirms—and this is critical—that, contrary to reductionist theories of style (Marxist, culturalist, sociological), there exists an autonomous functioning of the symbolic, such that state x of a combination y of a number z of variables at moment t is explained necessarily by the evolution and transformation of variables out of a previous state x', at another moment t'. Approaching the organization and evolution unique to a given symbolic form is, then, methodologically necessary,[9] *before* we attempt to explain music's structure and history by reference to external criteria (class, ideology, culture, gender). A symbolic form possesses an autonomous physical existence whose variables one can analyze. This preeminently material aspect of symbolic functioning—which, indeed, lends the faintest tinge of vulgar materialism to my semiological approach—is yet another argument, obviously, in favor of the necessity of analysis of the neutral level.

Molino's theory, as well as Meyer's—and it is important to make this distinction—does not imply some evolutionary determinism, or a teleology of any kind (something along the lines of "you cannot but end in tonal stability"). One of the merits of Richard Norton's book on tonality is its demonstration of how one must attempt to describe what tonality (in his general sense) *was* at each moment of its evolution, without interpreting it in terms of what was to follow. "The medieval musician . . . did not hear a triad as a triad . . . a textbook definition of tonal coherence is not the same as the phenomenon of tonal cognition as experiences" (Norton 1984: 125).

I would like to add two nuances to Norton's thesis. On one hand, he lets it be understood at several points that all "developmental theory" is necessarily teleological (for example, ibid.: 15). One might well confirm that "tonality has run the course of its usefulness and must be abandoned," if, as we could say using Meyer's terms, the tonal idiom has exhausted its possibilities for combination. In the same way,

---

[9] It would be pointless to claim that with these few lines I cannot solve the problem of the culturalist approach to music. I shall return to it at some length in Volume 2, concerning ethnomusicology.

the idea of the organic development of a musical element (like tonality) is not necessarily explained by recourse to the overtone series (ibid.: 203). There is a place for a nontelic conception of the organic life of symbolic forms: stylistic change if always effectuated through a variable, or more precisely, a constellation of variables present at a given state in its history. But this does not mean that evolution itself is accomplished in terms of an end predetermined for all eternity, or inscribed in nature. Only retrospective thinking interprets a variable in terms of what that variable becomes. As for the rest, there is certainly an area of agreement between Norton and myself, seeing that he writes, "the problem in current musicology and music theory is to establish and understand the *logic of this development*[10] without also subordinating it to the interests of the remarkable efficiency of key-centered music in its classic phase" (267).

It is also one of Norton's great merits that in suggesting a *cognitive* theory of tonal development, he resituates analysis *on the poietic side*. To be sure, he is correct in criticizing the way in which the period of "common practice" between 1600 and 1900 has been hypostatized. But musicians and musicologists also have the right to *perceive* retrospectively certain traits common in musical practice of the past two or three centuries. I am less disturbed than Norton by Webern's misreading of the Renaissance and the *Art of the Fugue* since a composer is not responsible for some analytical "truth," and since an historically false interpretation made by a composer (and I admit that Webern's is false) furnishes us with factual testimony about his *perception* of past music, and thus also furnishes us with critical information concerning Webern's *poietics*.

To account more precisely for the dialectic between perception and creation in the case of Webern and the Renaissance, it is of course necessary not only to make a distinction between the poietic and the esthesic, but also to *link them diachronically*. This can be expressed as in Figure 6.3.

This schema shows how Webern's poietics integrates a perceptive stance toward Bach and Renaissance composers, how Boulez in turn is the heir of Webern and a certain Webernesque understanding of Bach, and so forth.

The word "variable," so far as I know, does not appear in Meyer's work. On the other hand, in a more recent text he introduced the word *parameter*, in a spirit very close to Molino's theory of autonomization of *variables*: "on the highest level of style change, the history of western music can be understood as consisting of the successive dif-

---

[10] Emphasis is mine.

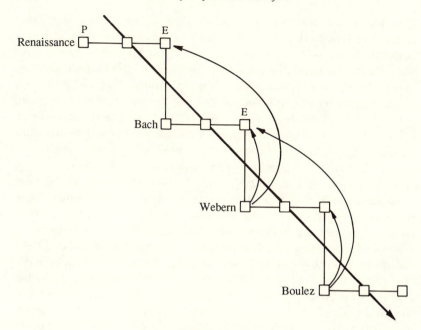

Figure 6.3

ferentiation of parameters, and the increasing autonomy and the eventual syntactification of those parameters differentiated" (1979: 25; reprinted in 1989, chapter 1). In fact, in the course of the history of tonal music, we have witnessed the integration of the timbral parameter, to a point where timbre could become the basic strategic variable of electronic and computer music. Total serial music applies operations that once concerned pitch alone, to rhythm, duration, and timbre. In writings attempting to justify his search for total serialization, Boulez (1966) continually insists upon the dissociation of parameters, even if he uses this notion in terms of an aesthetic sensibility (i.e., a taste for atonal music) that is wholly opposite Meyer's own aesthetic preferences for neo-classic music.

In the twentieth century, there has been an autonomization of parameters, but the attempt to syntactify them seems to have failed. This way of approaching the evolution of musical styles, characterized by the concepts of autonomy and syntactification of parameters, seems crucial within the framework of basic thinking on problems of twentieth-century music. (This is a question to which I hope someday to return.)

For the moment, however, we must link the theory of autonomi-

147

zation of variables to the more general conception of semiology that I have espoused. If I have preferred to describe semiological processes in terms of Peirce's infinite chain of interpretants, rather than the relation between signifier and signified, it is because the terms chosen by Saussure reveal themselves to be misleading and restrictive about the nature of symbolic functioning in general and of music in particular. Far be it from me to deny that music has the capacity to refer extramusically, to have "signifieds" (as we saw in the previous chapter). But studying musical history shows us how the formal substance of music evolves *intrinsically*, autonomously. A proliferation of *formal* interpretants is, indeed, also characteristic of symbolic phenomena basic to domains otherwise saturated with the indisputable presence of "signifieds," domains such as literature or discursive thought. Do not the rhymes at the end of a line of verse depend on symbolic functioning of a musical type? Is it truly for the sake of their meaning alone that one opposes the phrases "the theory of practice and the practice of theory" (Bourdieu) or "the poetry of grammar and the grammar of poetry" (Jakobson)? It is interesting to look at the functioning of our so-called "associations of *ideas*," which are more often than not dictated by assonance or purely phonetic or rhythmic connections. If this is so, then cannot the formal aspect of the semiologic functioning of music serve as a model for other symbolic domains, at least preventing us from downplaying, within these other domains, dimensions that are utterly essential to them?

By now my point should be clear. One cannot grasp the import of an analysis unless one takes into account:

— the dimensions of the corpus studied (connections between an isolated work and a series of works);
— the level of stylistic relevance: between the particular properties of a work and musical universals, where is the analyst situated?
— the analytical situation that has been adopted;
— whether the parameters being considered are within a work or a corpus of works.

We might add another variable—the analytical style adopted, which can range from cloudy impressionism to the most rigid formalism. This is a topic taken up in Chapter 7.

The combination of these particular choices gives to any analysis its unique physiognomy. This also explains why there have been in reality very few strictly comparable analyses (this must be kept in mind whenever we take a critical stance *against* a particular piece of analytical work, and *for* some other). But this combinational concept of analytical writing is not merely valid for studying existing analyses. If (as I have tried to do) we are able to thematicize the components of an analysis, this enables us to make explicit the import and the limits of analyses yet to be made, whether semiological or not.

7

The Semiology of Musical Analysis

1. Analytic Discourse as a Metalanguage

Musical analysis is not simply a symbolic fact like all others, since it draws its legitimacy and its right to exist solely from its link to another symbolic fact. (This point was made at the beginning of Chapter 6). The question concerning the metalinguistic position of discourse on music in general and musical analysis in particular is not often touched upon in musicological literature. Charles Seeger was able to write, without much exaggeration, that "while during the last 150 years linguists have developed a superb discipline of speech about speech, musicologists have done nothing at all about a discipline of speech about music" (1977: 38). This rather abrupt formulation is a bit more comprehensible if we locate it within the general context of Seeger's thought, since he was one of those rare musicologists who systematically undertook a metareflection on his own discipline. His essential notion seems in fact to underline the dilemma of the musicologist: while the musician "speaks in music" of purely musical things, the musicologist must necessarily pass through the intermediary of language—what Seeger calls the *bias of speech*. He never stopped wishing for a "comparative semiotics of the two compositional processes" (ibid.: 50), since for him the metalanguage of the musicologist also resulted from a creative act. He defined the "immediate aim of musicology" as follows: "(a) to integrate musical knowledge and feeling in music and speech knowledge and feeling about it to the extent this is possible in speech presentation, and (b) to indicate as clearly as possible the extent to which this is not possible" (48). In his last text, he demanded a "general theory . . . with the least distortion by the inescapable bias in the system in which the presentation is made—the art of speech" (1976: 1); this theory would permit establishing "the musicological juncture" between language

150

and music (1977: 19). For Seeger, there was indeed a level of musical experience that could not be reduced to language. Even if he expected the musicologist "to use a language, and the resources of speech, to treat music more expertly than can the professional musician" (45), he emphasized the inevitable complementarity of the two modes of knowledge: "gaps found in our speech thinking about music may be suspected of being areas of musical thinking" (49). "We must admit the limitations of speech and stay with them" (61). "Music communicates something that speech does not" (107). He stressed once more that music cannot speak of language, even when the converse is possible (67), even though certain remarks lead us to suspect that he dreamed secretly of a rapprochement between the two media: "speech sings and music talks to a greater extent than we realize" (131). He invited research on musical aspects of speech and linguistic aspects of music. The imaginary dialogue that Seeger published as "Towards a Unitary Theory of Musicology" (1977: 102–138) summarizes in the clearest and liveliest possible fashion the broad lines of his thought:[1]

S: Look at the job as an exercise in comparative semiotics. Speech communicates referent to what is not speech. Doesn't music communicate referent to what is not music?

K: Of course it does.

S: What, then, is the relationship between the two kinds of reference? And the two kinds of referents—between what is not speech and what is not music?

K: That is precisely what we all want to know.

S: Yes. We all say "music is this, music is that." We try to *say* how music does what it does. But that puts us right back in the linguocentric predicament. How do you know music is *this* or *that*? Doesn't it do *what* it does? Can't you check?

K: Against what?

S: Your musical knowledge.

K: But that would be pure subjectivity.

S: No, merely inexpressible in words . . . it is true that speech and music are very unlike in many ways, but they are very like in others. One can try to use the agreement upon the

[1] Although Seeger may be well known among musicologists and ethnomusicologists, there have been few systematic studies or critical commentaries on his thought. He expresses himself in a very abstract, paradoxical manner, rather as Gregory Bateson had. But certain basic ideas of Seeger's, notably his model of systematic musicology, are well worth being reexamined and discussed.

latter to help agreement upon the former's *account* of the latter. (1977: 104)

Seeger's reflections on the subject underline one critical fact: that musicological and analytical discourse, because it is *language*, has a semiological nature quite different from that of music. The statement clearly begs for further elaboration. Because analytical discourse is a metalanguage, it has a particular semiological specificity: to what does it refer?

Lamentations over the insufficiency of analytical discourse in comparison to the "real" music that we all love are quite numerous. We might cite this testimonial from 1966, more or less representative of what was being said and thought at that time in France: "taken as a whole," Pierre Schaeffer writes, "the copious literature devoted to sonatas, quartets and symphonies has a hollow sound. Only our getting used to it can mask the impoverishment, the ill-assorted nature of these various analyses . . . when all explanation is stripped down—whether that explanation is notional, instrumental, or aesthetic—we would do best to acknowledge that all in all we do not know a lot about music. Worse still, what we know is by nature more likely to lead us astray than to guide us" (1966: 19). There is doubtless some exaggeration in this, typical of a man who blamed himself for not reinventing music and music theory. We could put together an anthology of remarks more subtle, yet always pessimistic. Sachs, one of the pioneers of ethnomusicology, wrote, "descriptions of musical works and styles are hard to put into words, even harder to read and absorb, and almost impossible to translate into actual images" (1962: 49). More recently, Blacking commented, "as soon as we analyze music with speech, we run the risk of distorting the true nature of nonverbal communication with both the structural conventions of verbal discourse itself and the analytical categories of grammar which all educated speakers have assimilated" (1984: 364). We might cite the anecdote told by Gottwald: "when Stockhausen published his analysis of Nono's *Canto sospeso* (Stockhausen 1963: 157–66), Nono decreed, 'it is all wrong' " (Gottwald 1985: 97). Varèse wrote of *Density 21.5*, "I am sure that if you have read what is written in the score, following the various indications, you can ignore the analyses by Wilkinson and all the others" (Varèse 1983: 169). In other words, the musicologist is a nasty, scavenging vulture, and obviously of no use whatsoever. Behind all this, we seem to hear *sotto voce* the composer's cutting reply: "artist, you must create, not talk" (Hindemith). Lurking behind all these statements is a latent assumption: that music itself is capable of speaking about itself, without the mediation of a metalanguage. Hans Keller's musical analyses, in which music examples are juxtaposed in a wordless commentary (cf. Keller 1985, and 1958, 200) attempt to realize this assumption. Keller, of course, has simply transferred to the listener any responsibility for constructing analytical conclusions.

We reproach discourse about music for its inadequacies precisely because we have not reflected on the semiological and metalinguistic status of that discourse. Because it is a metalanguage, musical analysis cannot substitute for the lived experience of the musical. If analysis should achieve this substitution, that would mean that discourse *is* the musical piece itself. The relationship between experienced musical reality and discourse about music is necessarily an oblique one. The musical metalogue is, moreover, always full of gaps.

Metamusical discourse refers to a reality that is distinct from that discourse. Ian Bent defined musical analysis as "the means of answering directly the question 'how does it work?' " (1980: 342). Stated more clearly: in attempting to describe how a work functions, analysis is in effect a *simulation* (in the most rigorous cases, a *model*), but never a reproduction.

But if notions like model and simulation are current coin in epistemology and the history of science, what is not so common are the semiological implications that one might draw from these notions. From a tripartitional point of view, what, metalinguistically speaking, *is* an analysis? I would claim, with Molino (1975a: 48), that it is a *surrogate symbolic behavior*—that is, a symbolic behavior that feeds upon another, primary symbolic behavior. To analyze the processes of creation, interpretation, and perception, and to analyze the structures of the work in addition, is to establish, on an analytical plane, a web of interpretants that proposes itself as a *model* for interpretants "natural" to the work in the *real* processes of composition, interpretation, and perception.

If analysis has the status of surrogate symbolic behavior, then we can bring into final focus one aspect of the theory of tripartition that invariably leads to confusion. Consider this new version of the diagram from Chapter 6:

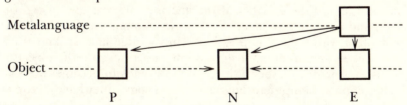

Metalanguage

Object

P   N   E

Semiological discourse is concerned with the poietic, the neutral level of analysis, and the esthesic. The investigator him- or herself occupies an esthesic position in relation to the object studied. Yet he or she occupies this esthesic position on a second, metalinguistic plane. The difference is significant, because we should not confuse[2] the perceptual process of listeners *in real time*, which is the object of esthesic analysis strictly speaking, with the very different perceptive process in which the musicologist is implicated *as would be any scholarly researcher*. Stated another way, the difficulty stems from the fact that music-analytical discourse (in order to *explain*) must simulate behaviors of production, performance, and reception, whose own purposes culminate in *perception* of a sound-trace. Now, there is a big difference between a physicist's act of perceiving a natural phenomenon (the solar system was not made to be perceived), and perceiving a musical phenomenon, which is made to be perceived: what would a "work" be if it were *not* musically perceived? Passing through an analysis of the neutral level is necessary—among other reasons—because the perception of the musicologist must not be confused with the *natural* perception of listeners. The importance of this distinction between musicological and natural perception of music—which at this point may seem merely anodyne, but which I believe to be fundamental— will be confirmed in Volume 2, in discussing the status of analyses conducted within the framework of cognitive psychology, such as those by Lerdahl and Jackendoff.

Once we acknowledge that the metalogue is an irreducible, anthropological given of human behavior, we must try to answer the following question: how should we talk about music? This is one of the most serious problems raised by semiological investigation.

I should stress from the outset that there is a physical mode of existence for music analysis, just as there is a physical mode of existence for music. Analysis is spoken or written down (and it is not saying exactly the same thing in one case as in the other). Certainly analysis is most often aural, but then by definition few traces will remain to facilitate examination of its properties. When one asks Messiaen's pupils about his famous class in analysis at the Paris Conservatory, a striking fact emerges—that the composers shaped by these classes have memories primarily of Messiaen's *attitudes*, his style of dealing with music, not the specifics of the analyses. We are able to return again and again to statements made in written analysis; we need not be content with a mere impression. Thus written analysis knows its own unique and autonomous evolution with respect to the object it discusses. For this reason, written analysis tends to become increasingly complex. Computers, linguistics, semiology—they have all come

[2] *Fondements* seems to have engendered a similar confusion between the two in the minds of reviewers, though page 409 does clarify the matter: "because musical semiology, by the same rights as scientific discourse, or musical phenomena, is a symbolic fact, it is answerable (in the second degree) to the very tripartition that is the basis of its working hypothesis in its analysis of musical works."

rushing into the fray; some have begged for mercy! Nettl could already claim in 1964 that "analysis must, above all, be communicative, must make some concessions to the reader's frame of reference" (1964: 132). More recently, he laments:

> What has happened to the effort of ethnomusicology to establish comprehensive, all-encompassing ways of describing a variety of musics for the purpose of comparison? Those [methods] most easily applied are also the least satisfactory because they simply give little information. As the music-specific characterizations by Hornbostel and Herzog, and for that matter Lomax, are replaced by the semiotics of Nattiez and Boilès and others, the methods are more and more complex; in a sense they give more information but are harder to read, lend themselves more easily to comparison, and are more difficult to apply by someone who did not originate them. Despite the universalist intention, they turn out to culture-specific, or at best scholar-specific. (1983: 95)

Analysis in fact cannot be prevented from evolving in terms of its own problematic, its own laws. The autonomization of parameters discussed in the previous chapter occurs within the musical work, but equally in analysis itself. Let Nettl, however, be reassured: I am aware that problems are posed by the analytic sophistication that musical semiology might bring. (This question will be considered in Volume 2, in discussing specific analyses).

Still, the increased complexity of contemporary analysis is the result of dissatisfaction engendered by the impressionistic or historicist style prevailing in analytic discourse up to the 1960s. When discourse about music came into contact with more formal disciplines such as logic, mathematics, information theory, and linguistics, its fuzziness and inaccuracy were once more called violently into question.

In undertaking a semiology of musical analysis, I will almost certainly be scolded for making the analytical landscape more complex still. Benjamin Boretz, another writer concerned specifically with the nature of musical metalanguage, asks, "what does one hope to gain by talking about talk about music when even just talking about music uses a language that is itself 'metamusical'?" (1969: 8). There is in effect an infinite number of metadiscourses and meta-metadiscourses (and so forth), even as there is an infinite number of interpretants.

Since musical analysis is the product of human activity, there is no reason why it should escape semiological investigation. Even if analysis makes no sense except in relation to the works that it examines, it constitutes a special human activity, one that tends toward autonomy, one whose specific characteristics can be studied. We will presently sketch a semiology of musical analysis in terms of the tripartition, beginning with a study of analysis's immanent properties.

2. *The Neutral Level of Analytical Discourse*

Let us take our vocabulary for melodic analysis as an example. Despite Abraham's and Dahlhaus's efforts to prove the existence of a *Melodielehre* in music-theoretical history (1972), it must be acknowledged that Hindemith was right after all: "there is no explicit *Melodielehre*" (1937: 209). Of course, we can agree with Ratner that "eighteenth-century theories of phrase and period structure . . . have not received as much attention as have harmony, performance practice, and other aspects of the music of the time" (1956: 439), yet even writers studied by Ratner complained, as early as 1777, about terminological inconsistency. For instance, Sulzer wrote, "the names used to indicate the smaller and larger sections of a melody are still somewhat indefinite. One speaks of *Perioden, Abschnitten, Einschnitten, Rhythmen, Cäsuren,* etc. . . . in such a way that one word will have two meanings and two words will have the same meaning" (cited in Ratner 1956: 441). I have deliberately avoided giving a history of musical semiology, yet it would be interesting nonetheless to see how and why definitions of terms like *phrase, cell, figure, motif,* etc., in works by important eighteenth-century theorists like Mattheson or Koch, were based upon more or less metaphorical analogies between music and language—interesting because very soon thereafter music itself was being considered as language endowed with a rhetorical force.

Ruwet, in his seminal article "Methodes d'analyse en musicologie" (1972: 100–134), asks us to compare definitions of (apparently) elementary musical terms drawn from different analytical treatises and encyclopedias:[3]

From the *Encyclopédie Larousse* of 1957:

> *Cell*: a small rhythmic and melodic design that can be isolated, or can make up one part of a thematic context. A cell can be developed independent of its context, as a melodic fragment. It can be the source for the whole structure of the work; in that case it is called a generative cell.
>
> *Motif*: a small element characteristic of a musical composition, which guarantees in various ways the unity of a work or a part

[3] I owe the list of definitions, which was already published in Nattiez 1972a (107–109), to my colleague Louise Hirbour. The discussion in this work is adopted and expanded from pages 93–99 of the *Fondements,* but I have brought the list up to date.

of the work (a motif can be assimilated into a cell, and can have three aspects that may be dissociated from one another, rhythmic, melodic, and harmonic).

Cell, motif, and figure are (for the *Encyclopédie Larousse*) a more or less single, identical thing, with one exception: there is no mention of harmony for "cell" and "figure." In getting down to details, though, can we speak of a difference between cell and motif? The cell can be the source for the entire structure of the work; the motif ensures the unity of the work or a part. Are we not talking about the same thing? The *Encyclopédie Larousse* also offers as a definition of theme, "a musical idea which is the melody (or the melodic fragment) on which the structure of a musical composition is based." This definition is pretty close to that of "cell." The difference is in the dimensions; the cell, like the motif, is a small unit. But when do we begin to have a theme? If we go to the *Encyclopédie de la Pléiade*, we can see how little the vocabulary is standardized: motif is there defined as a "melodic, rhythmic, or harmonic *cell*,[4] characteristic of a musical work" (Roland-Manuel, ed., 1960: 2052).

This Tower of Babel increases in complexity when we move from French to English. For instance, the "old" *Grove's Dictionary* (1964) gives as "figure" "any short succession of notes, either as melody or group of chords, which produces a single complete and distinct impression. The term is the exact counterpart of the German 'motiv' and the French 'motif.' It is the shortest idea in music." But is the French "motif" so precise that one can speak of exact counterparts? In the *New Grove* (1980), we read that *phrase* is "a term adopted from linguistic syntax and used for short musical units of various lengths; a phrase is generally regarded as longer than a *motif* but shorter than a *period*," and that *motif* is "a short musical idea, be it melodic, harmonic, or rhythmic, or all three. A motif may be of any size, though it is most commonly regarded as the shortest subdivision of a theme or phrase that still maintains its identity as an idea. It is most often thought of in melodic terms, and it is this aspect of the motif that is connoted by the term 'figure'." We could multiply infinitely such examples of definitions that refer to one another.

The second problem posed by these definitions is more important by far, because it calls traditional musical analysis into question. We are obviously dealing with units, with a beginning and an end, but what exactly are the criteria that allow us to articulate [découper] these musical units? The *Encyclopédie Fasquelle* (1958) offers the following definitions:

[4] Emphasis is mine.

Cell: a term in musical composition, used to discuss cyclic works. It is the smallest indivisible unit; the cell is distinct from the motif, which can be divided; the cell can, itself, be used as a developmental motif.

Motif: In classical musical syntax, this is the smallest analyzable element (phrase) within a subject; it may contain one or more cells. A harmonic motif is a series of chords defined in the abstract, that is, without reference to melody or rhythm. A melodic motif is a melodic formula, established without reference to intervals. A rhythmic motif is the term designating a characteristic rhythmic formula, an abstraction drawn from the rhythmic values of a melody.

Theme: Any element, motif, or small musical piece that has given rise to some variation becomes thereby a theme.

Phrase: This term, borrowed from *grammar*,[5] designates a collection of sounds, delimited by two pauses, with a complete sense . . . of all musical systems, tonal rhetoric assured precise delimitation of phrases, by means of hierarchized fixed points of harmonic cadences, which are modelled on articulations in spoken discourse. In modal monody, a pause coinciding with a pause in the text most often occupies the position of phrase-ending . . . the length of the phrase is quite variable.

Period: A complex phrase, in which the various parts are enchained.

We can put this inventory side by side with examples drawn from other works:

Phrase: A series of notes that display a complete musical sense, and that form a natural division of the melodic line, comparable to a phrase in discourse, and constituting a complete whole (a melodic phrase subdivides into various parts that correspond to the indices of discourse). (Larousse)

Phrase: A musical phrase is a developed idea, having a complete sense. (Falk 1958: 11)

Sentence: The smallest period in a musical composition that can give *in any sense* the impression of a complete statement is that called the *Sentence*, which may be defined as a period containing two or more phrases, and most frequently ending with some form of perfect cadence. (Macpherson n.d.: 25)

Phrase: In its most frequent manifestations, it is a passage of four bars culminating in a more or less definite cadence, and

---

[5] Emphasis is mine.

possessing as a consequence some degree of completeness within itself. (ibid.)

Satz [sentence, phrase, movement]: *Satz* is any single member of a musical piece, which in and of itself displays a complete sense. (Riemann 1976: 841)

Phrase: Phrases vary in length from three to six bars . . . the four-bar phrase is by far the commonest. (Davie 1966: 19)

Phrase: The term phrase is one of the most ambiguous in music. Besides the fact that it may validly be used for units of two to eight measures (sometimes even more) in length, it is often incorrectly used for subdivisions of multiple or single phrases. (Stein 1962: 37)

Period: In traditional music . . . a group of measures comprising a natural division of the melody; usually regarded as comprising two or more contrasting or complementary phrases and ending with a cadence. (*Harvard Dictionary of Music* 1969)

Phrase: A division of the musical line, somewhat comparable to a clause of a sentence in prose. Other terms for such divisions are period, half-phrase, double phrase, etc. . . . there is no consistency in applying these terms nor can there be . . . only with melodies of a very simple type, especially those of some dances, can the terms be used with some consistency. (ibid.)

Just what does it mean, however, to have a "complete sense"? "Complete" means being articulated by a cadence, of course: "a phrase is a rhythmic pitch unit marked off by a cadence" (Christ 1967: 77). But do phrases alone have "completed sense," and are cadences the unique criterion for delimiting musical units? The musicologists writing for the dictionaries clearly sense the insufficiency of such definitions, since they all add other criteria for determining the articulation of phrases: in Fasquelle, the pauses; among the English-language writers, the number of measures (though they do not always agree about that number, as Stein's reservations show). In discussing segmentation, Ruwet has asked, "do I obtain the same results, for example, if I base the segmentation on the rests and then on the cadences—a correspondence that is found especially in the chorale—or, on the contrary, does recourse to different criteria establish different segmentations which introduce ambiguities into [our perception of] the structure?" (1972: 106; English trans. by Mark Everist, in Ruwet-Everist 1987: 14).

Juxtaposing definitions, as I have just done, raises the question of analytic *criteria*. In practice, analysis operates on the basis of fuzzy and ill-defined terminology—so much so that, when all is said and done, motifs, themes, or phrases will often be identified intuitively, based on ideas born of historical knowledge, familiarity with a period or body of work, and personal perceptive reactions combined.

It is important to stress that this kind of intuition can result from a *very deep and learned contact* between the researcher and his or her subject, but, in the cases that concern me, *it is precisely this familiarity that substitutes for more scientific criteria for segmentation.* It is easy to wax ironic over definition-collecting as a source of "predictable amusement" (Osmond-Smith 1975: 185), but the exercise does encourage us to examine a real problem with the attention it deserves.

If I criticize the metalanguage of melodic analysis, this is because so many writers have behaved as if the *idea* that *they* might have about phrase or cell were sufficient to determine (for each particular musical text) this phrase or that cell. But the *word* "phrase," the *word* "cell," are both semiological units. They are linked to interpretants that (in a very general, very rough way) set in opposition the phrase as a longer unit and the cell as the shortest unit—and who is to say that this is wrong? Of course, it is nowadays quite normal for us to appeal to terms that themselves refer to a past usage; this may be adequate in certain scientific or pedagogic exchanges. What I object to here is substituting some intuitive, vague feeling about the nature of a phrase for a precise methodology that would delimit and define "phrase."[6]

In taking melodic terminology as my example, I have naturally chosen a particularly thorny case. Various metalanguages are from the outset more developed, or less so, *depending on the particular type of analysis.* Rhythmic analysis has not been much luckier than melodic analysis. On the other hand, harmonic analysis, since the advent of figured bass, has seen considerable development and refinement, doubtless because it originated as a *practical* (compositional, that is, poietical) necessity. We must not, however, jump to the conclusion that harmonic analysis is self-evident. It is astonishing to read, in an article devoted to analyzing the Tristan Chord, that "the analysis as such ceases with the choice of the tonic; once this has been made, the assignment of degree numbers to the chords is pure description" (Cone 1960: 35). It is a bit more complicated than all that, especially when we are dealing with Wagner, dealing with *that chord.*[7]

---

[6] In David Lidov's semiological work, the notion that it is possible to operate with an intuitive conception of the phrase recurs like a leitmotif. For Lidov, the opposition between phrase and motif is "a distinction that is central to intuitive experience" (1975: 36; cf. also 47, 79, 93; and 1978: 33; 1980: 36, 68).

[7] Deciding whether the G♯ is part of the chord is, from the beginning, an analytical problem. See Chapter 9.

The subtlety of the metalanguage depends, obviously, on the analytical criteria that support it. Thus, for instance, harmonic analysis does not describe the workings of individual voices, and can confuse the structure of a chord with its function. Having a flexible metalanguage at one's disposal is not enough. We must know what principles guide the analysis. The criteria of analysis, the development of a language proper to analysis, are two problems that are partially connected, but nonetheless distinct.

These critical reflections on analytical metalanguage bring us to a crucial question: what kind of language should be used in talking about music? In analysis above all, do we not need to have recourse to special signs, diagrams, tables, and so forth? Ian Bent was correct in proposing "media of presentation" as one of the axes in his typology of analysis (1980: 370).

For the moment, let us stay within the melodic domain. If we examine theories of melody, and the analytical techniques that are associated with them, we can tentatively classify different modes of using language—modes that seem, to me, representative of musical analysis in general.[8]

First of all, we can distinguish between analyses that (for the sake of simplification) we will call *nonformalized*, and those we will call *formalized*.

(1) *Nonformalized Analyses*

We can distinguish three subtypes: *impressionistic* analyses, *paraphrases*, and *hermeneutic readings* of the text [explications de texte].

(a) Impressionistic analyses explain the melody's content in a more or less high-literary style, proceeding from an initial selection of elements deemed characteristic. The following example describes the beginning of the *Prelude to the Afternoon of a Faun*:

> The alternation of binary and ternary divisions of the eighth notes, the sly feints made by the three pauses, soften the phrase so much, render it so fluid, that it escapes all arithmetical rigors. It floats between heaven and earth like a Gregorian chant; it glides over signposts marking traditional divisions; it slips so furtively between various keys that it frees itself effortlessly from their grasp, and one must await the first appearance of a harmonic underpinning before the melody takes graceful leave of this casual atonality. (Vuillermoz 1957: 64)

---

[8] The following recapitulates, with some changes, pages 1059–61 of my article on melody for the *Enciclopedia Einaudi* (1979).

(b) In paraphrases, it is basically a matter of "respeaking" a musical text in (plain) words, without adding anything to that text. One instance is Warburton's analysis of the beginning of the Bourée of Bach's *Third Suite*:

> An anacrusis, an initial phrase in D major. The figure marked (a) is immediately repeated, descending through a third, and it is employed throughout the piece. This phrase is immediately elided into its consequent, which modulates from D to A major. The figure (a) is used again two times, higher each time; this section is repeated. (Warburton 1952: 151)

This type of discourse in addition will allow a student, for instance, to become sensitized to the various melodic elements.

(c) The third type of verbal description might be called a hermeneutic reading of the text [explication de texte]. The term is, of course, derived from literary theory, but is not (to my knowledge) a standard expression in musicology.[9] Hermeneutic reading of a musical text is based on a description, a "naming" of the melody's elements, but adds to it a hermeneutic and phenomenological depth that, in the hands of a talented writer, can result in genuine interpretive masterworks. Such discourse involves grasping the melody's full richness, extricating the salient points, without being excessively systematic, and with the explicit or implicit purpose of grasping some textual "essence." It all depends, of course, on the analysis's particular hermeneutic orientation. All the illustrations presented in Abraham's and Dahlhaus's *Melodielehre* (1972) are historical in character; Rosen's essays in *The Classical Style* (1971) seek to grasp the essence of an epoch's style; Meyer's analysis of Beethoven's "Farewell" Sonata (1973: 242–68) penetrates melody from the vantage point of perceived structures. Hermeneutic reading of a musical text often leads to larger comparisons, whose horizons encompass the whole of the work being considered, or the composer's style in general, or the style of an entire era—and all this without giving up enthusiastic literary outbursts. We might cite, as one example among many, Tovey on Schubert's *Unfinished Symphony*:

> The transition from first to second subject is always a difficult piece of musical draughtsmanship; and in the rare cases where Schubert accomplishes it with smoothness, the effort otherwise

[9] Even less so in English, which tends occasionally to incorporate the French expression (*explication de texte*), as in Steven Feld's *Sound and Sentiment* (1982). [Translator's note: Despite the currency of the French phrase in English, I have used a standard English version of the phrase; one might also speak of "hermeneutical reading."

exhausts him to the verge of dullness (as in the slow movement of the otherwise great A minor Quartet). Hence, in his most inspired works the transition is accomplished by an abrupt *coup de théâtre*; and of all such *coups*, no doubt the crudest is that in the Unfinished Symphony. Very well then; here is a new thing in the history of the symphony, not more new, not more simple than the new things which turned up in each of Beethoven's nine. Never mind its historic origin, take it on its merits. Is it not a most impressive moment? (Tovey 1978: 213)

I have called these three analytical types "nonformalized" because, beyond musical and analytical terms, they do not appeal to resources other than language in translating melody. Things are quite different in analyses that propose constructing *models* for melodic function.

(2) *Formalized Analyses*

In this case it is not a matter of speaking about music, but of *simulating* music with sufficient exactness, so that (in principle) it would be possible to use the model to reproduce the natural configurations of the original object.

Modelizations have an advantage over nonformalized, verbal descriptions. Given any single variable, modelizations by nature proceed to a complete analytic sweep of an entire corpus vis à vis that variable. Modelizations cannot cover the whole of any corpus (since the number of variables and their possible combinations is infinite), but at least they avoid the serious epistemological lacuna that is characteristic of verbal description. This is what Elizabeth Bertrand, one of my students, called "the piecework effect" [pigisme]—that is, analyzing an object through discontinuous selection of a few elements deemed representative.

There are two large families of models, which we shall call "global" and "linear."

(a) *Global models.* By "global models" we mean descriptions that provide an image of the whole corpus being studied, by listing characteristics, classifying phenomena, or both; they furnish a statistical evaluation. We can distinguish *analysis by traits* from *classificatory analysis.*

Analysis by traits has been done most often in ethnomusicology: one identifies the presence or absence of a particular variable, and makes a collective image of the song, genre, or style being considered by means of a table. The "trait listing" done by (among others) Helen Roberts (1955: 222, for instance) is the classic example.

Classificatory analysis sorts phenomena into classes. Thus Kolinski (1956, 1961, 1965b) suggests a universal system for classifying types of melodic contours, in which the number of pitches in the scale is related to a hierarchy of pitches based on the circle of fifths. By these means, he generates 348 types. Melodic movement is also sorted into 100 types (Kolinski 1965a); all these types are treated statistically. Kolinski's classificatory analysis is merely one type among many.

More recent analytical methods that are based on systematic paradigmatization of units are fundamentally classificatory as well. They often specifically style themselves *taxonomical*. Making the basis for the analysis explicit is a fundamental criterion in this approach, so *delimiting* units is always accompanied by carefully *defining* units in terms of their constituent variables. This is important. Many melodic analyses come to grief because they do not specify why this or that variable is retained in defining this or that unit. Thus in "classificatory" analyses, a contour is always defined, for instance, in terms of constituent segments. But the variables that segmentation brings to light, the variables that govern the making of a given segmentation, are innumerable.

(b) *Linear models*. The analytical approaches described above are called *global* because they do not try to reconstitute the whole melody *in order of* real time succession of melodic events. *Linear* models, on the other hand, describe a corpus by means of a system of rules encompassing not only the hierarchical organization of the melody, but also the *distribution*, environment, and context of events. Chenoweth (1972, 1979) explains the succession of pitches in New Guinean chants in terms of distributional constraints governing each melodic interval. Herndon's attempts at transformational analysis (1974, 1975) describe types of events (specified in advance) in terms of their succession within a melody. We owe to Baroni and Jacoboni (1976) a remarkable grammar for the soprano part in Bach's chorales; when tested by computer, it allows us to generate melodies in Bach's style.[10]

3. On Intermediary Models

One question is immediately raised by all this. In moving from impressionistic analyses to formalized model, we seem to be establishing a qualitative hierarchy. There is certainly a difference in quality between paraphrasing and impressionistic discourses (low quality), and all the others. There is also a qualitative difference between global and linear models. For an art such as music (which is, fundamentally,

---

[10] A chapter devoted to generative grammar will appear in the next volume.

inscribed in time), it is better to have a model that can simulate the succession of component parts and structures, than to operate solely by means of a taxonomy. Nonetheless, one does not always choose one's model: the data at our disposal can dictate one particular treatment of the musical material more than some other (as we shall see later on). But it is still an open question whether we should favor formal models above exegeses. All in all, is it not better to have a good hermeneutic reading of the text than nothing at all? Moreover, do we not often feel that a deep and sensitive commentary, like Tovey's, goes a lot farther than the most elaborate system of generative rules? Such questions reflect in brief a much larger problem: what *cognitive value*[11] do we ascribe to these two large analytical types (hermeneutic, linear model)?

Formalist reductionism's great mistake is to proceed as if gaining precise knowledge of a work were possible only by working through the constraints of formalization. The contemporary intellectual landscape, however, persuades me that the opposite is true: if, in the course of an elegant hermeneutic reading, a writer allows him- or herself critical appreciations and aesthetic judgments, this does not preclude discovering and describing configurations that (without possessing the rigor of a collection of formal rules) nonetheless constitute the germ of some systematic organization, one whose force and cognitive value should not be denied.[12] Thus between reductive formal precision, and impressionist laxity, there is a place for "intermediary models."

Among these, we should assign a specific place to analyses that make use of graphics without appealing to a system of formalized rules (those of, for instance, Schenker, Meyer, Narmour, or Lerdahl-Jackendoff). Here the graphic element is a complement to verbal expression, and does not replace the verbal (as is the case, for instance, with formal models). Of course, one could attempt to formalize Schenker in order to make his analyses more precise (and a number of scholars have attempted to do this), but one cannot deny that graphics in themselves make the functioning of the musical object quite explicit. I am thinking in particular of Meyer's proposed classification of melodic structure (1973: Chapter 7), which speaks of gap-

[11] I would like to thank Jean-Claude Gardin for providing me with a forum, in April 1980, for reflecting and elaborating upon this problem, on the occasion of a seminar in epistemology held at the École Pratique des Hautes Études.

[12] Jean Molino has suggested to me that, in admitting the possibility of a rigorous musicological discourse that is not necessarily a formalized discourse, I am paralleling a trend in philosophy of mathematics that, contrary to the positivist view, recognizes the existence of "informal rigor."

fill melodies, triadic melodies, complementary melodies, axial melodies, changing-note melodies, prolongations—the graphics give us a model of perception, and of the composer's and listener's expectations.

Ten years ago, I would have come down on the side of formalized models without any hesitation. We should remember that it was the imprecision of a certain style of analytical discourse that fostered, even provoked, the birth of the musical-semiological enterprise. Imprecision provoked the flight to linguistic models, which partook of the prestige of scientific rigor—a prestige that distinguished linguistics from other humanistic disciplines. And in fact analysis by traits, paradigmatization, generative rules for recreating a text, do bring to musical analysis a dimension that it had lacked. They force us to explain the variables we choose, the musical units under consideration, the analytical methods: something once unknown. Linguistic tools (and it is not coincidental that we are speaking here of *structural* linguistics) function efficiently for an analysis of the *neutral level*. They do not, however, seem to work as well when we get down to matters poietic and esthesic. I have stated time and time again that these other two dimensions, the poietic and esthesic, are equally important in the total musical fact. Poietic and esthesic information brings us into contact with the entire *lived experience* of "producers" and "consumers" of music; analysis of textual *structures* does not. There could be a hermeneutic dimension in analysis of structures; we could have modelizations of poietic or esthesic information. But in both these (hypothetical) cases it seems clear that the phenomena being examined are by their very nature out of phase with the analytical method being used. (To evoke a more specific example: one can succeed in constructing a generative grammar for a particular style, but no one has ever succeeded in constructing a formal model of historical causality.)

We must therefore judge the value of different metamusical modes of discourse in terms of the poietic, neutral, and esthesic poles and their respective properties. Given some of my arguments here, I might be expected to subscribe to the principles animating Boretz's *Meta-Variations*. Boretz, taking as his point of departure a critique of analytical metalanguages, seeks (as I do) to minimize linguistic ambiguities (1969: 17) and laxity in analytic vocabulary (24). He extolls the superiority of formalized languages, inspired by logic (23). Nonetheless, there are some problems. First, this is all done at the cost of eliminating the emotive dimension of music (23–26), a dimension that is, of course, the province of the poietic and esthesic. Second, Boretz seems to be confusing his own formal, logical model with an immanent essence he then *ascribes* to music. He transmutes the virtue of logic into the formal "nature" of music (ibid.). In taking note of problems such as these, we ask ourselves whether what we gain in precision, in undeniable scientific rigor, is not lost in a distinct normativism, and in a total disregard for certain essential semiological and anthropological dimensions of the musical fact.

The same problems can be found in the work of another (indeed, seminal) theorist of the Princeton School of the 1960s and 1970s. When Milton Babbitt (1972) defines a musical theory as a hypothetical-deductive system, one might think that he is operating in strict conformity with the epistemological exigencies of logical empiricism. But if we look closely at what he says, we quickly realize that the theory *also* seeks to legitimize a music yet to come; that is, that it is also normative. Such a model cannot account for certain sorts of music (some types of electro-acoustic music, for instance). And there is a danger that in transforming the *value* of the theory into an aesthetic *norm* (by means of a subtle shift), one utterly denies certain musical genres their right to exist. From an anthropological standpoint, that is a risk that is difficult to countenance.

In other words, the tripartition seems to me the best guard against a neo-positivism that would inevitably lead to conclusions about the "essence" of its object. At the same time, a tripartitional approach would not in any way deny the necessity for a rigorous analytical approach—a kind that (as will become evident) I consider perfectly legitimate, a kind to which I myself devote considerable attention.

Boretz enthusiastically embraces logical formalism, while evading the question of knowing how the data—whose formalization he proposes—have been obtained. In my first writings (Nattiez 1971, 1972a, 1972b, 1973a, 1973b, 1974), I claimed linguistic rigor as an absolute panacea. I would no longer make that claim today. Seeger dreamed of a universal and rational metalanguage; he gave us some hint of it in his essay "On the Moods of a Musical Logic" (1977: 64–101), but he looked at mathematics with an envy mixed with caution (111, 117).

One can, of course, strike a balance (though this is difficult), a delicate tightrope act—one that I shall try to perform. The tripartitional model will force us to bring together quite different music-analytical models and discourses (in a way that is, perhaps, an epistemological hybrid). What is nevertheless certain is that this conjunction enables us to become conscious of, to understand more fully, the musical facts that we confront.

4. The Poietics of Analysis

An analysis is always made by someone: the analysis, then, inscribes itself in history and culture; at the same time, it is shaped by certain authorial a prioris, like those cited by Bent in his article on analysis in the *New Grove*: "the analysts's view of the nature and function of music," as well as "[his or her] underlying aesthetic approach" (1980: 370).

What does knowing these three factors—insertion into history, into culture, and the a priori assumptions of the author—mean for understanding a particular analysis? The *meaning* of a word (as I shall have occasion to repeat in my discussion of musical semantics), like all symbolic forms, depends in part on the *situation* in which a complex of signs is emitted. These three factors comprise an integral part of a *situation*; understanding analysis also depends upon recognizing this situation.

If I return here to the poietics of analysis, it is because I am concerned with explaining divergences within analyses—notably those dealing with the same work. Poietic factors account for many of these divergences.

Only rarely will a musicologist allow outright that an analysis other than his or her own is acceptable. In fact, when a musicologist takes the trouble to suggest a new analysis of a work, it is because that musicologist believes that he or she has discovered the truth. The thesis that I would like to defend is, however, precisely that there is never *only one valid* musical analysis for any given work. This may seem startling. John Blacking, for instance, stated without hesitation that "there is ultimately only one explanation and . . . this could be discovered by a context-sensitive analysis of the music in culture" (1973: 17–18); "everyone disagrees hotly and stakes his academic reputation on what Mozart really meant in this or that bar of his symphonies, concertos, or quartets. If we knew exactly what went on inside Mozart's mind when he wrote them, there could be only one explanation" (93). To explain them fully, we would need to reexamine Blacking's remarks in the context of his culturalist conception of ethnomusicology. But while recognizing that an explanation of a work could be *reduced* to its poietics alone (or to one particular sector of poietics— "what Mozart was thinking"), it is nevertheless doubtful that there could be a single explanation of a musical work.

Let us take a look at various strategies for explaining the poietics of music analysis.

(a) *Historico-cultural explanation: the example of Lomax.* Let us take a case study: how can ethnomusicologist Alan Lomax's cantometric project be explained in historical terms? Before trying to explain it, we need to describe it (though only briefly). Stated another way, we need to proceed from an analysis of the neutral level of his *Folk Song Style and Culture* (1968), to reconstitute the thematic articulation of Lomax's ideas.

His objective is twofold: his first goal is to establish on a global scale, from a comparative point of view, stylistic characterizations of 233 specific musical cultures, belonging to 56 cultural areas. In pursuing his second goal he tries to relate the music-stylistic traits he inventories to cultural traits proper to limited areas, to arrive at an explanation of each style in terms of the culture to which it belongs. In both cases, the methodology employed is similar. He bases his approach (1968: 28) on the idea that a culture's stylistic specificity is manifested more in style of performance than in any immanent musical system at work (scales, pitches, rhythms, and so forth). Lomax asked trained experts to fill out a "coding sheet" that characterized each song according to thirty-seven parameters, that ranged from the register or ambitus of the piece to the properties and volume of the voice. Further, Lomax borrowed a characterization of cultures by traits from the analysis in Murdock's ethnographic atlas (1962–1967). Bringing these two *clusters* of traits into conjunction leads him to explain the music style proper to each region in terms of culture, in *interpreting* the analogies between musical and cultural traits as a symbolic analogy, in which the former *represent* the latter.[13]

Here, briefly summarized, are the main lines of Lomax's approach. The summary is no doubt subjective, full of lacunae, but it remains on the neutral level of the author's text inasmuch as it attempts neither to explain Lomax's approach in terms of its context (its poietic aspect), nor to examine its influence or significance for posterity (its esthesic aspect).

What, however, would a poietic explanation of *cantometrics* look like? From a historical angle, semiological work undertakes to reconstruct what I have called the *poietic space* of the text (Nattiez 1984: 23; English trans., 7); that is (in this case), the web of scientific paradigms that existed prior to the advent of the cantometric project, because the project implicitly or explicitly situates itself in relation to those paradigms. Lomax's case lends itself well to demonstrating a poietic space, particularly because Lomax was emerging from a crossroads

---

[13] All the evidence (and I am not being ironic) points to the existence of a semiological theory in Lomax's work, but I do not intend to pause at this point to examine it.

where most preceding ethnomusicological currents were meeting. He also emerged at a crucial historical moment, during which the discipline was experiencing a far-reaching transformation: the explicit integration of anthropological perspectives.

Lomax takes up the old comparative and universalist orientation long defended by the German school, but this time on the basis of an empirical documentation much greater and more diverse than that available to someone like Hornbostel. Historical interpretation (the sort to which Curt Sachs was partial) was not cantometrics' major preoccupation[14] however, it was never wholly absent from Lomax's perspective (1968: 3, 75, 110). Cantometrics' comparative perspective—based on analyzing style in terms of traits—inscribes itself in the tradition of Helen Roberts, George Herzog, and Bruno Nettl. In this seminal work, grouping of traits was more or less systematic (Nettl enumerates them verbally; Roberts uses tables), but was intended to characterize pieces according to specifically defined properties.

Cantometrics would not be what it is without the notion of the musical areas, derived by Helen Roberts from Kroeber's idea of cultural areas, which she illustrated in books such as *Musical Areas in Aboriginal North America* (1936). The concept is also present in Nettl's doctoral thesis, *North American Indian Musical Styles* (1954), which appeared only shortly before Lomax published his initial cantometric hypotheses (1959).

In the end, the cantometric project's attempt to establish a link between stylistic traits and cultural traits is its primary original feature. How original? As Nettl has reminded us (1983: Chapter 10), ethnographic description has never really been wholly lacking in ethnomusicological monographs. Many ethnomusicologists view David McAllester's *Enemy Way Music* (1953) as the first study to deal with a *single* given musical area in terms of a systematic juxtaposition of analysis of a musical repertory with a cultural context in which that music is practiced. Lomax goes one step farther: he attempts to explain the first by means of the second.

A fully developed ethnomusicological-historical chapter on Lomax would, of course, provide detailed textual evidence of the various components of his "poietic space," and would identify each original departure from each of those components. A poietic inquiry would be concerned with a more specific matter. We would seek to identify what one could call the catalyst that engendered the specificity of can-

---

[14] It has a more central position in Erickson 1969, a doctoral thesis by a member of the cantometrics project.

tometrics, that lead to research into correlations between stylistic traits and culture. I believe I have identified this nodal point or catalyst (an identification confirmed by Lomax's own testimony [1968: viii]): Lomax's being struck by an analogy between stress of the singing voice and rigid sexual customs in Spain. (Sex, after all, is the most important thing in life . . . after musicology and semiology.)

The historian of ethnomusicology can, at this point, attempt to make a *cultural* characterization of cantometrics. He or she will be struck right from the start by the analogies between Lomax's approach and two typical western humanistic modes of thought—Marxism and structuralism. In Lomax's idea of a relation between culture and musical style, how can we avoid being reminded of the Marxist notion of infrastructure's influence on superstructure? To Lomax, cultural determination plays the same role as economic structures in the Marxist model. Does Lomax not make an association between two layered stages of a single unique structure (as Lévi-Strauss did with language and kinship), two stages—music and culture—that are inextricably entwined within one whole? It should be noted that I am not attempting to explain Lomax in terms of some sort of Marxist or Lévi-Straussian *influence* (for which I see no evidence),[15] but merely suggesting that this comparison allows us to hone in on the cultural specificity of cantometrics. A structuralist without knowing it, Lomax resembles a Lévi-Strauss who wants to get himself some rigorous empirical tools, supported by computer, to validate an intuition concerning correlations between music and culture. In this sense, Lomax's approach seems to a French reader characteristically *American*, seems to use the methodological and technological tools supplied to *prove*, and not merely affirm, a relation (i.e., between music and culture) that otherwise might give the impression of being a vague, literary speculation.[16]

(b) *The underlying principles of an analysis: the example of the Pelléas prelude.* Let us shift our grounds and compare different harmonic analyses of the first few measures of the prelude to Debussy's *Pelléas:*[17]

[15] An explication of the similarities betweeen Lomax and Lévi-Strauss is a matter of an esthesics of their theories, as will be shown presently.

[16] This does not mean that there might not be analogies between the epistemological difficulties of Lévi-Straussian structuralism and those of cantometrics—but a critique of Lomax's work cannot escape bearing upon the specific procedures that Lomax uses to disentangle and correlate the traits retained by his analysis.

[17] The following passage, concerning the harmonic analyses of *Pelléas*, summarizes a section of an article written in collaboration with my colleague Louise Hirbour (Nattiez,

Example 7.1 Debussy: *Pelléas et Mélisande*

For Leibowitz (1971a), the "initial measures" are in D minor. The first fifth does not have a third; one cannot invoke the B♭ belonging to the scale until measures 5 and 6. Moreover, the F♯ in measure 5 erases the sense of minor mode and the A♭ is an alteration of the dominant degree of D.

From the viewpoint of scale-step motion, Leibowitz proposes the succession I–VII–V for the first few measures. He does not take the horizontal movement of the voices into account, and integrates all pitches into his harmonic analysis. But at measure 9, there is a sudden change in his criteria: the D (which one could consider a fourth added to the chord A–[C]–E–G) is designated a passing note between E and C. Now, in short, Leibowitz does take account of melodic movement.

Leibowitz also sees precise tonal functions operating from measures 4 to 5: the bass progression from A♮ to D♮ in the bassoons and cellos would confirm a progression from I to V. But we are talking

Hirbour–Paquette 1973); it recapitulates and fleshes out pages 90–93 of the *Fondements*.

about inner voices: the lowest notes of the progression (C♮ to A♭) are given to the basses. And can we claim, as he does, that the first chord in measure 5 is a seventh chord with a diminished fifth (in second inversion, with a root of D)? This appears to confuse the chord's function with its structure. Can we really speak of that seventh chord as a secondary dominant built on D? To see the chord as a secondary dominant, we need to wait until measure 12 to find the IV.

A harmonic analysis, like all human productions, is a semiological fact. This means that Leibowitz, in a *perceptive* position in relation to his object (cf. the diagram on page 153), selects a certain number of salient traits. But what are the terms by which the opening of *Pelléas*, for Leibowitz, gives rise to one set of harmonic interpretants rather than some other? The terms, of course, are those of Leibowitz's own poietics. Behind his analysis lurks a philosophical project that we can reconstruct by reading his text in its entirety: for him, *Pelléas* invariably submits to the dictates of a dialectic between real and unreal. Thus, one can explain that chords may be built on the usual scale degrees (II, IV, etc.) but that actual harmonic syntax may be unusual, or that a passage is based on the whole-tone scale, while still being grounded in D minor, and so forth. Obviously in this particular case the analytical a prioris can be traced back to a single, dominant concept. (There is no reason to believe that this would be true for all analyses.) Semiological criticism of an analysis must nonetheless, in establishing the presence of certain categories of interpretants, attempt to arrive at what I suggest we call the *transcendent principles* of that analysis. (Nattiez 1977b: 853)

This notion of transcendent principles is not unrelated to what American theoretical physicist George Holton calls *themata*:[18] "the imagination of men and women of science can, at certain crucial moments, be guided by an allegience—eventually, an explicit one—toward some *thema*, or to several *themata*" (1981: 8). It seems to me that, most of the time, these *themata* (above all when they are of a metaphysical, religious, or ontological order) are in fact all but explicitly thematicized by the scholar; this is why I hesitate to adopt Holton's term. What I am suggesting tends, however, in the same direction: it is a matter of observing what types of interpretants intervene in an analysis of the musical fact—and, moreover, observing all the (more or less) conscious assumptions that are orienting the analytical operation.

This does not mean that a semiologist could work without transcendent principles of this kind just because he or she recognizes the ne-

---

[18] I would like to thank Célestin Deliège for bringing Holton's work to my attention.

cessity of thematicizing such principles. Obviously the tripartition is a transcendent principle, based on an ontological prejudice concerning the nature not merely of music, but of all human symbolic productions. This book begins with the theory of the tripartition for this very reason, in an attempt to explain the underlying axioms that inform my own enterprise.

Musical semiology thus touches upon this "transcendental" dimension, present in all manner of musical analysis. Precisely because semiology is concerned with all symbolic forms, it can put its finger on an aspect of the problem that few musicologists, with the laudable exception of writers like Ian Bent, have thematicized explicitly.

The term "analysis of the neutral level" does *not* (cannot) mean that the musicologist is neutral with respect to his or her object,[19] but that he or she *neutralizes*, for methodological reasons, the poietic and esthesic dimensions *of the object*. It is hardly a matter of putting parentheses around the individual doing the analyzing.

As soon as we parse out our musical units, specify variables, and conclude that both are organized according to certain rules, we have already *constructed* a piece-image; the *constructed* objects thus obtained are, so to speak, isomorphous with choices effectuated by the musicologist. These choices are guided by his or her cultural presuppositions, past experience, knowledge of the musical domain, and individual esthesic reactions. Analysis of the neutral level is "dirty" because the musicologist is never neutral vis-à-vis the object being analyzed. But the great virtue of such analysis is that it produces (by means of an explicit and reproducible procedure) a set of possible schemas, whose poietic and/or esthesic relevance will, eventually, be explored in turn.

Let us return, then, to the *Pelléas* prelude.

The a prioris of analysis are often more obvious to the older writers (who can be forgiven their sins on account of their antique status); I cite them here merely as one illustration in my argument. For Louis Laloy, the first two measures of the prelude give us the progression I-V, the G of measure 2 being an ornament. To show that Debussy does not contradict the aesthetic principles of his time (prohibition against parallel fifths), Laloy writes, "here, the second fifth does not

---

[19] Even if, in the *Fondements*, the expression "neutral analysis" (*analyse neutre*) tended more than "analysis of the neutral level" to lead to confusions, there was never any question of the neutrality of the researcher. In the diagram on page 60, I spoke of the "cultural presuppositions of the analysis of the three levels," and one can read in my conclusion (page 409) that "the entire [analytical] process is based on a *determined cultural knowledge*." The following text paragraph is borrowed from page 56 of the *Fondements* (see also note 12 in Chapter 1, above).

seem to collide brusquely with the first, because the G is heard as a provisional note, and the phrase is not ended, the sense is not complete, until after the resolution of the G to A" (1902: 116–17). The G *must* be ornamental.

In van Appledorn (1966), the first chord of measure 5 is not a dominant seventh with diminished fifth, but a French sixth made up of D–F#–Ab–[C], in the usual second inversion. Now, as musical theorists generally agree, if one places the French sixth on the second degree (D), within a modal framework whose tonal center is D, one must slip in a reference to the first degree (C). Van Appledorn discovers this reference in measure 2, since with C–E–G, we pass momentarily (according to her) to the pitch C. This C major chord, then, is equally as important as the D–(F)–A of measure 1. Not only the *position* of the chord C–E–G, but the *need to explain* the chord in measure 5, establishes that C–E–G is "equally as important" as the D–(F)–A of measure 1.

Finally, we can compare the analysis of the second chord in measure 5 in Leibowitz—the type of chord is not given, but the bass is E—to the analysis in Christ (1967)—an augmented eleventh with a bass of Bb. In the first case, we have the harmonic progression I–II, not common but "unreal"; the second shows that many chords unique to the impressionist period might be pedigreed in terms of classic concepts of the superimposition of thirds.

In Roger Scruton's review of the *Fondements*, a piece as spiteful as it was lapidary and inexact, we read on the subject of analytic comparisons: "describe it as you like so long as you hear it correctly . . . certain descriptions suggest *wrong ways of hearing* it [emphasis is mine] . . . what is obvious to hear is the contrast in mood and atmosphere between the 'modal' passage and the bars which follow it." After having discussed the role of the whole-tone scale, Scruton goes on to say that "all this can be heard without describing it" (1978: 175–76). If I pause for a moment on this point in his critique, it is not because I am eager for vengeance, but because the position presented appears to me typical of all I have been trying to refute. It is hardly surprising, then, that Scruton did not understand me.[20]

Scruton commits a number of errors. First of all, he hypothesizes that a description must correspond to hearing. But this is not necessarily true. Description can evoke the *poietics* of a work—how it was composed—as well as the esthesics of a work—how it is heard by a

---

[20] If the tone Scruton takes in his review seems to me unworthy of a scholar, I would be denying quite nicely the spirit of the tripartition if I were to take offense at "not being understood"!

given listener. We can assign merely esthesic relevance to descriptions, but this will not necessarily be identical to poietic relevance. If the two were identical (as Scruton's formulation might imply), then history could effortlessly be read in the work's structures: historians of musical language could take a permanent nap. Second, what exactly does "hearing correctly" mean? Scruton sets himself up as a universal, absolute conscience for the "right" perception of the *Pelléas* prelude. But hearing is an active symbolic process (which must be explained): *nothing in perception is self-evident*; if this were not so, then all those researchers currently racking their brains to understand the mechanisms of auditory perception could simply lean back and fold their arms. What is interesting in Scruton's text, beyond an egotistic pretension to perceptive truth, is testimony about *his* (incidentally, debatable) perception—evidence that is supplied by his remarks.

Let us return to the divergences among our various analyses and descriptions. What is happening in each one? On the basis of his or her personal baggage, ideology, philosophical points of reference, and knowledge, the musicologist is effectuating a particular selection of traits *that he or she arranges according to a plot [intrigue]*. I introduce "plot" as a term of *central importance*, borrowed from epistemological historian Paul Veyne, who defines *plot* in the following way:

> Facts do not exist in isolation, in the sense that the fabric of history is what we shall call a plot, a very human and not very "scientific" mixture of material causes, aims, and chances—a slice of life, in short, that the historian cuts as he wills and in which facts have their objective connections and relative importance . . . the word plot has the advantage of reminding us that what the historian studies is as human as a play or a novel, *War and Peace* or *Anthony and Cleopatra* . . . then what are the facts worthy of rousing the interest of the historian? All depends on the plot chosen; a fact is not interesting or uninteresting . . . in history as in the theater, to show everything is impossible—not because it would require too many pages, but because there is no elementary historical fact, no eventworthy atom. If one ceases to see events in their plots, one is sucked into the abyss of the infinitismal. (1971: 46–47; English trans. by Mina Moore-Rinvolucri 1984: 32–33)

We can easily transpose this concept of plot to the domain of music analysis. Our sense of the component parts of a musical work, like our sense of historical "facts," is mediated by lived experience. An infinite number of traits, therefore, is available for selection by the musicologist. Confronted by this multiplicity of interpretants, the musicologist effectuates a selection in terms of a *plot*, which he or she has chosen in order to explain the work.

Given an already *existent* analysis or *an analysis yet to be done, thematicizing* the analytic criteria used—general principles as well as detailed methods—seems essential. My point in emphasizing contradictions among authors who analyze the same work is by no means to plead for construction of an analysis that would be the *only true analysis*. On the contrary, my goal is to have at my disposal elements that explain *the how and why of their differences*.

All analysis with a semiological orientation should, then, at least include:

(a) *a comparative critique of already-written analyses*, when they exist, so as to explain why the work has taken on this or that *image* constructed by this or that writer: all analysis is a representation;

(b) *an explanation of the analytical criteria* used in the new analysis, so that any critique of this new analysis could be situated in relation to that analysis's own *objectives* and *methods*. As Jean-Claude Gardin so rightly remarks, "no physicist, no biologist is surprised when he or she is asked to indicate, in the context of a new theory, the physical data and the mental operations that led to its formulation" (1974: 69). I see no reason why it should not effectively be the same for the humanities and for musicology. Making one's procedures explicit would help to create a *cumulative progress in knowledge*, and consequently the emergence of an analytical discourse that would be more satisfying, because it is more controlled.

I have always insisted—repeatedly—on the necessity of making analytical criteria explicit, and this is of course (since Ruwet[21]) one of musical semiology's distinctive features. We must realize, nonetheless, that these analytical criteria focus on phenomena that have always, typically, been the subject of classic music-analytical writings.

In effect, a musical analysis is characterized on one hand by *what* it intends to seek, within musical material, in order to explain the phenomenon it wishes to explore. This is what Bent terms "approaches to the substance of music" (1980: 370), in which musical parameters or facts are seen through the lens of a given (pre)conception. On the other hand, musical analysis also relies on "methods of operation" (ibid.), which I would suggest be differentiated into *methods* properly speaking (comparisons, techniques of reduction, statistical tallies, and so forth) and *conceptual tools* for analysis (thematicization of such things as level, hierarchy, unity, rules, and so forth).

---

[21] Ruwet thematicized the question of "discovery procedures" in music analysis in an important article of 1966 (reprinted in 1972: Chapter 4).

In some respects, musical semiology is not, in comparison to "traditional" approaches, asking radically new questions. Semiology always asks: what is a work made of, what is its form, what is its main theme, how does the piece develop from a single generative cell, what are its stylistic properties, and so forth. My musical semiology asks familiar questions about music. But since semiology has been influenced by linguistics, it is always self-questioning about the methodology of analysis (methodologies of other analyses, as well as its own). For this reason too, semiology is more demanding: how do we define those phenomena considered relevent in the work? What exactly are the models that explain the organization of those phenomena?

Because it is a *critical framework*, as remarked at the beginning of this chapter, musical semiology examines what other musicologists select from their musical material, how they make their selection, how they discuss it, and what principles form the basis for the discussion:

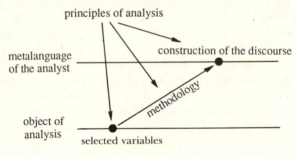

Figure 7.1

Because it is a *program for analysis*, semiology takes up each of these questions, and attempts to answer them with control and rigor—but not, of course, definitively.

5. The Esthesics of Analysis

Up until now, we have looked at musical analysis solely in terms of its descriptive dimensions (it takes account of an object), and its poietic dimensions (it comes from somewhere). But because analysis is a symbolic fact, analysis is itself read and commented upon; it has an influence. It has an esthesic dimension.

Let us return for a moment to Lomax. The cantometric method, once released on the market, no longer belongs to its author. It is the object of criticism, of interpretations. Critiques of cantometrics? They have hardly been lacking. Lomax has been reproached for using too small a sample, for defining musical traits imprecisely, and for bringing music and culture too easily and too quickly into association with one another. But we can at least agree, as a tribute to the importance of Lomax's work, that his work brings together many basic issues in ethnomusicology: comparisons between musical cultures, descriptive analysis of styles, and research into the link between culture and musical artifacts. Shall we *interpret* Lomax? We will be tempted to see the farthest, Utopian horizon of ethnomusicology in *Folk Song Style and Structure*, to see that dream of total, definitive description of all cultural factors, perceived as a whole, related to a whole, and integrated within a whole. Lomax wanted to fulfill ethnomusicology. There is something eschatological, something of a Marx or a Lévi-Strauss in him. The analogy between Lomax's approach and the structuralist approach was discussed above—though because I have no evidence for direct influence of any sort, I did not pursue this analogy in the section on poietics. But one can, certainly, assign Lomax to the same epistemological bailiwick as Lévi-Strauss; the concept of layering of structures, and research into correlations between those layers, is a common basis between them.

Here, I seem to hear a few readers muttering under their breath, "here it comes—we've had two sections in which he's been dealing with history of sciences, and he hasn't yet talked about Foucault!" Though it may entail certain deceits, at this point I do need to explain my reservations. A Foucauldian approach to Lomax appears to me impossible. For one thing, with Foucault, the author has disappeared. (1969: 264) For another, the history of ethnomusicology is doubtless too short for the purpose; according to Foucault, "from the very first" we must have "large enough domains, chronologies that are vast" (1969: 42–43). From Foucault's perspective, we would probably need to add anthropology (at least) to ethnomusicology, then add acoustics and linguistics, to be able to grasp movements and ruptures in the collective history of these disciplines. Foucault's *position* must, however, be understood—and here the tripartition once more can help us. What classic history of science (that of Bachelard or Canguilhem) traditionally suggested was a *poietics* of authors and science; Foucault, furiously divorcing himself from them, develops an *esthesics* that speaks of discontinuities, thresholds, limits, sequences, and transformations. In this sense, his project erases all symbolic relations between science and those who practice it. On the other hand, the Foucauldian project hypostasizes (without ever calling by name) a privileged perceptive position: Foucault's own.

What? Has Foucault taught us nothing? Of course. As soon as we

look at ethnomusicology's entire historical development, we can identify a transformation of ethnomusicology's objective. Foucault teaches
us to see this break in all its radicality. "Music" is not at all the same
thing to an ethnomusicologist of the Berlin School—keen on transcriptions, acoustic analyses of scales, or vast evolutionist constructions—as it is to a musical anthropologist, for whom all reference to
the dimension of sound tends to melt away, in favor of a cultural-
contextual interpretation. Rupture, discontinuity: so Foucault would
say. Foucault insists that one not ignore long stretches of time (1969:
9), and points to various "ruptures" in historical continuity, for instance: "medicine before the clinical phase had only its name in common with medicine after 1800" (Foucault, summarized in Veyne
1979: 230). But we must go farther, ask *why* the word "medicine" has
endured; *why*, given that they have such different objectives, Hornbostel, Sachs, Blacking, and Zemp are all recognized as "ethnomusicologists." To do this, we need recourse to a theory of symbolism that
acknowledges certain component parts of semiological phenomena as
stable, even though the reciprocal rhythms of permanence and transformation may not coincide. (as established by Braudel [1949]) Lomax's intermediary position in the history of ethnomusicology helps
us to understand what is happening within the discipline: in his com-
parativist and universalist objectives, Lomax is a product of his ethnomusicological precursors. But in his research into correlations between style and culture, he is already a musical anthropologist. The
objectives of the latter soon seemed radically opposed to the work of
the former. But this eventual opposition does not emerge *without a
transitional phase*. If rupture there was, then a given group of scholars
stopped perceiving the work of their *immediate* predecessors. History of
science is not some merely transitive operation—but it is never, at any
stage of its development, entirely free from an esthesic component.
This process can be represented in a supplementary schema (Figure
7.2.). By modifying the schema first introduced at the end of Chapter
6, it could be suggested that this or that writer, in a poietic position
in relation to his or her own work, is at the same time in an esthesic
position in relation to the work of predecessors.[22] In the end, history
of science cannot disregard symbolic functioning.

Musical analysis, then, is the object of interpretations and readings.
But its esthesic dimension turns out to be more active than would

---

[22] All schemas . . . schematicize, simplify. This one gives the impression of a linear
development. We would need to be able to represent in graphic terms things like net-
works of influence, to have available more axes that cross over one another. In any
case, the schema explains how writer (3) can no longer be in contact with the thought
of writer (1), even if (2) has played the role of an intermediary.

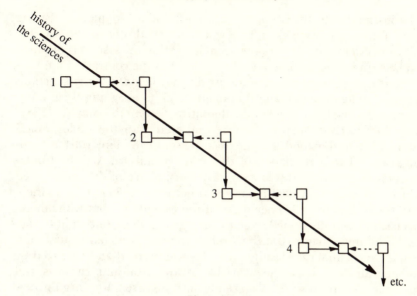

history of
the sciences

Figure 7.2

appear at first: the esthesic dimension intervenes in the *evolution of music itself*. Musical analysis obviously shares with economic theories this ability to transform, once they have been released, the phenomena that they examine. Apparently, we need only *talk* about "inflation" to provoke it (this is a nice example of the importance of symbolic facts in social life, an example of their *constructive* force). A theorist explicitly forbids parallel fifths; a composer transgresses this interdiction of his own free will; Brahms writes sonatas in a form that had been explicitly theorized: this is what reorients musical language.

As symbolic facts, analyses and musical theories constitute a far from negligible factor in the poietics of musical *works and practices*. This means that semiology, which deals with musical discourse, cannot evade its own esthesic impact. This—the semiological aspect of the metadiscourse—doubtless explains why the best-intentioned *descriptive* analysis or theory can be easily taken as *normative* discourse, without it being intended as such. It also explains why many theorists and analysts, while imagining that they are speaking the Truth, cannot rid themselves of a simultaneous desire to reshape notions of the Beautiful—the confusion between descriptive and normative is common coin in the history of music theory. As Marie-Elizabeth Duchez so justly observes, "musical structures are more imposed than made" (1980: 181). To adopt her terminology, musical theories are at once cognitive and operative, or reflexive and prospective. The move from the normative to the absolute occurs with some frequency. (Seeing that a given theory is true, why would we need others?) So says the voice of Riemann: "it does not seem likely that my system is destined to be supplanted by others in the future. On the contrary, I am convinced that in respect to grounding all chords in the three functions of tonic, subdominant, and dominant, (even in assigning them numbers) my work has provided the definitive view on the subject" (1887: xii). Fétis writes, "many of those endowed with the philosophical spirit have understood that the doctrine set forth in my work is nothing more than a revelation of the secret of musical Art, the fundamental law; without this law works of musical art, of the sort created during the last four centuries, would not exist" (1844: 1). The theorist these days has a keener sense of the ridiculous—but who among us has not secretly hoped to be the one giving voice, once and for all, to the ultimate truth? But the symbolic nature of metadiscourse precludes such finality. Alas, our writings will be read and criticized by others; and new traits, new variables drawn from musical facts, will provide the impulse for suggesting new analyses, for forging new theories, and for inventing new plots.

8

The Musician's Discourse

1. Analyses by Composers

IF the musical fact gives rise to a multiplicity of discourses, meta- and perimusical discourses, this is because commenting on music is a universal anthropological given of the musical fact. We could in this context paraphrase Paul Ricoeur: as soon as someone dances, sings, or plays an instrument, someone else gets up and talks about it.

But musicologists, or semiologists, do not have a monopoly on discourse about music. If I have been examining the semiology of the metalogues, this is because the total musical fact includes *verbal symbolic forms that are closely tied to the sonorous event* in a strict sense: reactions of listeners, critical commentaries from the esthesic angle, arguments, letters, and analyses of composers who supply poietic information. My musical semiology is, then, concerned with an *intrication of symbolic forms* that can, themselves, be made the object of a tripartitional analysis. One never relies on a *single* semiological description in analyzing a symbolic form. We need to move on to multiple semiologies, and to make (with as much care as possible) an inventory of the elements that are at stake.[1]

For example, we might ask ourselves: where should we situate those analyses that are offered by a special category of musicians, the composers themselves? On a metalinguistic plane, of course. But they also, above all, constitute an esthesic testimonial.[2] This can be expressed by Figure 8.1.

When Pierre Boulez untangles the rhythmic structures of the *Rite*

---

[1] This is what will be shown in some detail in the chapters in Volume 3 devoted to poietics and esthesics.

[2] The remainder of Section 1 is borrowed from my article "La relation oblique entre le musicologue et le compositeur" (1985).

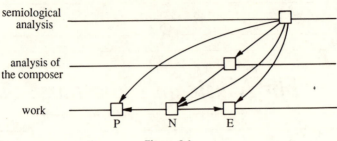

Figure 8.1

of Spring, he states specifically that he has not "pretended to discover a creative process" (1966: 142); that he considers the "mathematical relationships as the only tangible relationships [in the piece]" (ibid.). Nevertheless, his research into mirror forms, retrograde rhythms, and inversion structures owes more than a little to serial thinking in general, and to Messiaen's teachings in particular. When Berg analyzes Schumann's *Träumerei*, we are no longer dealing with the formal, thematic, and harmonic analysis of classical musicology: "the entire first section of the phrase," he writes concerning the piece's opening, "already constitutes a variation—and what a variation!—on that initial interval of the fourth. This will appear several times in the little descending phrase that follows it; it will transform itself, at the whim of the harmonic turns, into ever-changing intervals" (1985: 85). The same type of description could apply, *mutatis mutandis*, to the first measures of his own sonata for piano. Why did Pousseur devote an entire book to Schumann's *Dichterliebe*? We need quote only the beginning of his analysis of *Im wunderschönen Monat Mai*: "the first piece, and with it the entire cycle, begins with the most sustained dissonance, in a distribution that for a brief instant is literally Webernian" (1981: 96). A bit further, he sees the key succession of each piece as being "practically a row" (104–113). When he analyzes the "Étude pour les quartes" by Debussy, Boulez (1981a) shows how Debussy departs from minimal material, developing and transforming it: the author of *Notations* and *Répons* recognizes himself in Debussy's *Étude*. On the other hand, Guy Reibel, a composer of the Groupe de Recherches Musicales, will deal with Debussy's harmonic aggregates as "musical objects" in Schaeffer's sense (cf. the analysis presented at the Paris Conservatory in 1975).

What, then, is the contemporary composer doing when he or she confronts the works of the past? Does the composer, perhaps, seek to inscribe him- or herself within a given historical tradition? Without necessarily wanting to, the composer reveals the origins of certain inspirations, and above all, shows us how music can be subject to a marvelous and erratic alchemy within the confines of the atelier, an alchemy that bears upon the origin of contemporary works.

We say erratic because, in some ways, a "serial" or quasi-serial analysis of *Dichterliebe* possesses little sense in terms of conventional musicology. In my book on the centennial production of the *Ring* at Bayreuth, I included a conversation I had with Pierre Boulez concerning musical analysis. He said:

> I prefer that someone analyzes four measures of a work for me, just four measures, at the moment that something of the future can be drawn from that work. In that, I can judge his imaginative power. If he doesn't put anything into the inquiry, he could analyze three years worth of music, and come up with nothing. I would hope that, as a composer, he sees something in this music, *even if it is wrong in relation to the original.* There is an analysis of Stockhausen's (1963) that is a joy to me: he is interested in a passage in Webern's quartet, not in terms of counterpoint, but in relation to *density.* From Webern's point of view, that's nonsense, obviously. But I am sure that Stockhausen profited greatly by it. Wrong analyses are more revealing of a personality. (in Nattiez 1983: 239–40)

In comparison to a musicologist, the composer deliberately strikes a *delinquent* stance. Does this mean that musicologists should feel uneasy when confronted by such analyses? Not in the least. Insofar as composers draw past works toward the future in reading them in terms of their present, their analyses are *testimonies*, bearing upon an engaged hearing of works by contemporary artists—a document, in other words, for the musicologist, in the study of musical perception. These analyses cannot pretend to objectivity; they are not privileged; they constitute a particular symbolic form that maintains a specific rapport with their analytical object.

But from an epistemological point of view, they represent what is perhaps the extreme case of a trait manifested in all works that bear upon past works or actions. Whether we are talking about philosophers such as Heidegger or Gadamer, or epistemologists of history like Aron, Marrou, or Veyne, or music historians like Dahlhaus, all have emphasized the *historicity* of historical work, that is, the influence exercized upon the historian by the epoch in which he or she lives. I speak of an "extreme case" because, in a composer's analysis, historicity is not merely assumed, but constitutes the very basis of the approach. It is also its chief point of interest.

Chapter Eight

2. The Discourse of Musical Producers

We have just spoken of the composer's discourse in his or her approach to others' music. But composers also discuss their own music. We therefore need to expand our investigation—especially since ethnomusicologists have (finally) recognized that "primitive" man can also possess music theory, possess what is elsewhere called ethnotheory.[3] We can express the relationship of a producer's discourse to his or her own music in a new schema, similar to Figure 8.1. We can see that this type of discourse is one component part, one piece of information at our disposal for a semiological analysis: the musical producer can speak of his or her own compositional strategies, the elements of the music produced, how it is (or should be) played and heard. But the schema once more keeps the reader in a metalinguistic position.[4]

Our first task is to ask questions about the status of *ethnotheories*. Smith writes, for instance, in the context of her research on the Panamanian Kuna:

> The organization, content, and structural function of music theories are articulated on four levels of experience: (1) mythical and historical explanations of the origin and function of music; (2) semantic fields used to identify musical elements and activities; (3) patterns of sound and motion used to form recognizable domains of expression; and (4) structural and functional interrelationships between music theory and theories of other expressive forms. (Smith 1982: 1)

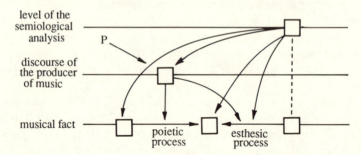

Figure 8.2

---

[3] A short bibliography of ethnotheories would include Feld 1982, Keil 1979, Powers 1980, Sakata 1983, Smith 1982, Stone 1981, Tedlock 1980, and Zemp 1978, 1979.

[4] The essential matter in the remainder of this chapter recapitulates, with certain revisions, my article "Paroles d'informateurs et propos de musiciens: quelques remarques sur la place du discours dans la connaissance de la musique" (1981d).

We shall deal only with the second and third propositions.

Proposition (2) is not in itself dangerous, but it could imply, in the context of the whole paragraph, that music theory is located in some way *behind* the words, that it is underneath another discourse. Certainly one can always reconstruct the tenets and results of a system of thought, the main lines of its organization (as some people would say, its structure), on the basis of a series of arguments of any kind (whether strongly or loosely organized)—it is the musicologist's job to move toward this *exegesis*. (This reconstruction is equally possible in the case of so-called "civilized" societies as in societies of the oral tradition.) But this exegesis can be more accurately regarded as *hermeneutic* work, in which the researcher takes *interpretive* risks. This is why, rather than supposing that the theory is somehow hidden behind the discourse, we must take it as axiomatic that the theory is produced by the musicologist *out* of the discourse. The musicologist's work must begin with recognizing, with observing, particular modes of organization for thinking about music *as mediated by discourse*. It is only *afterward* that it will be possible (and much easier) to determine the gap between what is written or said, and the underlying system of thought manifested in that discourse. If we lose sight of the fact that the researcher is moving toward a *reconstruction* of thought-systems, we would run the risk of erasing the difference between what almost certainly belongs to the indigenous peoples themselves, and what is a result of the musicologist's intervention.

Smith's third proposition also reflects a real situation: again, that behind the sounds there is a system of thought. But we must note at once that this is only one potential case. As we know from Rameau, from the academic fugues of the classical era, from the history of the idea of sonata form, theory can long outlive its time. It would be interesting to know (if this were possible) the *histories* of the more elaborate discourses studied by ethnomusicology, like Irisipau's remarks on his own people the "Are" are, remarks collected by Zemp. Did Irisipau, too, deduce the theory from the musical practice of his people, or was it handed down to him? To establish a theory on the basis of sonorous configurations . . . is not always to untangle an ethnotheory. It means reconstructing the structural organization of a musical style, by means of methodological and conceptual tools belonging to an occidental knowledge, and with or without the help of remarks made by indigenous peoples. The connection between this reconstructed organization and a native mode of thought remains to be established—carefully.

When Smith elsewhere speaks of nonverbalized domains of music theory, is this not a contradiction in terms? We have no way of speaking of theory except as verbalized and explicit. It might be suggested in response that theory in fact could exist in oral societies, in forms or modalities that we cannot recognize in our western mode. But to suggest this would be to entrap ourselves in an aporia. We will always define the word "theory" even in its loosest sense[5] (as the *Dictionnaire Robert* states, a "collection of ideas, abstract concepts more or less organized, applied to a particular domain") according to its usage in *our* societies. If it is defined otherwise elsewhere, would we still have the right to speak of "theory" (our word)? I might be permitted to observe that the most remarkable instances of ethnotheories that have to date been recorded [presented] are quite close, when all is said and done, to our western theoretical discourses. That Irisipau speaks through the expedient of metaphors, in Zemp's film on the "Are" are, is not a problem.[6] On the contrary, for Zemp has been able to translate these metaphors in terms of western theory.

Actually, as soon as musical ethnotheories are discovered, we should undertake a classification of different types of ethnotheories, from ground zero (where after the most extensive investigation, it is clear that the ethnotheory amounts to only a few words) to the most sophisticated elaborations on the subject. Even in the first case, the paucity of words does not mean that the indigenous person is not thinking, but if we are to avoid the difficulties noted above, it would seem necessary to distinguish among three orders of reality: the musical corpus, the metamusical discourse, and the reconstruction of indigenous systems of thought. The direction of the arrows in Figure 8.3 is intended to summarize what has been said previously: the words, as much as the musical corpus, constitute *data*; they have their own symbolic configurations whose specific articulations must be respected. The indigenous discourse bears on the corpus (1). Our job is to examine the nature of the relation between this ethnotheory and music (2). From study of this relationship (2), of the words themselves (3), from analysis of the musical corpus (4) one can deduce something like a "thinking about music," but this is a *reconstruction* whose connection to the *data* that allow its elaboration must be established with great care.

As metalanguage, discourse about music *is not* music. As a specific symbolic form, it is an *autonomous* object, even if it has no meaning except in relation to the object it interprets. This explains why musi-

---

[5] In opposition to a more stable epistemological conception of theory, "a methodical, organized intellectual construction, of a hypothetical and (at least in certain parts) synthetic character" (*Dictionnaire Robert*).

[6] It is a matter of metaphors to which we are not accustomed, which is something different again.

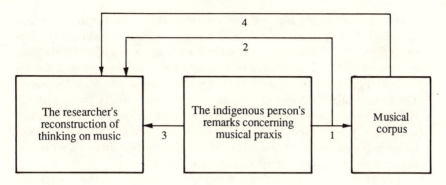

Figure 8.3

cology can be an activity in itself, whose history, and whose sociology and ethnography as well, can be written. The *attitude* of musicologists and musicians often betrays their recognition of this autonomy, but in terms quite different from mine. There is, first of all, the usual musician's rejection of musicological discourse, a discourse considered parasitic. There is the usual musicologist's rejection of the musician's discourse: "the composer doesn't know what he's talking about. He's the last to know anything about the results of his creative activity. Only the result counts." In ethnomusicology, it was thought for a long time that the indigenous peoples were not capable of metamusical conceptualization, and they were simply not asked about such conceptualizations.[7] On the other hand, historical musicology has been able to develop a virtual fetishism for musicians' writings and remarks: in the worst case, collecting and editing letters and texts of composers comes to be a substitute for musical analysis. A similar situation exists, now, in more recent ethnomusicology. Though I doubt that it has ever been stated so brutally,[8] developments in cognitive anthropology and ethnoscience have encouraged certain ethnomusicologists (traumatized by the specter of ethnocentrism) to believe that the indigenous informant's word is always and necessarily more "true" than that of the external observer.

Of course it is epistemologically more reasonable to adopt an intermediate position: discourse is a piece of *testimony*. Rosen writes concerning sonata form: "I have not relied entirely on eighteenth-cen-

---

[7] See the statements by ethnomusicologists collected by Feld (1982: 163): "In primitive music a scale does not exist in the mind of the native musicians, so the musicologist must deduce it from the melodies" (Nettl 1956: 45). "The Flathead [Indians] simply do not verbalize about music" (Merriam 1967: 45).

[8] I have already, again, heard it said that "analysis must be made by the people," which is epistemologically absurd, and politically demagogic.

tury theorists (they misunderstood their time just as we do ours) although I have often found their views stimulating and useful" (Rosen 1980: ii). In his edition of Berg's writings (*Écrits*, 1957), Belgian composer Henri Pousseur sets into relief the contradiction between what Berg says, and what we observe, about his music. His discourse, Pousseur states, is "behind the times" in comparison to his profound musical innovations, which, in retrospect, we are better able to evaluate. It is hard to see why the discourse of an indigenous informant in societies of the oral tradition must necessarily supply us with our only totally adequate image of what his music is.

As an autonomous symbolic form, the discourse of the composer, or the indigenous musician, has its own poietics, and for this reason I have drawn a "P" with a slanted arrow, a level of the producer's discourse, in Figure 8.2. How do we describe that discourse? For the most part, by making an ethnography.

This ethnography is necessary in evaluating the distance between discourse and what it discusses; in other words, the ethnography allows us to judge how far the discourse of the composer, of the native musician, "adheres" to the musical fact, to judge at what point it becomes unreliable. The ethnography of discourse about music includes at least four dimensions:

— attitude toward language in general;
— attitude toward discourse about music;
— circumstances of the discourse;
— the speaker's personality.

(a) *Attitude toward language in general.* We know, for instance, that language is not used the same way, within the same linguistic group, in urban and rural milieus. Although they speak the same language, the Québecois do not assign the same value to language as the French, in whom a certain logo-chauvinism anchored in the culture has led to a virtual fetishism of speech and writing. Since Genviève Calame-Griaule's fine book *Ethnologie et langage, la parole chez les Dogon* (1965), we no longer need to plead that the existence of a cultural conditioning of discourse be recognized; the systematic research on the ethnography of language in the collection by Bauman and Sherzer, *Explorations in the Ethnography of Speaking* (1974), along with essays by Dell Hymes, presents initial evidence. What we must stress, however, is the need to recognize the specific status of language in a culture, to judge the exact scope of discourse about music.

(b) *Attitude toward discourse about music.* The content of the thought conveyed by metamusical discourse depends greatly on the social norm, according to which a certain type of discourse about music is tolerated, accepted, encouraged; this norm will vary, moreover, from one group to another within the core of the same society. Boulez and Messiaen are anything but sparing of commentaries on their own works, and (apart from their individual personalities) their linguistic behavior is quite typical of the fashion for commentary characteristic of French society. It is manifested in that particular genre of literary "explication de texte," in the format of the lecture-recitals of the *Jeunesses Musicales*, the broadcasts and debates on books, films, and theater on radio and television, and so forth. But various personality types can coexist within the core of the same society. Parmegiani[9] discusses music because he is asked to, and because, in France, one has to talk about music, but in his heart of hearts he detests it: he belongs to a group of artists who would gladly say "I said it all in my music, listen to that."

(c) *The circumstances of the discourse.* Culture does not only determine the activity of talking about music; it also dictates how one speaks of it and what one talks about. In Wagner's writings, there is, practically speaking, no musical analysis whatsoever. We find a few rare musical examples in the "Anwendung der Musik auf das Drama" (Wagner 1879). What was important to him was sustaining a discourse that situated itself on the same level as the great philosophies of the time—philosophies that he had made his own, first those of Feuerbach, and then Schopenhauer.

The context in which one speaks about music is, then, decisive. This context is at once, as we shall see, social and cultural in the largest sense. A second context, however, is that of the particular circumstances in which the discourse is conducted. The press did not miss the chance to point out the great diversity of Boulez's approaches in my recent edition of his collected writings (Boulez 1981b). The truth is that one does not, in fact, talk the same way about music in giving a summer course at Darmstadt, in granting an interview, or in writing up an analysis, a program note, or liner notes for recordings. In the field, the native informant—all ethnomusicologists know this—changes his or her style from spontaneity in a conversation among friends, to a very cool stance in the systematic interview with the researcher.

(d) *The speaker's personality.* It is, in the end, a matter of knowing who is talking. Margaret Mead, among others, has taught us not to regard societies of the oral tradition as well-regulated clocks. Even in

[9] He is one of the most important French composers of electro-acoustic music, and the author of a superb piece, *De Natura Sonorum*, that was the object of a poietic inquiry in Mion, Thomas, Nattiez 1983.

a small community, not everybody thinks the same way. Zemp detailed it well when he wrote of his informants: "not every 'Are' are musician is aware of these denominations [i.e., indigenous terminologies]" (1979: 6) and we would do well to acknowledge that, within a group, some will possess more wisdom than others, like Ogotomele in the case of the Dogon (Griaule 1966: 209).

I am not necessarily a great partisan of systematic quantification of data, but it is critical all the same to specify the number of informants on which an ethnotheory is based. And if we are able to (or must) trust only one, it is still necessary to explain why. We have been sensitized to this problem by Edward Sapir: "Apparently, Two-Crows, a perfectly good and authoritive Indian, could presume to rule out of court the very existence of a custom or attitude or belief vouched by some other Indians, equally good and authoritive." (1949: 570)

The sage may be *right* in opposition to the entire community, but he may also be crazy. Each piece of testimony must be subjected to critical evaluation. First, on the personal level: what is the part played by lapses of memory, lying, bad faith, or reticence in the testimonies collected? When there is some discordance within the information gathered, what role is played by perception, point of view, age, or geographical origin?

Thus we see that a piece of testimony has the status of a document, whose validity must be evaluated by comparisons and cross-checking. Analysis of discourse about music begins with an ethnographic hermeneutics, one that bears certain similarities to the methods of a historian.[10]

To evaluate the content of meanings conveyed by metamusical discourse, we must also study the *possibilities* of this discourse: of what is it able to speak?

(a) What is important, first, is to redo an inventory of the domains that are dealt with in speech (or writing) about music. These include history and socio-cultural context, psychology of the composer or the performer, compositional processes, musical structures themselves, interpretation, and musical perception. It is a trivial list, of course, but it forces us to remember that the best-intentioned informant in the world cannot simultaneously speak about *all* the characteristic domains of the total musical fact.

(b) Metamusical discourse has a lesser or greater bearing in relation to each of these domains. It may happen that the composer reveals the mechanism of his creative process in some detail (again, in compositional styles that lend themselves to it, such as serial music and

---

[10] On the connection between history and anthropology of music cf. Volume 2.

stochastic music), but it is rare, not to say impossible, that he or she is able to explain the process in its entirety. This is even more true in ethnomusicology. From the side of perception or evaluation, the *scope* of the discourse is larger still, more global. The discourse is able to get close to the musical material only with respect to structural elements of music. Depending whether we are dealing with composition, structure, or perception, and according to possibilities for apprehending the musical facts that are being considered, metamusical discourse effects a more or less extensive *focalization* in relation to the data.

(c) The possibilities of discourse do vary between those that are riddled with lacunae, and those that are continuous. In the best of cases, the person who engages the musical substance does so from the beginning to the end of a piece. But I do speak of continuity, not totality, since no discourse can ever cover the whole "reality" of musical structures. Any structural trait can, in effect, be related to any other trait, and thus give rise to a new combination. Musical analysis (as mentioned previously, in Chapter 6, note 5) is interminable (Molino 1975a: 58–60).

Discourse about compositional processes and perception is, itself, far more discontinuous. To speak with Gushee (1976), who is concerned with compositional processes in music of the oral tradition, as well as medieval music, we need a "gapology," a science of lacunae, an analysis of the empty spots.

(d) The usefulness and validity of the metamusical discourses of our informers will ultimately depend on the *nature of the analytical approach into which we wish to integrate those discourses.*

At present, musical ethnotheories have an autonomous status in the strategy of ethnomusicological research. We have just discovered their existence and their importance, and we have studied them for themselves, in themselves. But no one, so far as I know, has yet published a systematic confrontation of ethnotheories with analysis of musical structures. In Zemp's film, Irisipau gives us terms that correspond to the equiheptatonic second, the major second, the third, and the octave, which are important intervals for length of bore in panpipes. But what about the other intervals? One could ask Zemp the question that Molino asked about Steven Feld's book (1982): "does the fact that there is no conceptualization of these intervals have any consequences for musical practice itself, or for the perception of music? To limit ourselves to one example: could we not imagine that the absence of terms to designate the 'wide, ascending jumps' that appear in *gisalo* derives from the fact that the Kaluli make their musical segments begin with the high notes, and do not thematicize the transition from one segment to the next?" (Molino 1984c: 298). This *absence* of terms must lead to inaugurating new questions. Far from discouraging study of the structure of recorded pieces, it should stimulate such study. It seems critical to me to emphasize at this point that in no case (for the danger is that we hypostasize the word of the indigenous person) should presentation of the musical ethnotheory think of substituting itself for analysis of the music. The indigenous discourse cannot cover all aspects of the musical fact; this justifies yet again the *necessity of undertaking an analysis of the neutral level.*

In the near future, the problem will be to determine how we can use knowledge of the ethnotheory in our analysis of structures, how that knowledge will influence those analyses. But we should not think of dispensing with structural analyses. By means of an interaction between the ethno-information and the analytical tools of the researcher, a richer study of the musical fact will become possible. This study would be at once reverent of indigenous data, while aspiring by means of a detailed elaboration of structures on the different levels, to a maximally complete view of the works considered. The forms of this interaction can take on different guises. Norma McLeod (1966) was not able to find an indigenous terminology in Madagascar for the names of musical phrases; she moved on to an inventory of criteria for analyzing these units. In the generative grammars proposed by David Sapir (1969) and Judith and Alton Becker (1979), the informants' categories (though not for all the units) are available to us,[11] but it is clear that the "final product" of the analysis, as well as the setting up of the rules, results from observing the behavior of various musical units, and the use, on the western researcher's part, of a particular (western) analytic technology.

What has been said here about ethnomusicology can be transposed to the study of the western repertory. Without going into detail, I would say that the possibility of connecting information concerning history of music, social and psychological data of creation, the composer's background, and perceptual processes, with an analysis of musical structures, depends on the possibility of *controlling the constituent variables* of these different fields of human knowledge.[12]

---

[11] For *srepegan*, the Beckers have noted the term *gongan*, which designates a phrase that ends with a gong stroke, but there are apparently no names (within the culture) for the units of four pitches on a low level—units that a paradigmatic analysis immediately brings to light, and that no analysis of this music should pass over. For the Diola-Fogny, Sapir allows the intervention of abstract labels (phrase, interjection, and so forth), that have no equivalent in indigenous terminology.

[12] This crucial problem in music analysis will be the object of a detailed examination in Volume 2.

I indicated in Chapter 7 that a whole gamut of metamusical discourses exists, from "close readings of texts" [explications de texte] to formal models. Depending on the type of commentary chosen, the indigenous informant's or the composer's discourse will integrate itself more or less smoothly into the whole analysis. If we remain at the level of a general exegesis, smooth integration is not a problem. But if we wish to undertake a detailed analysis of structures, there will certainly be problems in adjustment.

One should not think of doing without analysis of musical substance, analysis coolly done, so to speak, even when—in the best cases—this analysis is also adopting and integrating indigenous categories.

But: would analysis of the neutral level be more "true," more "objective," than the musician's word? The preceding discussion enables us to hone in on the problem. The difficulty stems from the fact that the "view from inside" is not necessarily more "true" than the view from outside. A culture is nothing other than a style: a style of beliefs, customs, behaviors. It was not simply fortuitous that Montesquieu, at the dawn of western anthropology, entrusted the task of observing French society to a fictitious Persian narrator. In making comparisons to his own society, Uzbek perceives and little by little understands the *differences* that he observes. Only by leaving his own country can a German make himself realize that respect for pedestrian crossings, and other marks of collective discipline, are a matter of cultural habit and are not necessarily shared by other people.

Metaphor is currently high fashion in the social sciences.[13] After having drawn up a history of different definitions of metaphor, a group of scholars (Molino, Soublin, Tamine 1979: 38) showed that, beyond conceptual divergences, what remained as an irreducible element of "metaphor" was the opposition of the literal and the figurative. Transposed into an ethnographic context, the question becomes: are the indigenous informant's metaphors "wrong" in comparison to the western researcher's "truth"? We can ask it in other terms: if we deem a given ethnotheory metaphorical, is this not because we compare it with a form of knowledge that we consider more positive? In speaking of "indigenous metaphors," I mean the opposition of masculine and feminine themes in writings by Riemann and d'Indy, as much as the use of vocabulary connected with water and birds in the Kaluli studied by Feld. Actually, in the social context

[13] As a representative work in this line, see Lakoff and Johnson, *Metaphors We Live By* (1980). For a critique of Feld's use of the concept of metaphor, see Molino 1984: 299–300.

of the Kaluli or the historical context of Riemann, these metaphors are experienced perfectly well—within the respective thought-frame-works—as *models* of musical reality. I am quite ready to acknowledge that mathematical or linguistic models introduced into music analysis are, for us (as Paul Cardin suggests[14]) metamusical scientific meta-phors. There are, in science, numerous metaphors (Molino 1979a, 1979b); the problem is evaluating their capacity for simulation. In societies of the oral tradition, it would be a matter of knowing (from a perspective that ethnoscience cannot impugn) where exactly *is* that border between the literal and the figurative in the society or epoch being examined.

In practice, we are of course obliged to accept the idea that the researcher (through his or her work of observing) is capable of re-vealing *facts*. This, too, is irreducible. When an Inuk says that the throat is the point of origin of sound in *katajjaq*, but modern articu-latory phonetics (Ladefoged) states that there are no guttural sounds as such,[15] I am hard put to imagine what guilt complex about ethno-centricity could allow privileging the informant's illusion above a well-established physiological fact. Obviously, it is quite another thing to take the informant's conception literally in order to resituate it within a larger symbolic context. Smith, for example, notes that "an analysis of the hocket parts [in the Panamanian Kuna] shows that the terms 'leader' and 'follower' are somewhat misleading, because the follower part leads the leader in many ways" (1982: 9). A divergence between ethnotheoretical discourse and the researcher's observations (similar to those discussed above) thus opens the way to new investi-gations: if the one who follows in some way leads, why use this ter-minology? What else does it encompass? What exact meaning do these terms have in their context—this language, this culture? We should always keep in mind that excessive culturalism should not pre-vent us from recognizing, from accepting, the existence of *facts* and *truths* (Bouveresse 1984: 109–129).

We have been brought to our conclusion: to outline the nature of the relationship between the indigenous discourse and the research-er's discourse. It is a question of *dialogue*, and dialogue alone, for there can be no purely emic or purely etic analysis. I have always been struck that Judith Becker was able to show the emic relevence of the scale-units she analyzed (1969: 269), but that she put her trust in her own analytic tools to describe the hierarchical levels above the musical

---

[14] Personal communication with the author.

[15] Here, I am referring to a yet-unpublished study by Claude Charron.

structure:[16] emic data and etic data are juxtaposed in her work, and rightly so. Ethnomusicological research, like historical or anthropological research, consists of *translation*: we explain—in our language, according to our categories (which are themselves culturally determined)—what the informant tells us, and the musical facts we observe. I espouse, definitively, Geertz's position: "we are not . . . seeking either to become natives or to mimic them. Only romantics or spies would seem to find a point in that. We are seeking . . . to converse with them . . . the whole point of a semiotic approach to culture is . . . to aid us in gaining access to the conceptual world in which our subjects live, so that we can, in some extended sense of the term, converse with them" (1973: 13, 24).

In summary: the metamusical and ethnotheoretical discourse of our informants is only *one* of the possible sources that allow us to understand the musical fact in its totality—just as this discourse is itself no more than one component part of the total musical fact. Of course it is a strategic part, in the sense that it must be through the intermediary of discourse that protagonists' thoughts reveal themselves; but for the same reason, metamusical and ethnotheoretical discourse is no more than one trace of this thought-system among others, a piece of testimony, an index of compositional and perceptive processes. It is neither reflection nor image of those processes. Knowledge of music on the most global scale would presuppose an exchange, an interaction among the documents that are at our disposal: the words, the musical praxis, the works themselves.

I have insisted with some force on the cultural conditioning of metamusical discourse. In my various schemas, semiology has always appeared at the "peak" of a succession of metadiscourses. Does the semiologist, then, take him- or herself to be God? I should repeat once and for all that all the principles proposed here can also be applied to semiologic theory itself. I had a particular education, in a particular country. I belong to a particular culture. In the end, however, it is not up to me to add to the pile of accreted metadiscourses by analyzing my own. But it should be clear that I am perfectly well *aware* of the semiological and cultural nature of my own remarks. I do not offer them as a *doxa*, but as elements in a dialogue—with my critics, with my readers.

[16] Cf. 1969: 272: "the segments combined into patterns, combined into verses, combined into songs make Burmese music a multileveled hierarchical system. How the Burmese musician manipulates the various levels of the hierarchy to create the song has eluded objective investigation and remained within the mysterious realms of the intuitive. But with sharper, more effective tools of investigation this mental operation itself should begin to be revealed."

Conclusion

9

Theory and Analysis as Symbolic Constructions

M Y PURPOSE in Part II was to insist (perhaps more than is cus-
tomary) that the musicologist's persona is present behind his
or her discourse. For this reason, an analysis, like a musical work (or
like any product of compositional labor) is a *symbolic construction*. As
such analysis in its own turn is subject to tripartite scrutiny; thus in
Part II I have discussed discourse about music both as a semiological
and as an anthropological fact.[1]

In the course of Part II, I have suggested that we highlight two
concepts: the notion of the transcendent principle, and that of plot.
In concluding, I would like to show how, in the case of harmonic
analysis, different *variables* are retained in a description of harmonic
phenomena, that these variables are chosen from among an enormous number (perhaps an infinite number) of possible variables.
Moreover, I would argue that these variables are selected according
to a *transcendent principle* (or even principles) that dictates the choice
of a theoretical framework, and according to a *plot* that orients the
way the analysis unfolds. This examination brings us face to face with
a difficult question, one that will always recur in our minds, even

[1] This final chapter draws material from various sections in Chapter 9 of the French
edition, which was itself a reprint of the article *Armonia* in the 1977 *Enciclopedia Einaudi*. I wish to thank M. Pietrangeli, director of Einaudi Editions, for permission to
use it here. I have added to this a revised version of my article "Plot and Seriation in
Music Analysis" (1984) [which has been retranslated from the French text of the revi-
sion]. In the present version, I have attempted to respond to questions and observations raised in the course of a particularly fruitful conversation I had with Jonathan
Dunsby, Esther Cavett-Dunsby, Craig Ayrey, and James Ellis. I have also heeded various suggestions by Jean Molino; I thank all these.

201

when we try to avoid it: is one analysis more *true* than others; is there truth in analysis?

1. *Harmonic Theories and the Transcendent Principle*

One need only read a sufficient number of treatises, in different languages and from different eras, to realize that a given classification of chords, a given way of explaining their succession, will be based upon some general explanatory principle of tonal harmony. Most often this principle is signalled within the first few pages. This principle will also be a generative principle, since the author will need to explain how chords are created. Rameau, for instance, based his theoretical work on the natural overtone series—and until quite recently, most harmony treatises began with a description of the harmonics generated above a low C:

Example 9.1

As we know, the "overtone" theory fails to explain the minor chord. This is why Riemann and d'Indy appealed to the theory of the "undertone series" proposed by Zarlino in the *Instituzione armoniche* (1558), which is based not on the harmonic division (1, 1/2, 1/3, 1/4, 1/5, 1/6) but on the arithmetic division of the string (1, 2, 3, 4, 5, 6):

Example 9.2

It is greatly to Fétis's credit that in a work conceived in 1815 (though not published until 1840), he refused, in juxtaposing the systems in music of the oral tradition with traditional tonality, to ground harmony in any natural law. This was, for its time, revolutionary in the extreme. He preferred to speak of a "law of tonality," applicable to harmony as well as melody, that defines the laws of attractions among the scale degrees.

These basic principles constitute typical instances of *transcendent principles*: they explain the global functioning of tonal harmony, above and beyond the practical activities of this or that composer. Rameau is quite clear on that point, from the first pages of his *Traité*: "even if experience can enlighten us concerning the different properties of music, it alone cannot lead us to discover the principle behind these properties with the precision appropriate to reason. Conclusions drawn from experience are often false, or at least leave us with doubts that only reason can dispel" (1722: 1; Gossett 1971, xxxiii). Riemann considers harmony a *pure* and theoretical science: its goal is to "define the laws that govern how our mind conceives of relationships between different sounds" (1926: 1). According to Riemann, however, only professional musicians are interested in knowing these laws, so theoretical study of harmony is mixed with practical study.

Knowing the transcendent principle at work in an analysis is fundamental to explaining analytical details, and explaining decisions made by the authors of the treatises. Given a particular analysis, we must not only go back to the theory of reference, but to the transcendent principle of that theory (if it exists)—a principle that generates certain theoretical consequences.[2] For instance, Fétis allows only the perfect triad and the seventh as "natural chords": all others are obtained through the application of three essentially melodic procedures, justified by the law of tonality: substituting one interval for another, prolonging one or several pitches, or chromatically altering pitches (either sharp or flat). Though d'Indy attributes the origins of minor chords to the "undertone series," he cannot follow Rameau in ascribing a dominant role to the fundamental bass, and he explains the formation of other chords in terms of the perfect triad alone, as the results of melodic phenomena: "all the combinations we call 'dissonant chords' originate in *dynamic* melodic successions, and can always be traced back to one of the three tonal functions, I, IV, or V . . . contemplating chords in themselves, for themselves, is foreign to music" (1903: 116–17). D'Indy even comes to reject the very idea of classifying chords. We see from these brief examples that what one might call the "taxonomical stock" of each harmonic theory—that is,

---

[2] I say "transcendent principle" and not "axiom" in order not to imply that the results of a transcendent principle have the same character of necessity as a formalized theory's theorems. These results are actually reconstituted by the epistemologist or the historian of music theory, and thus relate to a hermeneutic approach.

the collection of chords that the theory recognizes, classifies, and describes—depends heavily on a transcendent principle.

But an analysis does not depend only on the transcendent principle at work behind the theory. On the basis of these unchallenged principles, the musicologist does his or her best to explain the harmonic material in a coherent way. This is done according to a *plot*.

2. *Plots and Tripartition*

There is no limit to the number of possible plots. With the help of semiology, we shall linger a bit over three large plot-families. Harmonic analysis can strive to correspond to the composer's *poietics*, to correspond to his or her categories of thought, explaining the organization of the works. Such analysis might, on the other hand, try to explain ways of perceiving harmonic phenomena; it adopts an *esthesic* standpoint. It might, however, simply begin from a given "taxonomic stock," and describe what the composer has created (without asking about the poietic or esthesic pertinence of the facts thus brought to light). This is analysis of the harmonic *neutral level*.

Transcendent theories, even when they do not explicitly thematicize these three aspects, almost invariably justify their positions by adopting a poietic or an esthesic criterion, or perhaps both. Thus Rameau admits near the end of the *Traité* that "knowledge cannot suffice for perfection unless good taste comes to its aid . . . the only rule we have for good taste demands variety in composition" (1722: 323; Gossett 1971: 341). Here, the criterion is essentially esthesic. For d'Indy, chords *result from* melodic motion: the criterion is implicitly poietic.

Nonetheless, certain harmonic theories espouse in a more radical way either the standpoint of compositional strategies, or that of the listener. I shall deliberately borrow my examples from *textbooks* that have exercised considerable influence on respectable numbers of students in two different cultures (in France and in the U.S.), those of Chailley and Goldman. In so doing, I want to underline the fact that choice of plot is not merely a purely theoretical question, but has concrete pedagogical effects. (The most influential music-analytical paradigms—particularly those of Schenker—will be examined extensively in Volume 2.)

(a) *A Poietically Oriented Approach to Harmony*

Jacques Chailley's *Traité historique d'analyse musicale* is characteristic of theories based on poietics. Chailley writes, for instance, that "since consonance is a subjective phenomenon, our fundamental duty is to put ourselves into an analytical environment that corresponds exactly to a notion of consonance that might have been entertained by the composer we are analyzing" (1951: 11). To achieve this goal, the musicologist (in my opinion) would have to take into consideration such things as the music the composer heard during his or her years of apprenticeship, mentors and their advice, composition textbooks used, the theories they preached. But Chailley takes a shortcut, by appealing to a well-known transcendent principle: that throughout music history, new chords were gradually allowed as harmonic entities; that is, that (in his view) the addition of new "consonances" matches the series of natural overtones. Hence his diagram (in 1951: 12):

Example 9.3

Thus he refuses to recognize ninth chords in Bach: "this chord does not have any currency at the time" (ibid.: 11), and states concerning an example from Rameau that "chords that appear to be premature examples of ninth chords are in reality no such thing" (45).

One could make two objections to this approach. First, can we blindly follow this transcendent principle that is an oft-evoked setting for poietic-historic analysis? Koechlin's *Traité*, although written twenty-five years earlier (1928), offers a powerful antidote to such thinking:

In this evolution [of dissonant sonorities into consonant ones], is there any general, or even vaguely *scientific* law at work? Many fine minds believe so; above all, they hope so. In every case, it seems that musical language is going from the simple to the complex. Theorists have seen this historical march of progress as duplicating the march through successive harmonics of a single pitch. Of course, there are points of coincidence between this theory and historical developments. The fifth (the third overtone) appeared before the third (the fifth overtone),[3] the third before the dominant seventh (the seventh overtone), and that be-

[3] These numbers refer to the overtones.

fore the major ninth (the ninth). But we should also take note of the chronology of chords, which is not explained by the harmonic series. The minor triad appears rather late in the harmonic series (the sixth, seventh, and ninth overtones) but music history shows it to be more or less contemporary with the major triad (built on the first, third, and fifth overtones). To get the *minor* ninth of the dominant, we need to wait for the seventeenth overtone (or the thirteenth at the very least), and this is also true for the diminished seventh, which is a ninth without the root. The diminished seventh and the minor ninth chords, however, come before the major ninth chord. Moreover, the diminished seventh chord is older than the seventh built on the leading tone in major (i.e., the half-diminished seventh), but the harmonic series suggests the opposite. The diminished fifth chord (overtones five, six, and seven) was being written in common practice before the dominant seventh (overtones four, five, six, seven), a thing not suggested by the harmonic series. The augmented fifth (overtones seven, nine, eleven) appeared among musicians before the major ninth (four, five, six, seven, nine). Where in the series can we find seventh chords like D–F–A–C? We find them in Monteverdi, prepared no more elaborately than the dominant seventh ... in short, there is undoubtedly a certain analogy, a certain parallelism between the intervals in the overtone series, and intervals gradually permitted to make up chords. The correlation, however, seems to me too fragmentary to be seen as an "exact law." (Koechlin 1928 II: 106)

Second, Chailley's transcendent principle functions as a substitute for philological study of all those poietic factors listed above. Now, it is not impossible to reconstruct or at least to suggest hypothetically what composers conceptualized as their notion of consonance. Chailley cites Rameau; yet we could ask how Chailley's interpretation (that Rameau did not recognize ninth chords) can possibly be compatible with the *Traité III*, Chapter 30, entitled "On the Ninth Chord"—in which this chord is described as a harmonic entity in its own right! As for the eleventh chord, whose origins Chailley relegates to the period between Wagner and Debussy, it is analyzed in Chapter 31 of the same book, even though Rameau considers it to be "seldom used, because it is extremely harsh" (1722: 278; Gossett 1971: 297). It is a question of defining what is meant by *real* ninth or eleventh chords.

In his preface to Schenker's *Harmony*, Jonas reminds us of C.P.E. Bach's letter to Kirnberger: "you may announce it publicly that my father's principles, and my own, are anti-Rameau" (cited in Schenker 1973: xii). This means that an analysis of Bach's music that is guided by a theory rooted in Rameauian doctrine cannot be *poietically* pertinent to Bach. Chailley's entire perspective (even when it appears not to take Rameau's writings into account in analyzing his music) is based on a theory of vibration that, in the French tradition, goes back to 1722. We are quite correct in supposing that C.P.E. Bach's *Versuch über die wahre Art das Clavier zu spielen* (1762), even though it was written after J. S. Bach's death, can supply us with clues about the father's categories for music.

We must differentiate between two phases in analysis: recognizing harmonic configurations according to a given classificatory "stock," and considering their poietic relevance.[4] Koechlin devotes himself to the neutral level of harmonic facts in the historical part of his *Traité d'harmonie*: "I do not dwell upon 'theories,' nor upon discovering whether there are scientific causes for one chord's appearance prior to some other. I shall endeavor to make this study come alive by means of copious musical examples" (1928 II: 107). Koechlin is particularly sensitive to the stylistic importance of the link between chord and context: "it is not always the chord, not even the sequence of that chord and some other, that determines the music's character, but rather the way in which this sequence is realized, its relation to melody and rhythm" (ibid.: 171–72). A little later, he writes, "I do not attach much significance to a *chord in itself*, because *everything depends on what the composer makes of it*. Its relation to context, to *melody* (which remains the essence of music), to the harmony of a given passage (tonal or atonal, it matters little which): these are paramount" (263). Recognizing harmonic entities—on the basis of a classification adopted by the musicologist—makes little sense, unless it is integrated within a stylistic description that embraces all constituent parts of musical substance. The poietic pertinence of this material description will emerge afterward, perhaps simultaneously—but judgments about poietic pertinence do not involve the same decision-making tools. Once again, we have been brought to the point where we must differentiate between a *description* of the neutral level, and poietic *interpretation*.

---

[4] Nicolas Ruwet has suggested using the principles of generative grammar to study harmony: in analyzing Rameau, there is no reason not to use Rameau's own theories, to formalize them, and (by means of trial and error) to add rules that can account for Rameau's practice (1975a: 24). This approach will reveal differences between explicit poietic strategies and stylistic configurations (on the neutral level) that may be empirically observed.

(b) *An Esthesically Oriented Approach to Harmony*

Richard F. Goldman, professor of theory at the Juilliard School from 1947 to 1960 and author of the textbook *Harmony in Western Music*, deliberately chooses the perceptive standpoint, in a context that seems to me to introduce a new note in the history of harmony manuals. He writes, "the student today is in all probability not going to compose in the idiom of the Bach chorales or, for that matter, in any idiom based on conventional usage of the eighteenth or nineteenth centuries. In some respects, he no longer needs traditional or classical harmony *as a technique*. What he does need is an understanding of, and a feeling for, the harmonic principles that form the basis of his artistic heritage" (Goldman 1965: ix–x). Of course, the ground had been prepared by other American harmony manuals, like Piston's (which first appeared in 1941, and has gone through numerous revisions and modifications); his is among the most frequently used in North America. He proposes systematic rules, deduced from observing composers' practices in the eighteenth and nineteenth centuries. The viewpoint to which Piston subscribes no longer pretends (or no longer attempts) to reconstruct what the composer had in mind in writing; rather, it situates itself quite deliberately *post festum*. Goldman makes a similar claim: "the conventional harmony book is aimed in the wrong direction; its end is too often the properly completed exercise rather than the understanding of principles" (1965: xi). The transcendent principle here is no longer the natural overtone series, but, as we shall see, the underlying existence of a circle of fifths. The analytical plot itself is controlled by esthesics: "it is what one hears . . . that makes sense of harmonic progression" (Goldman 1965: xii). Piston had been quite clear on this point: "the variety of chords built upon these roots is of secondary importance, and no change in the makeup of the chords can remedy an inappropriate root progression" (Piston 1941: 17). In certain sectors of the American harmonic school, function becomes the weightiest variable. Piston was undoubtedly one of the first writers on harmony who did not begin his treatise with a ritual invocation of the natural overtone series. With Piston, there is no explicit announcement of a transcendent principle; he observes the "common practice" of the eighteenth and nineteenth centuries and takes functions as a basis for his arguments. Goldman is more radical: for him the overtone series "leaves unexplained the *selection* made by art from arithmetical or acoustical data . . . almost any arithmetical or proportional division might be used as a basis for creating a usable scale within the octave" (1965: 5). The functional explanation, which is explicit in Goldman, is derived from the transcendent principle of the *circle of fifths*. As he himself says, there is no natural basis for the dominant-tonic motion; "the force of the dominant, that is, our sense that it requires resolution, or movement toward a tonic, is arbitrary. It rests on no law of acoustics, but is an acquired meaning. It is the single most important fact in what we shall call the *syntax* of music . . . but other periods, and other cultures, have used other formulas" (30). An arbitrary force, yet a critical one. In his textbook, Goldman introduces the dominant seventh in the course of Chapter 2, and Chapter 3 stresses the role of secondary dominants (V of V). Any scale degree may be preceded by its own dominant, without weakening the principal tonic. Throughout the remainder of Goldman's work, the dominant plays a key role.

If, by way of comparison, we look at the treatises in the French tradition (Reber, Dubois, Koechlin), we see nothing like this. Not unexpectedly, French textbooks state that the chord progression must be constructed according to the roots. This progression is not in any way based upon a series of formulaic prescriptions (as it is in the American textbooks, which speak of I–IV–vii°–iii–vi–ii–V–I, or I–V–vi–V–I, or I–vi–V–IV–V–I, and so forth). Rather, the progression is grounded in a series of practical, poietical recommendations:[5] intervals between two roots can be good, satisfactory, or bad, and are listed as such (Reber 1842: 20; Dubois 1920: 36; Koechlin 1928 I: 108). With Koechlin, nonetheless, we get an explanation of all chords and scale degrees that can precede the V–I;[6] the emphasis is no longer exclusively on the interval, and we come closer to a functional approach.

The differences between the two traditions stand out in particular relief when we use the treatises as reservoirs of analytic concepts. Are there secondary dominants in the French treatises? They are mentioned (a tradition that goes back to Jelensperger) solely to explain augmented sixth chords as derived by means of a flatted fifth. Goldman, on the other hand, explains augmented sixth chords as *variants* of V of V,[7] or as chords without roots that proceed to the fifth scale degree (1965: 88). Piston prefers, in the case of Italian and German sixths, to speak of a raised fourth degree (1942: 278) whose origins are contrapuntal, and, for the French sixth, of a raised second degree.

When I speak of a transcendent principle in Goldman, I do not

---

[5] Conforming to Rameau's propositions in other respects. His thinking is not functional, but intervallic.

[6] They are: IV^5, $^6_3$, $^6_4$, 7; II^5; II^7; sixth chords $^6_5$, $^6_5{+}$; a seventh chord on the raised forth degree; VI^5, VI^6 (cf. 1928 I: 108).

[7] Strictly speaking, a chord with an augmented sixth is not a seventh chord, but acoustically it is quite close to the minor seventh—hence the assimilation.

mean "metaphysical." Goldman's idea is that from Bach to Wagner, tonal harmony can be *explained* in terms of a gradually more complex overlapping of basic function-formulas, and that our *ear* is receptive to these formulas. This much said, we can discuss Goldman's thesis by beginning with three observations:

(1) An *a posteriori* explanation of harmony in terms of the circle of fifths leaves one question open: whether composers of the tonal era consciously realized that (1) music is governed by this principle, and (2) works are constructed from basic function-formulas. The "circle of fifths" may exist, but its reification—did the concept exist at a given historical period?—is much more difficult to determine. Does this transcendent principle, then, have any sort of poietic pertinence?

Fétis does not mention the circle of fifths in any of the authors cited in his documentary chapter devoted to harmonic theories; he classifies theories into three groups—those that declare themselves to be based upon acoustic considerations, those based on an arbitrary choice of basic chords, and those based on an arbitrary division of the monochord.

The situation is all the more difficult in that there is no reason to suppose that the poietic strategies of all composers in a given era are identical. There is no such thing as a totally false theory, there are only theories situated at a certain level of abstraction, and pertinent with respect to one (or many) privileged aspect(s) of musical phenomena. When they compare their theories, are musicologists always talking about the same thing?

Goldman's principle, while a perceptual one, at the same time wants to cover the entire tonal period: he seeks to reconstruct "the continuing logic of traditional harmony" (1965: 163). He further states that "the style of Bach differs clearly from that of Schubert or Wagner, but . . . the syntactical principles on which style has evolved remain fundamentally the same in all cases" (3–4). There is a certain amount of Hegelianism here: if harmonic evolution is teleologically oriented, what is the pertinence of these principles to hearing? The "aural understanding" (100) that he proposes is in fact that of a musicologist of the sixties, who hears every work of the tonal period in terms of his knowledge of the *entire* period.[8] This is a retrospective perception, and tells us nothing about the way in which styles were constructed as one advances through the history of tonal language.

(2) We need to acknowledge from the outset that the perception of

---

[8] The relevence of Goldman's analysis is located on the level of "tonal style" (cf. my pyramid of styles, p. 136.

a musicologist or listener today is not necessarily the perception of a Beethoven. Koechlin is in this respect admirably cautious: "today, when we accept all sorts of consecutive seventh and ninth chords . . . it is hard to understand the *state of hearing* in 1830" (1928 II: 176). We can only collect indirect testimonials about the perception of classical works in their own time. *Rezeptionslehre* may be of some aid, as we recall how certain works were received when they were first written. In Paris, Beethoven's symphonies were reproached, in having their "harmonic errors" (those Habeneck hunted down) corrected. It would be interesting to know which "errors" were thus rectified (cf. Koechlin: ibid.). Fétis devoted acid critiques to certain passages in the Fifth Symphony; they make us smile nowadays, but they are an important document. Olivier Alain states that "understanding the history of harmony means trying to rediscover the different stages in western hearing. It means acknowledging the relativity of sonorous *language,* but also the ear's indefinite adaptive capacities" (1965b: 6). The difficulty is in reconstructing this dialectic between habituation and transgression: a given state in harmonic language does not necessarily correspond to the musical perception of the time; musical theories in particular often lag behind in comparison to contemporary practice.

On the other hand, one can attempt an experimental study of current perception of Beethoven's symphonies. Goldman's analyses attempt to be *perceptive,* but they are only *hypotheses* about the ways in which we perceive tonal harmony. They are dependent upon what I called *inductive esthesic analysis.* Goldman is in other respects quite aware that not everybody hears the same piece in the same way; he is one of those rare writers who thematicize the ambiguities of analysis (cf. 1965: 104–106), and who leave open possibilities for multiple analyses of the same passage. (163)

Now, the difficulty of the esthesic position in the case of harmonic analysis is that knowledge and a priori theories are one of the controlling factors in perception. We run the risk of being trapped in circular reasoning: from the moment that functional formulas based on the circle of fifths satisfactorily explain harmonic progressions, are we not going to *hear* in terms of the theory? By necessity, analytical thematicization always influences perceptual orientation.

(3) Goldman rejects harmonic analysis of phenomena that cannot be heard. (1965: 163) This is a radical position, because considering the harmonic aspects of a passage can bring to light musical facts that the ear (but whose ear?) does not take in—facts that are pertinent on a more or less abstract level of stylistic description, or in connection

with some poietic factor.[9] In effect, Goldman eludes the poietic question, or rather, he subsumes that question under esthesics:

> It is, in any case, the harmonic plan and movement of musical works, especially in the classical period, to which the listener must be sensitive. In the tradition of western music, the composer expects this of the listener, for it is only on this assumption that he can apply his skill or genius to the elaboration of this basic grammar of musical communication. (1965: 130).

His reasoning goes something like this: analysis must translate auditory understanding; the listener's perception above all must grasp the harmonic plan elaborated by the composer, because the composer constructed this plan in terms of the listener's perception. Here we encounter one of the most tenacious myths purveyed not only by musicology, but also by semiology and human sciences in general: in human intercourse (whether artistic, linguistic, or social), strategies of perception will correspond to strategies of production because the producer has internalized laws of perception. But to subscribe to such a *correspondence* is to interdict understanding how musical language *evolves*, an evolution that is generated by surpassing acquired perceptive situations.

3. Semiology of Harmonic Theories and Harmonic Practices

I am not disputing the perspicacity of existing harmonic theory. Rather, I am trying to show that construction of any harmonic theory corresponds to a principle that might be stated as follows: *Most harmonic theories are based on a transcendent principle that claims validity for the entire tonal era; analyses that one can develop within this theoretical framework relate either to the poietic, or the esthesic, or they assume that the two points of view are equivalent.*

There is never, as stated previously, an entirely false theory. As André Régnier stated, "they die of things about which they do not speak" (1974: 99). The theories with which I am concerned have perhaps one essential flaw: they never really try to encompass the *complexity of the symbolic phenomena* at work within the "harmonic fact." This complexity can, perhaps, be sorted out into three aspects:

(1) The composer's work (which can be the object of a combinatory stylistic analysis of the neutral level) is the product of various poietic

---

[9] An analysis of the harmonic neutral level is thus necessary.

strategies, in which all the composer's music-theoretical and practical knowledge are mixed with the socio-psychological determinants that interact with them. These works are in turn the object of diverse perceptions, on the part of listeners, other composers, and contemporary theorists.

Harmonic theories, as distinct from harmonic facts within musical works, are at once the result of works, and a motor for their composition, inasmuch as these theories codify the data associated with harmonic facts, and reorient creativity in directions that in turn reinforce the theory's positive and negative dictates. A harmony treatise is, itself, a symbolic construction, one that draws nourishment from the symbolic construction called music; I hardly need point out that the relationship between theory and practice is a dialectical one.

If, however, we privilege the aspect of "theoretical conceptualization" above all poietic and esthesic phenomena, we get Figure 9.1.

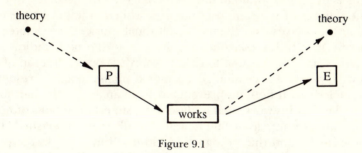

Figure 9.1

(2) Musical creation is not, however, a static phenomenon; a continuous fabric stretches from Bach to Wagner. This tripartite edifice must, then, be put on a temporal axis; Beethoven's poietics is based to a great extent on his hearing of his predecessors' works.

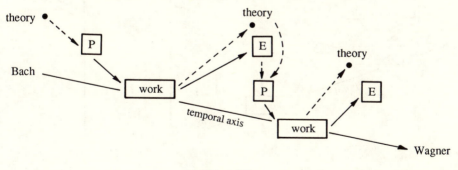

Figure 9.2

213

(3) Until now, my schemas have included those traits capable of (a) having influenced the works that we study, or (b) being an immediate reflection of those works. The whole of this complex, dynamic phenomenon is, however, being viewed from the "height" of the 1980s. Now, observations about all this, whether a matter of musical works or the theories associated with them, will be *filtered* for each musicologist, filtered through an individual system of musical knowledge and theoretical concepts. This is a product of his or her personal intellectual education—an education that, in general, is grounded in western musicology as practiced roughly since 1850.

This body of musicological thought since 1850 is, however, also a symbolic construction, but with a difference characteristic of nineteenth-century thought: a *historical* standpoint that encompasses all past centuries. The situation is particularly complex, because if harmonic treatises are simultaneously factors in harmonic evolution and products of it, they would in the "musicological era" become evidence of the poietics of the composer-theorist, while at the same time presenting themselves as a theory for all tonal music. The chapter on harmony in d'Indy's *Cours de composition* is to me both radical and revelatory. D'Indy's refusal to classify chords is one indication of his personal, poietic conception of harmonic phenomena, as resulting from melody. But nothing prevents us from analyzing the harmonic neutral level of his work; that is, describing superimpositions of notes empirically present, according to a given, culturally established "taxonomic stock," and thus recognizing within d'Indy's works the presence of this or that chord, chords that he himself would not have

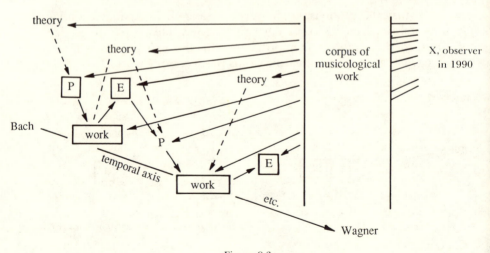

Figure 9.3

214

acknowledged. This is what Koechlin did, in his analysis of a passage from *Fervaal* (Koechlin 1928 II: 201). Moreover, no poietic analysis can ever be taken as *sufficient* to understanding a musical style. Were this not the case, then we would have to acknowledge that rules established in treatises by theorist-composers like Rameau, once thereby formalized, are fully able to account for the harmonic facts that we observe within his works. But they cannot.

A descriptive and stylistic neutral level is vital. Because music is essentially motion through time, this level may seem to turn out to be useless. Grasping musical movement is a question of esthesics, but such understanding cannot be explicit unless one is able to describe the configurations, the entities of which the movement is comprised.

But theoretical filters are not blindfolds; at most they are fogged-up glasses. Once we acknowledge the dynamic reality of the musical work's symbolic character, once we acknowledge the work's insinuation into the temporal axis, it becomes hard to conceive of current harmonic theory as any kind of unidimensional activity, based on a unique and sufficient principle, privileging a single kind of pertinence. In this respect, we are perhaps fortunate in entering into a privileged era. Many past harmony treatises, with the exception of Goldman and Piston, had to play a double game, and suffered because of it. They had to explain an established practice, that is, propose *descriptive* rules. But at the same time—because the tonal system had not yet run its course (true also for Koechlin, even if he had to talk about "modality" as well as tonality)—they had to fulfill a pedagogical and normative function, and impose *prescriptive* rules.[10]

Musicology was simultaneously the judge and the guilty party. Today, when harmony theorists are no longer personally implicated in harmony's evolution (*because* tonal harmony *has* run its course), it is no longer a question of learning to write tonal music according to a more or less academic norm, but of understanding tonality, of being able to produce tonal pastiches. Goldman is most eloquent on this point: "there are no [prescriptive] rules, only styles" (Goldman 1965: 127). But as we saw above, given any moment in the history of harmony, we must know how the language of a given composer was constituted, how tonality was experienced in Mozart's time, how Mozart understood tonality (to be able to write what he did), and how

---

[10] On these two kinds of laws, see Molino 1975a: 49. He insists on the "discrepancy between regularity of the norm, and the regularity of praxis." Koechlin's position is revealing vis-à-vis the ambiguity of harmonic laws. In the end, he is saying to his students: follow the principles I have taught in order to pass your exams, but tonal harmony does not work this way at all!

Mozart's works have in turn changed tonality's *image* in the minds of subsequent theorists and composers.

One might think that all this is already in place, that the "history of musical langauge" is known. In some respects, this is true. But if we acknowledge that creation is in part the consequence of a *conceptualization*, and that theory plays a greater or lesser part in any individual's personal conceptualization, we must recognize the need for a systematic study of the *interaction* between theory and creation. This has not been done. Fétis was certainly one of the first musicologists to have contextualized his own theory, by making a historical and classificatory study of theories that preceded his own. Koechlin gives us a fine chapter on the evolution of musico-harmonic phenomena, independent of any theory or attempt at scientific explanation. We must now reunite these two sorts of history, the history of musical material, and the history of discourse about music. We must resituate the conceptualization of harmony proposed by modern musicology within the intellectual context that engendered it. Finally, beyond identifying the general principles that inform that conceptualization, we must realize that such a conceptualization will always favor certain symbolic aspects of the musical data being studied; we should identify their poietic, neutral, or esthesic registers.

Concepts of tonal harmony are cultural concepts. The history of harmonic theories traces a succession of explanatory paradigms that, whether through transcendentalism, normativism, or reductionism, have often failed to grasp the complexity of the "harmonic fact" in its triple symbolic dimension. The least we can do is restore a semiological dimension to harmony, which will permit us to account for the insufficiency of the theories, the contradictions among different theories, the circumstances surrounding the evolution and construction of tonal harmony, and the theories that try to explain it.

4. Principles at Work in Constructing Harmonic Analysis

Obviously, the complex symbolic interactions described in the previous section lend a somewhat Byzantine air to my remarks; undoubtedly I will be reproached for not having renounced this kind of openly programmatic and speculative discourse. I have, however, always believed that it is better to acknowledge complexities *before* getting to analysis, than to lend some illusion of simplicity through the magic of reductionist theory. The time always comes when complexity takes its revenge, and will explode in one's face.

Instead of offering a tentative realization for propositions that we have just discussed, one can—especially in coming to the conclusion of a book—give an example of how transcendent principles and plots intervene in one specific case. If I opt for discussion of the Tristan Chord one more time, I do so because its ambiguity is so pronounced (it does not correspond to any classificatory label one finds in treatises) that the chord can function as a sort of test case for theories. In the various analyses that have been proposed, we can observe *in vivo* the *operations* that intervene in the *construction* of different, divergent explanations, and specify the *criteria* at work in elaborating discourse about harmony.

In 1962, German musicologist Martin Vogel devoted an entire book to this single chord—*Der Tristan-Akkord und die Krise der modernen Harmonielehre*. The title itself was a response to Ernest Kurth's seminal work, *Romantische Harmonik und ihre Krise in Wagners "Tristan"* (1920). Vogel in effect looked at the published analyses of the chord (since 1879) one by one, and concluded that "the crisis of romantic harmony is in reality the crisis of harmonic theory" (Vogel 1962: 82).

This claim seems critical to me, because it means that the harmonic language belonging to a given music-historical period or composer is not comprehensible *unless mediated by a metalanguage* that explains it. There are no musico-harmonic phenomena per se; they are accessible to us only because they have become the object of a *process of symbolization* that organizes them, renders them intelligible. To speak of a "crisis of theory" is to admit that the *tools* used to describe the phenomena of a particular era are, once the material has reached a certain developmental stage, no longer sufficient. Far from being a special case, the Tristan Chord becomes a real "touchstone" (Vogel 1962: 15) for all the writers I shall be discussing. After reviewing the different interpretations of the chord, and after studying (as in the preceding) the various harmony textbooks used in different national traditions, one comes to share Vogel's conclusion that "the critical situation of musical theory demands a viewpoint that is critical of theory's methods and concepts in a meaningful way" (ibid.: 83).

Nevertheless, what is missing in Vogel's book is *thematicizing* the reasons that explain divergences between the various writers. He collects all the necessary material. Yet before centering in on the semiological nature of processes at work when we grasp harmonic phenomena, we must answer the following question: how and why did a given musicological writer come to say what he or she did?

Examining various analyses (and I shall include a few analyses published since the appearance of Vogel's book) leads to singling out principles that serve as a basis for elaboration in harmonic theories.

The basic principle might be stated as follows: *there is no harmonic theory without recognition and identification of harmonic entities*. This proposition is less trivial than we might think. We can encounter "pure chords" in a musical work:

Example 9.4 Mussorgsky: *Pictures at an Exhibition*

But more often, we must go from a textual given to a more *abstract* representation of the chords being used:

Example 9.5 Debussy: *Première Arabesque*

Knowing the criteria for this process of abstraction is essential. The first principle seems to me to be the following: *for a sound configuration to be recognized as a chord, it must have a certain duration*. The *time factor* is not always accorded the weight it deserves in music analysis; Schenker's analyses can often be tricky, but at least they have the virtue of reminding us that music is movement in time.

In *Harmony in Western Music*, Goldman stresses the role of time, for example, in establishing a tonic, and (what interests me), in establishing the existence of a harmonic entity: "the sense of harmonic relation, change, or effect depends on *speed* (or tempo) as well as on the relative duration of single notes or triadic units. Both absolute time (measurable length and speed) and relative time (proportion and division) must at all times be taken into account in harmonic thinking or analysis" (1965: 26).

I insist on this point for one reason: if the Tristan Chord causes problems, it is because this "bizarre" configuration has a long enough duration to attain the status of a harmonic *entity*:

Example 9.6 Wagner: *Tristan und Isolde*

We can have fun finding the Tristan Chord in earlier works by Machaut, Gesualdo, Bach, Mozart, Beethoven, or Spohr (Vogel 1962: 12):

Example 9.7 Beethoven: *Sonata Op. 31, No. 3*

In this example, however, one sees how great the difference from *Tristan* really is: in Beethoven, the tempo is *allegro* (♩= 160), and the immediate resolution of the E♭ to D does not convey the same sense as that resolution in the Tristan Chord; in Wagner, the tempo is *langsam und schmachtend*. Beyond this, however, Wagner also places the chord at the opening of the work and repeats it three times (in measures 6, 10, and 12); it recurs frequently, and finally at the end of the last act. Dramatically and harmonically it has the character of a "statement."

Seen from this perspective, Jacques Chailley's analysis is one of the most curious of all those that have been proposed (though we shall see later that there are reasons that Chailley's *modus operandi* is also legitimate). He writes, "*Tristan*'s chromaticism, grounded in appoggiaturas and passing notes, technically and spiritually represents an *apogee of tension*. I have never been able to understand how the preposterous idea that *Tristan* could be made the prototype of an *atonality* grounded in destruction of all tension could possibly have gained

219

credence. This was an idea that was disseminated under the (hardly disinterested) authority of Schoenberg, to the point where Alban Berg could cite the Tristan Chord in the *Lyric Suite*, as a kind of homage to a precursor of atonality" (1962: 8). Schoenberg in fact did not know how to describe the chord's structure, but he placed it on the second scale degree in a completely tonal context. (1954: 77) Nowadays we know—thanks to George Perle's work (Perle 1977)—that the quotation of the chord in the *Lyric Suite* can be explained in terms of a romance between Alban Berg and Hanna Fuchs: this novel historical discovery throws Chailley's earlier "plot" awry. But we can continue with the passage from Chailley: "this curious conception [of the Tristan Chord as precursor to atonality] could not have been made except as the consequence of a *destruction of normal analytical reflexes* leading to an *artificial isolation of an aggregate in part made up of foreign notes*, and to considering it—an abstraction out of context—as an organic whole. After this, it becomes easy to convince naive readers that such an aggregation escapes classification in terms of harmony textbooks" (Chailley 1963: 8). For Chailley, the chord can be explained as follows: "it is rooted in a simple dominant chord of *A minor*, which includes two appoggiaturas resolved in the normal way" (1962: 40):

Example 9.8

The F in measure 1 is a sustained appoggiatura to E; in measure 2, the F is an appoggiatura to E, the D♯ is an appoggiatura to D, and the A is a passing note; in measure 3, the earlier appoggiaturas are resolved, except the passing note A, and the A♯ appoggiatura resolve to B. The G♯ is considered a harmonic tone.

Chailley's prejudice against serialism aside, this analysis has something fantastic about it all the same, because the Tristan Chord *is no longer a chord*, but an anticipation of the dominant chord in measure 3.[11] The chord's temporal duration, however, gives it the physical characteristics of a harmonic entity, and for this reason, musicologists

[11] Chailley's analysis has been the object of critical examinations by Dommel-Diény (1965) and Serge Gut (1981: 149).

have sought to name it.[12] At this level at least, that attempt is legitimate. The analytical melodrama results from the fact that the configuration F–B–D♯–G♯ does not, no matter what Chailley thinks, correspond (as such) to any of the labels provided by traditional harmonic theories.

Thus a second factor intervenes in the abstract symbolization of harmonic data; this factor may be described as follows: *for a given configuration to be described as a chord, one must be able to name it, in terms drawn from the chordal "taxonomic stock" suggested by a given harmonic theory.*

By "taxonomic stock," as suggested previously, I mean the general system of classification for units, to which a given configuration can be compared, in order to be characterized. In the case of the Tristan Chord, we must get by as best as we can; that is, we must ignore certain aspects of the configuration, thus bringing it as close as possible to a known harmonic entity. This means that a harmonic analysis will organize and "manipulate" the component parts of a chord in specific ways. These can be put together into the following schema:

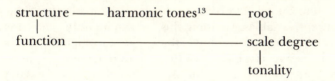

I have placed the two essential variables to the right of the diagram. All harmonic description in effect defines structure and function: we speak of an augmented sixth chord on the fourth scale degree, a dominant seventh chord, a sixth chord on the second scale degree, and so forth. Identification on the basis of these two variables, however, presupposes that, for a given case, we have already determined four other variables: in what key is the passage? On what scale degree is the chord built? What is its root? What notes are integral to the chord? This final question, moreover, touches upon a decisive point in defining the *harmonic* entity being analyzed, since it asks us to distinguish between properly harmonic notes that are integrated into a vertical configuration, and melodic notes that belong exclusively to the work's horizontal unfolding. We must realize that *decisions* concerning these variables could begin at any point in the schema (de-

[12] Since I agree with Goldman in saying that a chord implies a certain duration, I do not specify its length, because the temporal *feeling* that establishes the existence of a harmonic entity depends on a number of factors: tempo, context, dynamics, etc.

[13] And the chord's integration into a melodic unfolding.

pending on the particular musical situation being analyzed and the theoretical framework in which the analysis is conducted). In Germany since Riemann (1897), and in the English-speaking tradition, analytical reasoning takes place within the framework of functions; the key is defined first, then the scale degree and the root, from which the chordal structure is deduced. In the French treatises, one will look at the chord's structure and the voice-leading first off; function will be the end-product of the analytical process.

At this point, we can suggest an initial definition of *a theory* and *a harmonic analysis*. Early in this century, epistemologist Paul Duhem (1906) stated that a theory in physics is a classification of laws. I would say that a *harmonic theory is a hierarchical classification of data*. To understand why a certain analysis will give more *weight* to this or that variable, we need to *go back to the theory*, which will have organized variables in their relationship to one another, for all of tonal music. Thus we could suggest a third principle as follows: *harmonic analysis defines a chord by privileging a certain set of variables, according to the weight accorded them in the theory of reference.*

I want to illustrate this principle by classifying different analyses of the Tristan Chord, according to the decisions made about the chord's constituent variables. In doing this, we can identify *values* ascribed to the variables being examined; that is, we can identify the points of entry that serve as a basis for efforts to understand the chord.

There are four analytical decisions that define the Tristan Chord:

(1) What notes are specifically considered harmonic tones? (In this case, the only real question is whether G♯ is integral to the chord.)

(a) If so, then the chord being described is F–B–D♯–G♯.

b) If not, then the chord is F–B–D♯–A

The same question has been asked (though less frequently) of the D♯, as we saw in Chailley's analysis.

(2) Each of these two configurations in principle could generate four possible sonic structures, since each of the four notes could be taken as the chord's root.

(a) In the G♯ group, writers tend to keep two of the four possibilities: F or G♯.

(b) In the no–G♯ group, the A never appears in root position.

(3) Once the root is chosen, it is assigned a scale degree, depending (obviously) upon the key chosen as the point of reference for analyzing the passage, or the chord. In general, this is A minor, but there are, as we shall see, some exceptions.

(4) In A minor, the possible roots—F or G♯ (in the G♯ group), and F, B, or D♯ (in the no–G♯ group)—can be interpreted as one of four scale degrees: II, IV, V of V, or (less frequently) VII.

Finally, we should note that enharmonic factors sometimes come into play in determining the chord's interpretation.

This initial sweep through the variables that play a role in analyzing the Tristan Chord is by no means genetic; that is, the order I have adopted does not necessarily correspond to the chronological order each musicologist might adopt in his or her decision-making strategy.

The final analytical characterization of the chord depends upon choices that operate on the basis of a combinatorially established selection of variables—the status of G♯, the structure of the chord, its function, its tonality—which are "filled in" in one way or another in terms of the *weight*, the role assigned by the theory of reference to sequences of functions, structure of the chord, or integration into melodic context. Thus we might add a coda to the principle stated previously: *in making a harmonic analysis, one aligns oneself implicitly or explicitly with an analytical-theoretical family, one characterized by a given transcendent principle that orients the direction of a specific analytical plot.* It is these "plots" that I shall be untangling.

5. *Plots in Analyses of the Tristan Chord*

There are many analyses of the Tristan Chord, but they can be divided into two large families: those that ascribe some weight to the functional succession of chords, and those that do not.

(a) *Functional Analyses*

These are quite numerous; a single principle rules all of them: tonal music is composed of characteristic successions of chords. The chords' structures are of secondary importance. We must not, however, assume that all functional analyses reach the same conclusions, since the transcendent principles that govern these analyses will vary from one theory to the next.

(1) *The Fourth Scale Degree*

First, we have those analyses inspired by Riemannian doctrine; for Riemann (as we saw previously), all chords could be reduced to three functions: I, IV, and V. This single transcendent principle, however, will not necessarily generate a single, unique analytical solution. Different authors, faced with the chord's ambiguity, will play with the chord's constituent elements in terms of quite different plots.

Most functional analyses do not consider the G♯ as part of the chord. In 1901, Arend saw the Tristan Chord as "a modified minor seventh chord": he moves enharmonically from F–B–D♯–G♯ to F–C♭–

E♭–A♭, then to F–B–D–A. This F–B–D–A chord is a IV chord, according to Riemann, because it is actually a triad D–F–A, to which the "lowered seventh" has been added. Riemann (1909) explains the chord in the same way, keeping the D♯. What is important for these "plots," as we see, is being able to put the chord on IV, for the sake of conformity to the transcendent principle.

Taking an analogous transcendent principle as his point of departure, d'Indy arrives at a different chordal structure because he rejects the Riemannian theory of the added "lowered seventh." D'Indy, whose course in composition influenced many generations of French theorists and composers, summarized his conception of tonal harmony, in what amounts to a distant echo of the Latin *credo*, as follows:

> (1) There is only *one chord*, a *perfect* chord; it alone is consonant, because it alone generates a feeling of repose and balance; (2) this chord has *two different forms, major and minor*, depending whether the chord is composed of a minor third over a major third, or a major third over a minor; (3) this chord is able to take on *three different tonal functions, tonic, dominant, or subdominant*. (1903: 116)

For d'Indy, one arrives analytically at three basic chords by eliminating "all artificial, dissonant notes, arising solely from the melodic motion of the voices, and therefore foreign to the chord" (117). In converting the G♯ to A and the D♯ to D♮, the Tristan Chord is "no more than a subdominant in the key of A, collapsed in upon itself melodically, the harmonic progression represented thus:

IV6   V

Example 9.9

This is the simplest in the world" (1903: 117). It seems that the Tristan Chord is nothing more than a sophisticated sixth chord. Two ideas, as we can see, have controlled the analysis: discovering the progression I–IV–V (an idea borrowed from Riemann), and dismissing as "foreign" all notes that sully the purity of the perfect chord.

Lorenz's analysis (1926: 14 and 196) is also grounded in the central role of the fourth degree, but "omitting the B for the sake of clarity" reads the chord as an augmented sixth chord (F–A–D♯). More recently, Deliège reached the same conclusions as d'Indy, though apparently independently: he legitimizes the chord on the fourth degree by proposing that "in the end only one resolution is acceptable, one that takes the subdominant degree as the root of the chord, which gives us, as far as tonal logic is concerned, the most plausible interpretation" (1979d: 23). For Deliège (who has continued to insist upon this point; cf., 1989), the G♯ could only be seen as an appoggiatura to A. He states further that "this interpretation of the chord is confirmed by its subsequent appearances in the Prelude's first period: the IV⁶ chord remains constant; notes foreign to that chord vary" (1979d: 23).[14] As we see, Deliège brings another argument (one to which we shall return) to bear on *his* plot's construction: what happens to the chord on the fourth degree in the rest of the Prelude?

(2) *The Secondary Dominant*

One can, however, view the Tristan Chord as built on a root other than the fourth scale degree (D♮). By taking B as the chord's root, we might interpret it as V of V, or as a chord on the second scale degree. In 1912 Ergo proposed the secondary-dominant solution, a view that (in contrast to the II solution) favors the fifth motion B to E, and sees the chord as a seventh chord with lowered fifth (which explains the F♮). Kurth (1920) also saw the "real" chord as B–D♯–F♯–A, as did Distler (1940).

(3) *The Second Scale Degree*

Many of those in the functionalist camp prefer the II solution, probably because the V of V solution requires too many manipulations (e.g., sharping the F). For the proponants of II, we are dealing not with a seventh chord, but a French sixth (F–A–B–D♯, which preserves the F♮). This is the solution adopted by most American musicologists (cf. Piston 1941: 279; 1970: 285). The interpretation appeals not to the Riemannian transcendent principle, but to another, in which functional succession is explained by the circle of fifths (in which, therefore, scale degree II is closer to the dominant than scale degree IV). Goldman's *Harmony in Western Music*, discussed previously, seems to me to vindicate Piston's analysis without much difficulty: "the IV chord is actually, in the simplest mechanism of diatonic relationships, at the greatest distance from I. In terms of the circle of fifths, it leads away from I, rather than toward it" (1965: 68). For Goldman, then, the progression I–ii–V–I seems to comply with tonal

---

[14] After having pleaded for degree IV in 1979, Deliège has come to admit the II-solution (personal communication with the author).

logic based on the circle of fifths (ibid.: Chapter 3). The chord on the fourth degree occurs long before the chord on II, and the subsequent final I, in the progression I–IV–vii°–iii–vi–ii–V–I (Chapter 4). Goldman nonetheless points out that "historically the use of the IV chord in harmonic design, and especially in cadences, exhibits some curious features. By and large, one can say that the use of IV in final cadences becomes more common in the nineteenth century than it was in the eighteenth, but that it may also be understood as a substitute for the ii chord when it precedes V. It may also be quite logically construed as an incomplete ii^7 chord (lacking root)" (1965: 68). The circle of fifths had a narrow escape: only the theory of a ii chord without a root allows Goldman to maintain that the circle of fifths is completely valid from Bach to Wagner.

(b) Nonfunctional analyses

The functionalist perspective allows three different analyses of the Tristan Chord (as iv, V of V, or ii). The fact that this is possible is a bit suspicious: can we still maintain that function is relevant when (so to speak) the littlest shove can transport us from one function to another?

But the variability of the functionalist analyses justifies a move to other analytical possibilities, this time, nonfunctionalist analyses. They have one thing in common: they take the G♯ to be part of the chord, and (unlike the functionalist analyses) they privilege the chord's structure above its function. They take the G♯ as a characteristic element in the chord's acoustic specificity, and thus seek to explain not F–B–D♯–A, but F–B–D♯–G♯.

In the history of the Tristan Chord's analysis, all the same, one needs to differentiate between two important and quite distinct families of nonfunctionalist analyses: those that characterize the chord's structure *vertically*, and those that, influenced by Schenkerian teachings, are *linear analyses* that deal with the chord with respect to the melodic continuity that forms its context.

(1) Vertical Characterizations

Vogel's view summarizes the stance of those who integrate the G♯ into the chord: "who expects to hear over five beats the seventh of a chord which is missing a perfect fifth, whose root is different from its bass, whose bass is altered and cannot be integrated into the chord?" (Vogel 1962: 58). With Vogel, the criterion of duration reappears: "the nonharmonic tone must appear clearly as such, and should not cause a change in harmony, even if it has duration" (Goldman 1965: 26).

As soon as the analysis is no longer connected to the logic of functions, and structure takes precedence over function, the chord can be situated on degree VII, where functionalist practice would not dream of putting it. The first analysis of the chord, made by Kistler in 1879, deemed it a seventh chord "with minor triad" on the seventh degree in F♯ minor (E♯–G♯–B–D♯). Jadassohn (1899) saw it as a seventh chord (F–G♯–B–D♯ = E♯–G♯–B–D), also on the seventh degree in F♯ minor (!). Soon, however, the chord became a seventh chord on the second degree in A minor, with the G♯ resolving to A. Ward (1970: 181) speaks of a diminished seventh with an appoggiatura to D, again on the seventh degree. Sadai (1980: 404) made it an augmented-second chord on the seventh degree. Hindemith (1937: 247) did not specify the degree, but described the chord as a G♯ minor chord in A minor—G♯–B–D♯—to which the sixth is added (F–E♯). Schoenberg refuses to choose, and suggests therefore the idea of the "wandering chord" (*vagierender Akkord*): "it can come from anywhere" (1911: 284).

In being freed from functionalist constraints, musicologists can attempt to explain each of the notes actually *there*. Is there any reason to regret giving up a functionalist explanation? Goldman, a very functionalist man, seems to me best at justifying a nonfunctionalist approach. In *Harmony in Western Music* he does not analyze the Tristan Chord, but rather a chord in *Parsifal*, in which the same pitches occur, differently distributed (F–A♭–C♭–E♭), written F–G♯–B–D♯, and, reading it by paired thirds, B–D♯–F–A♭. He writes, "the chord in question from *Parsifal*, from the way it moves, should most accurately be spelled F–A♭–B–D♯ (or, reading in thirds, B–D♯–F–A♭), which would indeed be a new chord. The temptation to find a label for it is one to be resisted. We are justified in explaining it and understanding it only in terms of its dynamic properties—that is, the tendency of its components to move onward in aurally comprehensible steps" (1965: 159). In other words: if the functionalist view cannot be maintained, this is due to choosing an explicitly *perceptive* analytic pertinence. We shall return to this point.

(2) *Linear Analyses*

The Schenkerian approach to harmony, by thematicizing prolongational phenomena, has been led to attach great importance to voice-leading motion (which had been neglected by functionalist analysis and, *a fortiori*, by vertical nonfunctional analysis). William Mitchell adopts a Schenkerian perspective; he examines the chord in relation to the first three measures as a whole, and refuses to take the G♯ as an appoggiatura, since the melodic line ascends to the B. The A becomes a passing note. The ascending line in the oboe (G♯–A–

A♯–B) is mirrored by the descending line in the cello (F–E–D♯), which is completed by the English Horn (D). This enables him to argue that the D♯ should be accorded the same status as the A♯, as an appoggiatura. The melodic lines both fill out a third, which accentuates their parallelism:

3rd asc.

3rd desc.

Example 9.10

By making the D♯ an appoggiatura to D, Mitchell is able to view the Tristan Chord as a diminished seventh chord (G♯–B–D–F), which he refuses explicitly to characterize in functional terms. In his analysis, he extends Schenker's comparison of the Tristan Chord and a dissonant contrapuntal gesture in the E minor fugue of *The Well-Tempered Clavier*, Book I (cf. Schenker 1925–1930 II: 29; Schenker, we should recall, was the first to consider the Tristan Chord from a solely melodic standpoint). Noske, who is similarly situated within the framework of melodic analysis, refuses (as did Mitchell) to characterize the chord in functional terms (1981: 116–17). Gut has also discussed the contrary motion between the two melodic gestures, but draws different conclusions concerning the chord's integral notes: "if one focuses essentially on melodic motion, one sees how its dynamic force creates a sense of an appoggiatura each time, that is, at the beginning of each measure, creating a mood both feverish and tense . . . thus in the soprano motif, the G♯ and the A♯ are heard as appoggiaturas, as the F and D♯ in the initial motif" (1981: 150). Gut argues that the underlying harmony of measure 2 (and in this, he demonstrates his functionalist view) is fixed by the chord D–F–A–B (the minor chord with added sixth) on IV, but strictly speaking, for him, the Tristan Chord itself "is engendered by melodic waves."

A detailed discussion of Forte's analysis (1988) is beyond the modest scope of this chapter, since Forte integrates a Schenkerian perspective into his own set theory. He identifies the chord as an atonal set, (according to his terminology, 4–27); in other words, what traditional harmony would call a "half-diminished seventh chord." What is striking about his analysis is that not only the chord's function, but also its vertical structure, no longer interest him: his point is to show how the Tristan Chord is projected linearly through the entire Prelude:

> Although the "dominant seventh" may here display some functional significance with respect to an implied tonality and therefore demand attention from Roman-numeral addicts, I elect to place that consideration in a secondary, even tertiary position compared to the most dynamic aspect of the opening music, which is clearly the large-scale ascending motion that develops in the upper voice, in its entirety a linear projection of the Tristan Chord transposed to level three, g♯'–b'–d"–f♯"." (1988: 328)

As we see, discussion is now focused on the link established between the four notes of the chord as a totality, and their composing-out in different passages of the Prelude. One could hardly state more clearly that other analytic variables—function and chord structure—have been relegated to last place, but, in so doing, Forte excludes harmonic analysis in the usual sense from his field of inquiry.

6. Plots and Analytical Situations

We have discussed how each of these analyses inscribes itself within a given family, ruled by a given transcendent principle. We have already seen that sharing a transcendent principle is not sufficient to ensure analytical agreement, and that each writer manipulates the data in ways governed by different strategies. We thus need to look at the *plot* being followed, to identify the specific factors that have arisen in constructing that plot. One can explain the divergences of the plots in terms familiar from Chapter 6: there are three possible *analytical situations*, which involve the following factors in varying combinations:

— choice of a musical corpus
— choice of a level of stylistic relevance
— choice of a level of semiological relevance

By all this, I mean that these choices are explicit or implicit for each individual author, and in the latter case they can only be identified through a kind of epistemological investigation.

(a) *Choice of an Analytical Corpus*

The choice of the corpus to be analyzed is (in this case) not a big problem. Most writers focus on the Tristan Chord as it exists within the context of the first three measures, which enables them to locate it (as almost everybody does) in the tonal realm of A minor. Mitchell and Forte situate themselves within a larger context; these two propose less a characterization of the Tristan Chord than an analysis of all or part of the Prelude.

(b) *Choice of a Level of Stylistic Relevance*

Things start becoming a bit more varied if we look at how each writer constructs an analysis in relation to a *stylistic horizon*. All analysis actually assumes that the object under consideration exists in relation to a *series* of other objects, both dissimilar—this is what enables us to establish our object's unique properties—and similar (this is what enables us to detect recurrence). My point is to show that the writers cited above, in explaining the Tristan Chord, resort to different *ways of situating the object within the series* ["mises en série"] depending upon the *plot* they have chosen.

The term "seriation" [mise en série], which was proposed by Molino and derived from classic philological studies, invokes the idea that any investigator, in order to assign some plausible meaning to a given phenomenon, must integrate it within a *series* of comparable phenomena. One cannot interpret what philology calls a *hapax*; that is, an isolated phenomenon. Art historian Erwin Panofsky has explained this situation in very clear terms:

> Whether we deal with historical or natural phenomena, the individual observation of phenomena assumes the character of a "fact" only when it can be related to other, analogous observations in such a way that the whole series "makes sense." This "sense" is, therefore, fully capable of being applied, as a control, to the interpretation of a new individual observation within the same range of phenomena. If, however, this new individual observation definitely refuses to be interpreted according to the "sense" of the series, and if an error proves to be impossible, the

"sense" of the series will have to be reformulated to include the new individual observation. (1955: 35)

Or, in the words of the archeologist Gehrard, "whoever sees one monument has really seen none; whoever has seen a thousand has only seen one" (cited in Molino 1974: 87).

One can detect three levels of seriation in the analyses discussed above. D'Indy, Piston, Goldman, and Riemannian analyses, represent systems whose transcendent principles embrace the whole of tonal music. They claim that tonal music (from Bach to Wagner) is based on the circle of fifths, or on the natural overtone series, or on a hierarchy of modal degrees, and so forth. In this, incidentally, Riemann's, or d'Indy's, or Goldman's propositions constitute a *theory*; that is, a general principle of functioning that is supposed to enable us to explain all properties of tonal music. In Goldman, we also find a more limited instance of the seriation process—his observations on nineteenth-century cadences as compared to those found in earlier centuries. In the latter, the chord on II predominates; in the former, that on IV. These first two instances of seriation are *external* to the musical work being analyzed: the work is being put in perspective against a horizon that extends beyond it. The third example (that of Mitchell and Forte) involves seriation internal to the work. But there is nothing that logically prevents us from combining numerous seriations—which is what Deliège does when he exploits both "tonal logic" and the Tristan Chord's many recurrences within the Prelude, and what Goldman does when he compares all nineteenth-century music to tonal functioning in general.

Of course, seriation alone is not sufficient to shape an analysis. Everything will depend on the relative *weight* assigned to each of the object's constituent parts, a weighting that is made in terms of a plot.

(c) *Choice of a Level of Semiological Relevance*
Choosing a plot will, to a great extent, depend on our stance toward the analyzed object; by stance I mean one of the three levels of the semiological tripartition (poietic, esthesic, and neutral). All the analyses previously discussed involve a level of immanence: the structure of the chord. But this strictly immanent level is quickly abandoned. It is my belief that an initial decision about the G♯—whether it is integral to the chord or not—depends whether the poietic or esthesic point of view is the predominant one. As noted above, the great majority of functional analyses—based on the I–IV–V progression or the circle of fifths—consider the G♯ an appoggiatura. In what sense do these particular analytical seriations have poietic relevance?

By looking at the Tristan Chord in relation to tonal functioning in general, we can hypothesize that normal compositional practice before Wagner gives us an image of the "poietic space" that oriented his compositional decisions. What I mean by this is that a chord as new as the Tristan Chord does not suddenly appear *ex nihilo*, but is instead born of contemporary tonal logic and tonal practice. Among our *Tristan* analyses, the IV-solution predominates over the II-solution, though the Tristan Chord always occurs in the same distibutional situation (before the V): this fact suggests what Molino calls a "presumption of poietic relevance" (1988: 199). Systematic, intuitive, or implicit seriation brings to light what one might call the stock of possibilities from which composers draw their creations. The analysis may consider the chord to be on II or IV, but in either case the analysis characterizes the chord in relation to a *contemporary* tonal logic, that admitted chords with recognizable functions—chords in which the G♯ need be neither an appoggiatura nor a suspension.

As soon as we begin to deal with the chord's total configuration, however, structure prevails over function, and one moves from the poietic to the *esthesic* standpoint, with writers fascinated by the strangeness of this unknown chord, held for five beats. This fascination explains analyses in which the chord is built on degree VII, something utterly unthinkable from the functionalist point of view; or, on the other hand, how the melodic motion that forms the chord's context leads other analyses to privilege melodic gestures above functional harmony. In the latter, even if the tension spanning the G♯–A is acknowledged, it is no longer interpreted in terms of the "vertical" function of the chord, but in relation to horizontal melodic motion.

But the esthesic point of view is not in itself unequivocal. If Gut has reservations concerning analyses that take the G♯ as a harmonic tone, this is because they thereby "reduce the fevered attractive power that is so crucial, since the note G♯ is the first in the famous Desire Theme" (1981: 149). Leonard Meyer invokes the same argument (in what is probably the latest analysis to precede the present revision of this book): "I do tend to favor [the appoggiatura interpretation] for criticism, because the character and affective quality of the chord seem inextricably linked to its continuation to A" (1989: 283). But Meyer is careful to add that "the analysis of the G♯ as a structural element in an independent harmony is perhaps preferable historically" (ibid.). By invoking an historical point of view, Meyer is alluding not to the "poietic stock" that serves as Wagner's point of departure, but rather to the history of the chord in posterity: "what has been called the emancipation of the dissonance begins with unprepared appoggiaturas and continues with unresolved dissonances that are eventually transformed into acoustic entities (discords) in relation to which the notion syntactic resolution is meaningless" (ibid.). The second esthesic point of view to which Meyer appeals is analogous to the role I assign to perception in the progressive evolution of music (see Chapter 7, Section 4). For Meyer, as for Goldman, the syntactic function of the chord "has begun to give way to the claims of sonority and voice-leading" (ibid.) In emphasizing that "there is an inverse relationship between awareness of sonority and awareness of syntactic specificity" (284), Meyer provides the best illustration of the fact that Tristan Chord analyses are pulled between the poietic and the esthesic, and that this discrepancy *must* be explicitly thematicized.

7. Analyses and Truth

The multiplicity of these analyses forces us to consider certain inevitable questions: are all these analyses valid? Are we condemned to an absolute relativism? Need we privilege any single answer? I want to state right from the start (and as decisively as possible) that the Tristan Chord's own considerable malleability does not save the musicologists who analyze it from being *wrong*. Until now, I have been talking as if it were self-evident that the Prelude is in A minor. But at least one writer (Schreyer 1905) heard the whole beginning of the Prelude in E minor, making the chord in measure 3 a seventh on I (?!). Searle (1966), since he revoiced and spelled the chord enharmonically F–A♭–C♭–E♭, was forced to place it in the odd tonal context of E♭ minor, an interpretation that Gostomsky (1975: 25–26) proposed as an option beside A minor. We should not scruple to call the E major or the E♭ minor readings *wrong*.

When Veyne, in a work more recent than his 1971 study in historical epistemology, states that "truth is the daughter of imagination" (1983: 110), I am not sure I can agree with him, because in the end one can have reservations about the existence of Atlantis or the Loch Ness monster, but no one can question the existence of London. I admit that establishing the border between pure observation and an interpretive act is a delicate matter, especially in the present case. But when Edward Cone, in a passage already cited in Chapter 2, writes that "the analysis as such ceases with the choice of the tonic; once this has been made, the assignment of degree numbers to the chords is pure description" (1960: 35), I have the feeling that analysis—or at least analytical problems—begins precisely where Cone thinks it ends.

This having been said, we are still faced with opposing plots. Their coexistence brings us to relativism—yet does this relativism authorize us to say anything we want? When I presented a preliminary version of these remarks in London in 1984, one discussant compared my approach to Barthes's *S/Z*. This is a comparison that I must reject in the strongest terms. If Barthes has a plot (given that it could be made explicit), he nonetheless makes no *seriation*, and this same absence damages the credibility of many arguments elaborated by French "New Criticism." Between total interpretive freedom, and the kind of relativism that results from the multiplicity of possible seriations, is a barrier that I, for one, am not prepared to cross. Seriation allows us to control interpretation.

In addition, the plots compared here share two essential properties:

— they have been *constructed* on the basis of reasonable propositions that are subject to control;
— they can be compared and placed into a qualitative hierarchy; we can make our criteria for evaluating them *explicit*.

Riemann, as we noted above, believed that the basic precepts of his system of explanation could never be challenged. Yet it appears that the circle of fifths is nonetheless the more powerful explanation, even if we have no metatheory that would satifactorily explain its foundations. For this reason, I myself favor an analysis that places the Tristan Chord on degree II. But we must not hide this construction's flimsiness from ourselves, or that, in general, of resorting to seriation. Seriation is flimsy because of its statistical character. Goldman, as we saw, states that the cadence on IV becomes more frequent in the course of the nineteenth century. But to what extent? The only answer would be to move to computer-assisted seriation of all nonambiguous cadential progressions in all music for ten to twenty years before *Tristan*. But we should remember that, in the first flush of musical information-processing, we always said that we would "get to these sorts of things someday." Goldman's insight rests not on some rigorous statistical tally, but on a statistical intuition. His seriation is not systematic, but implicit. If we trust him, this is because we live in a scholarly culture that respects erudition (it alone, in the last analysis, guarantees validity, indeed, even the "truth" of a given suggestion: we know that total induction is an impossibility).

But a different factor inclines me toward the camp of the French sixth (though on degree II): the doubling of the descending second in the bass in measure 2 (F–E), which indicates a certain emphasis on Wagner's part. At least two other writers have discussed it (Cone 1960: 35, and Gut 1981: 150). In such an otherwise unstable context, this doubling is an indication of the chord's root (F). Three lines of argument combined (that the circle of fifths theory is true, that II is closer to I than IV is, and that Wagner's doubling suggests that the chord's root is F) bring me to privilege this one interpretation above the others. But is this the only possible option? My concept of semiology is in itself based on two transcendent principles, and if I strive to show how transcendent principles inform the work of others, it is to be expected that I make such principles explicit in my own, as I did in Chapter 1:

- — in symbolic forms, the poietic and the esthesic do not necessarily coincide;
- — all symbolic objects give rise to an infinite series of interpretants—the Tristan Chord bears eloquent witness to this—and one can never reduce them to a single, unequivocal meaning.

If this is, as I believe to be the case, a reasonable set of assumptions, then esthesically relevant analysis must be acknowledged and allowed to exist side by side with the poietically inflected analysis that has traditionally been favored. If, in following Goldman's arguments, one erases the functional characterization of the chord (i.e., the chord is so vague that one cannot, *in hearing it*, assign it to a stable scale degree) then it is enough to call it a diminished seventh chord with a raised fifth, defined by an empirical superimposition of thirds over five beats. This is, in terms of the taxonomical stock we know from the harmony treatises, an eccentric characterization, but it alone explains the notes actually heard and the chord's unique *sonority*. (Further on, we will see that, even from the Wagnerian point of view, recognizing the D♯ is not such a crazy idea.)

Until now, actually, I have been privileging two different and competing analyses on the basis of certain explicit principles, depending whether we are examining the poietic or esthesic side. Of course, we are speaking of *inductive* poietics or esthesics. I say *inductive* because I have neither made the Tristan Chord the object of some experiment in perception, nor made reference to some Wagnerian document external to the music.

Such a document in fact exists. We must, then, ask whether the inductive poietic analysis suggested above—on the basis of certain rationalizations—would be, in Wagner's view, reasonable. The answer may be surprising.

Mayrberger, a Czech professor, suggested an analysis of the Tristan Chord in his 1878 text *Lehrbuch der musikalischen Harmonik*; this analysis is remarkable for its originality. He initially suggests the roots A–D–B–E. He places the chord on the second degree, and interprets the G♯ as an appoggiatura. But above all, Mayrberger considers the attraction between E and the real bass F to be paramount, and calls the Tristan Chord a *Zwitterakkord* (a bisexual or androgynous chord), whose F is controlled by the key of A minor, and D♯ by the key of E minor.

Mayrberger's analysis was a supplement to an offprint published by the Bayreuth Patronatverein in 1881, "Die Harmonik Richard Wagners an den Leitmotiven des Vorspieles zu 'Tristan und Isolde'." In a preface to this publication, Hans von Wolzogen—editor in chief of the Bayreuther Blätter and best known for his inventories of Wagner's leitmotifs—reported Wagner's opinion of Mayrberger's analysis. According to Wolzogen, "[Wagner] with considerable delight believed he had found in this heretofore unknown man from faraway Hungary the theorist he had long been waiting for." Serge Gut, Professor of Musicology at the Sorbonne, drew from this report his own conclusion that Wagner (since he had endorsed Mayrberger's analysis) considered the G♯ an appoggiatura and not a chordal note. (Gut 1981: 149) If one accepts Wolzogen's report as a reliable poietic document, it seems that Wagner saw the Tristan Chord as built on the second degree in A minor (as Mayrberger had explicitly stated). This, incidentally, contradicts Gut's analysis—which, in fidelity to its Riemannian principles, describes the opening of Tristan as "the most classic succession in the world: Tonic, Subdominant, Dominant" (1981: 150). Since it had something to do with E minor by virtue of the D♯ (a point that practically nobody after Mayrberger would make), was the Tristan Chord—for Wagner as well as Mayrberger— an androgynous chord? I have examined this question elsewhere.[15]

No matter how relativist we may be, no scientific activity is possible without judgments about truth (*adequatio rei et intellectus*) seeping into our readings of literature. But I believe I have shown how judgments about truth devolve upon presuppositions that sustain their own elaboration. This is why the reader's sense of truth often depends both upon the confidence he or she places in the writer's *erudition*, and upon his or her sensitivity to the *rhetorical force* or *style* of the argument. When the reader's confidence and the author's plot meet, the consequence can be a certain *stability* of explanation: the history of science and the history of musical analysis are thus marked by *periods of a theoretical and epistemological consensus*. This stability allows us to accept an analysis or a theory as true so long as it endures for a suf-

---

[15] I have devoted an entire book, *Wagner androgyne* (Nattiez 1990), to the metamorphosis of the figure of androgyny in Wagner's work. A fuller discussion of the Tristan Chord, and Mayrberger's interpretation, appears in this volume. I thank John Deathridge for sending me a copy of the Mayrberger publication.

ficient time in history of thought. But should a new fact intervene, should a new theoretical paradigm emerge, then this stability is called once more into question. What was taken as truth becomes merely one possible plot, henceforth debatable and outmoded. Knowledge is a cumulative process; the quest for truth is asymptotic.

Must we, however, appeal to that epistemological monster, "relative truth"? Do we have to fall into the vertigo of absolute relativism, into which the partisans of deconstruction would draw us?[16] I do not believe this to be the case. It is important to stress that authentically scientific theories and analyses are *symbolic constructions*: *symbolic*, because (as we saw in Chapter 7) discourse about music is simultaneously the product of a creative process, a material trace, and the object of interpretation; *constructions*, because theoretical or analytical propositions are not products of a free, ethereal imagination, but instead result from arguments, observations, and decisions that can be controlled and defined explicitly. This is why, as soon as data are reinterpreted within the framework of a new plot, it is only rarely that nothing of previous plots will remain. I say this despite, even arguing against, Kuhn's concept of scientific *revolution*, and I am not the first to do so. Thus the idea of the Tristan Chord as androgynous, related simultaneously to A minor and E minor, does not prevent the retention of the II-solution. Rather, the notion of the androgynous chord simply adds a supplementary web of meanings that, moreover, nudge us well beyond technical musical analysis. It supplements and enriches what semiology strives to explain: the web of interpretants associated with the chord.

At the conclusion of this chapter, I am well aware that I have dealt with a rather "slim" phenomenon, and have chosen an object that is at once special and privileged. In submitting these four unhappy notes to the perverse game of analytical comparison, I realize that the Tristan Chord's malleability and ambiguity make it function as a kind of Rorschach test, revealing the bases and the analytical orientations unique to various concurrent theories and methods. Given that semiology is not necessarily the science of communication, that more detailed knowledge of symbolic functioning has everything to gain from inverting the generally accepted communication hypothesis, and that we must consider the poietic, neutral, and esthesic as having their own individual ways of functioning rather than deciding a priori that they coincide, I have sought to show by means of a radical example how categories that are normally confused must be kept sep-

---

[16] For a first exploration of this subject, see Nattiez 1990 (forthcoming).

arate. But I do not pretend, in studying this miniature, to have supplied the conclusive proof of the tripartitional model's validity. I hope merely to have shown, throughout this book, that these three semiological elements—poietics, the neutral level, and esthesics—are legitimate in thinking about or analyzing the properties of musical symbolism.

The essential work remains to be done, for ethnomusicology as much as for classical musicology: to examine how the important theories, those accepted and discussed, actually function; to interrogate the different methodologies practiced in music analysis; and to offer analyses guided by the principles that have been described in these pages. But this will be the task of future volumes.

References

Abbate, C. 1989. What the Sorcerer Said. *19th-Century Music* 12 (1989):221–30.

———. 1991. *Unsung Voices: Opera and Musical Narration in the Nineteenth Century*. Princeton: Princeton University Press.

Adams, C. 1976. Melodic Contour Typology. *Ethnomusicology*, 20, no. 2:179–215.

Adorno, T. W. 1976. *Mahler, une physionomie musicale*. Paris: Éditions de Minuit.

Alain, O. 1965a. Le langage musical de Schönberg à nos jours. In *La musique, les hommes, les instrument, les oeuvres*, vol. 2. N. Dufourcq, ed. Paris: Larousse, pp. 354–86.

———. 1965b. *L'harmonie*. Paris: Presses Universitaires de France.

Apel, W. 1944. Melody. *Harvard Dictionary of Music*. Cambridge: Harvard University Press, pp. 435–38.

Arend, M. 1901. Harmonische Analyse des Tristan-Vorspiels. *Bayreuther Blätter*, no. 24:160–69.

Arom, S. 1969. Essai d'une notation des monodies à des fins d'analyse. *Revue de musicologie* 55, no. 2:172–216.

———. 1978. Rythmique et polyrythmie centrafricaines: fonctions, structure. *Conférences des journées d'études du festival international du son haute-fidélité stéréophonique*. Paris: Éditions Radio, pp. 163–71.

———. 1985. *Polyphonies et polyrythmies instrumentales d'Afrique centrale*. 2 vols. Paris: S.E.L.A.F.

Attali, J. 1977. *Bruits*. Paris: Presses Universitaires de France.

Austerlitz, R. 1983. Meaning in Music: Is Music Like Language and If So, How? *American Journal of Semiotics*, 2, no. 3:1–12.

Babbitt, M. 1972. The Structure and Function of Musical Theory. (1965) In *Perspectives in Contemporary Music Theory*. B. Boretz and E. T. Cone, eds. New York: Norton, pp. 10–21.

Bach, C.P.E. 1762. *Versuch über die wahre Art das Clavier zu spielen*. Berlin: Henning.

Baker, T. 1882. *Über die Musik der nordamerikanischen Wilden*. Leipzig: Breitkopf und Härtel. New York: Da Capo Press.

Baker, N. K. 1976. Heinrich Koch and the Theory of Melody. *Journal of Music Theory* 20, no. 1:1–48.

Baroni, M., and C. Jacoboni. 1976. *Verso una Grammatica della Melodia*. Bologne: Antiquae Musicae Italicae Studiosi, Universita Studi di Bologna. English trans. Montréal: Presses de l'Université de Montréal, 1978.

Barthes, R. 1973. *Le plaisir du texte*. Paris: Seuil.

Bauman, R., and J. Sherzer. 1974. *Explorations in the Ethnography of Speaking*. Cambridge: Cambridge University Press.

Beaudry, N. 1978. Le katajjaq: un jeu inuit traditionnel. *Études Inuit Studies* 2, no. 1:35–53.

Becker, J. 1969. The Anatomy of a Mode. *Ethnomusicology* 13, no. 2:267–79.

Becker, A. and J. 1979. A Grammar of the Musical Genre *Srepegan*. *Journal of Music Theory* 23, no. 1:1–43.

Belvianes, M. 1950. *Sociologie de la musique*. Paris: Payot.

Bent, I. 1980. Analysis. *The New Grove Dictionary of Music and Musicians*, vol. 1. London, pp. 340–388.

Benveniste, E. 1966. *Problèmes de linguistique générale*. Paris: Gallimard.

———. 1969. Sémiologie de la langue. *Semiotica* 1:1–12, 127–35.

Berg, A. 1985. *Écrits*. Paris: Christian Bourgois éditeur.

Bernstein, L. 1976. *The Unanswered Question*. Cambridge: Harvard University Press.

Beswick, D. M. 1950. The Problem of Tonality in Seventeenth-Century Music. Ph.D. Diss., Chapel Hill, University of North Carolina.

Biton, P. 1948. *Le rythme musical, le rythme de la langue français, paroles et musique, le rythme en général*. Geneva: Henn.

Blacking, J. 1971. Deep and Surface Structures in Venda Music. *Yearbook of the International Folk Music Council* 3:91–108.

———. 1973. *How Musical Is Man?* Seattle: University of Washington Press.

Blacking, J. 1984. What Languages Do Musical Grammars Describe? In *Musical Grammars and Computer Analysis*. M. Baroni and L. Callegari, eds. Florence: Olschki Editore, pp. 363–70.

Blom, E. 1946. Rhythm. *Everyman's Dictionary of Music*. London: Dent, pp. 495–96.

Bloomfield, L. 1933. *Language*. New York: Rinehart and Winston. French trans., *Le Langage*. Paris: Payot, 1970.

Boilès, C. 1973a. Sémiotique de l'ethnomusicologie. *Musique en Jeu*, no. 10:34–41.

———. 1973b. Reconstruction of Proto-Melody. *Anuario Yearbook in Inter-American Musical Research*. 9:45–63.

———. 1975. Rev. of *Fondements d'une sémiologie de la musique*, by J.-J. Nattiez. *Yearbook for Inter-American Research* 9:242–44.

———. 1982. Processes of Musical Semiosis. *Yearbook for Traditional Music* 14:24–44.

———. 1984. Universals of Musical Behaviour: A Taxonomic Approach. *The World of Music* 26, no. 2:50–65.

Boretz, B. 1969–1973. Meta-Variations. *Perspectives of New Music* 8, no. 1 (1969):1–74; 8, no. 2 (1970):49–111; 9, no. 1 (1970):23–42; 11, no. 1 (1972):146–223; 11, no. 2 (1973):156–203.

Bouchard, G. 1980. L'A.B.C. de la sémiologie. A propos de "Silence, on parle: introduction à la sémiotique" par Jurgen Pesot. *Philosophiques* (Montréal, Oct. 1980):321–75.

Boulez, P. 1964. *Penser la musique aujourd'hui*. Paris: Gonthier.

———. 1966. *Relevés d'apprenti*. Paris: Seuil.

————. 1981a. *Matériau et invention musicale*. Cassettes IRACAM-Radio France, C.R.F. 080 (no. 1: Debussy-Varèse).

————. 1981b. *Points de repère*. 2nd ed. Paris: Christian Bourgois éditeur, 1985.

Bourdieu, P. and A. Darbel. 1969. *L'amour de l'art*. Paris: Minuit.

Bourgeois, P. 1946. Éléments d'acoustique. In *La musique des origines à nos jours*. N. Dufourcq, ed. Paris: Larousse, pp. 1–6.

Bouveresse, J. 1984. *Rationalité et cynisme*. Paris: Minuit.

Boyé, P. 1779. *L'esthétique musicale mise au rang des chimères*. Amsterdam.

Brailoiu, C. 1931. Esquisse d'une méthode de folklore musical. *Revue de musicologie* 12, no. 40:233–67.

Brandel, R. 1962. Types of Melodic Movement in Central Africa. *Ethnomusicology* 6, no. 2:75–87.

Braudel, F. 1949. *La Méditerranée et le monde méditerranéen à l'époque de Philippe II*. 6th ed. Revised and enlarged. 2 vols. Paris: Colin, 1985.

Brendel, A. 1976. *Musical Thoughts and Afterthoughts*. Princeton: Princeton University Press.

Brenet, M. 1926. Mélodie. *Dictionnaire pratique et historique de la musique*. Paris: Colin, pp. 243–47.

Bright, W. 1963. Language and Music: Areas for Cooperation. *Ethnomusicology* 7, no. 1:26–32.

Bukofzer, M. F. 1947. *Music in the Baroque Era from Monteverdi to Bach*. New York: Norton.

Butor, M. 1960. La musique, art réaliste. *Esprit*, no. 280:138–56.

Cage, J. 1969. *Notations*. New York: Something Else Press.

————. 1976. *Pour les oiseaux: entretiens avec Daniel Charles*. Paris: Belfond.

Calame-Griaule, G. 1965. *Ethnologie et langage, la parole chez les Dogon*. Paris: Gallimard.

Capellen, G. 1902. "Harmonik und Melodik bei R. Wagner." *Bayreuther Blätter*, no. 25:3–23.

Chabanon, M. de. 1779. *Observations sur la musique, et principalement sur la métaphysique de l'art*. Paris: Pissot. Geneva: Slatkine Reprints, 1969.

Chailley, J. 1951. *Traité historique d'analyse musicale*. Paris: Leduc.

————. 1954–1955. *Formation et transformation du langage musical, I. Intervalles et échelles*. Paris: Centre de Documentation Universitaire.

————. 1958. Rapport du groupe de travail—La révision de la notion traditionnelle de tonalité. In *Actes du septième congrès international de musicologie* (Cologne, 1958). Cologne: Bärenreiter, 1959, pp. 332–34.

————. 1959 (Dec.). Essai sur les structures mélodiques. *Revue de musicologie* 44:139–75.

————. 1963a. *Tristan et Isolde de Richard Wagner*. Paris: Centre de documentation universitaire.

————. 1963b. L'axiome de Stravinsky. *Journal de psychologie normale et pathologique* 40:407–19.

————. 1971. Rythme verbal et rythme gestuel, essai sur l'organisation musicale du temps. *Journal de psychologie normale et pathologique* no. 68:5–14.

Changeux, J.-P. 1983. *L'homme neuronal*. Paris: Fayard.

Charbonnier, G. 1970. *Entretiens avec Edgard Varèse*. Paris: Belfond.

References

Charles, D. 1967. Ouverture et indétermination. *La Pensée*, no. 135:182–92.

Charles, D. 1970–1971. L'empirisme de John Cage. *V.H. 101*, no. 4:20–29.

Chatman, S. 1978. *Story and Discourse: Narrative Structure in Fiction and Film.* Ithaca: Cornell University Press.

Chenoweth, V. 1972. *Melodic Perception and Analysis.* Papua, New Guinea: Summer Institute of Linguistics.

———. 1979. *The Usarufas and their Music.* Dallas: S.I.I. Museum of Anthropology.

Chion, M. 1975. Un langage pour décrire les sons. *Programme-Bulletin du G.R.M.*, no. 16:39–75.

Chion, M., and G. Reibel, 1977. *Les musiques électroacoustiques.* Aix-en-Provence: Edisud.

Chocholle, R. 1973. *Le Bruit.* Paris: Presses Universitaires de France.

Choron, A.-E. 1810. *Dictionnaire historique des musiciens, artistes ou amateurs, morts ou vivants, précédé d'un sommaire de l'histoire de la musique.* Paris: Valade.

Christ, W., et al. 1967. *Materials and Stucture of Music.* Englewood Cliffs: Prentice Hall.

Coker, W. 1972. *Music and Meaning, a Theoretical Introduction to Musical Aesthetics.* New York: The Free Press.

Combarieu, J. 1893. L'expression objective en musique d'après le langage instinctif. *Revue philosophique* 35:124–44.

Cone, E. T. 1960. Analysis Today. In *Problems of Modern Music.* E. Land, ed. New York: Norton, pp. 34–50.

———. 1974. *The Composer's Voice.* Berkeley and Los Angeles: University of California Press.

Cooke, D. 1959. *The Language of Music.* London: Oxford University Press.

Cooper, G., and L. B. Meyer, 1960. *The Rhythmic Structure of Music.* Chicago: The University of Chicago Press.

Costère, E. 1961a. Mélodie (B). *Encyclopédie de la musique*, vol. 3. Paris: Fasquelle, pp. 178–81.

———. 1961b. Tonalité. *Encyclopédie de la musique*, vol. 3. Paris: Fasquelle, pp. 802–3.

Creston, P. 1964. *Principles of Rhythm.* New York: Columbo.

Dahlhaus, C. 1980. Tonality. *The New Grove Dictionary of Music and Musicians*, vol. 19. London, pp. 51–55.

———. 1982. Musikwissenschaft und systematische Musikwissenschaft. In *Systematische Musikwissenschaft.* C. Dahlhaus and H. de la Motte-Haber, eds. Wiesbaden: Akademische Verlagsgesellschaft Athenaion, pp. 25–48.

Daube, J.-F. 1797–1798. *Anleitung zur Erfindung der Melodie und ihrer Fortsetzung.* Vienna.

Davie, C.-T. 1966. *Musical Structure and Design.* New York: Dover.

Delacroix, H.-J. 1927. *Psychologie de l'art, essai sur l'activité artistique.* Paris: Alcan.

Delalande, F. 1972. L'analyse des musiques électro-acoustiques. *Musique en Jeu*, no. 8:50–56.

———. 1974. "L'Omaggio a Joyce" de Luciano Berio. *Musique en Jeu*, no. 15:45–54.

———. 1977. L'objet virtuel. *Cahiers Recherche/Musique*, no. 6:71–74.

———. 1982. Vers une "psycho-musicologie." In *L'enfant du sonore au musical*. B. Céleste, F. Delalande, and E. Dumaurier, eds. Paris: INA-GRM/Buchet-Chastel, pp. 157–79.

———. 1984. *La musique est un jeu d'enfant*. Paris: INA-GRM Buchet-Chastel.

———. 1986. En l'absence de partition; le cas singulier de l'analyse de la musique de la musique électroacoustique. *Analyse musicale*, no. 3:54–58.

Deliège, C. 1974. Les techniques du rétrospectivisme. *International Review of the Aesthetics and Sociology of Music* 5, no. 1:27–42. (Reprinted in Deliège 1986, pp. 369–83.)

———. 1979. Théories récentes de la tonalité. *Degrés*, no. 18:1–26.

———. 1984. *Les fondements de la musique tonale*. Paris: Lattès.

———. 1986. *Invention musicale et idéologies*. Paris: Christian Bourgois éditeur.

Deprun, J. 1979. *La philosophie de l'inquiétude en France au XVIIIe siècle*. Paris: Vrin.

Distler, H. 1940. *Funktionelle Harmonielehre*. Kassel und Basel: Bärenreiter.

D'Ollone, M. 1954. *Le langage musical*. 2 vols. Paris and Geneva: La Palatine.

Dorflès, G. 1973. Objectalité et artifice dans la musique contemporaine. *Musique en Jeu*, no. 13:14–23.

Dubois, T. 1891. *Traité d'harmonie théorique et pratique*. Paris: Heugel.

Duchez, M.-E. 1974. Principe de la mélodie et origine des langues: un brouillon inédit de J.-J. Rousseau sur l'origine de la mélodie. *Revue de musicologie* 40, nos. 1–2:33–86.

———. 1980. La représentation de la musique. *Actes du XVIIIe Congrès des Sociétés de Philosophie de langue française*. Strasbourg: Université des sciences humaines de Strasbourg, pp. 178–82.

———. 1983. Des neumes à la portée. *Revue de musique des universités canadiennes*, no. 4:22–65.

Dufrenne, M. 1967. L'Art est-il langage? *Revue d'esthétique* 19, no. 1 (Jan.–March 1966):1–42. Reprinted in *Esthétique et philosophie*. Paris: Klincksieck, 1967, pp. 74–122.

Duhem, P. 1906. *La théorie physique*. Paris: Rivière.

Dumesnil, R. 1949. *Le Rythme musical; essai historique et critique*. Paris: La Colombe.

Dunsby, J. 1977. Rev. of *Fondements d'une sémiologie de la musique*, by J.-J. Nattiez. *Perspectives of New Music* 15, no. 2:226–33.

———. 1983. Music and Semiotics: The Nattiez Phase. *Musical Quarterly* 69, no. 1:27–43.

Durr, B. 1976. Valeur et plus-value. *Programme-Bulletin du G.R.M.* no. 17:50–56.

Eckstein, F. 1923. *Erinnerungen an Anton Bruckner*. Wien: New York, Universal Edition.

Eco, U. 1965. *L'oeuvre ouverte*. Paris: Seuil. English trans., *The Open Work*, A. Cancogni. Cambridge: Harvard University Press, 1989.

———. 1968. *La struttura assente*. Milan: Bompiani.

———. 1971. *Le forme del contenuto*. Milan: Bompiani.

———. 1975. *Trattato di semiotica generale*. Milan: Bompiani.

———. 1976. *A Theory of Semiotics*. Bloomington: Indiana University Press.

———. 1978. Codice. *Enciclopedia Einaudi*, vol. 3. Turin: Einaudi, pp. 243–81.

———. 1979a. *Lector in Fabula*. Milan: Bompiani.

———. 1979b. *The Role of the Reader, Explorations in the Semiotics of Texts*. Bloomington: Indiana University Press.

———. 1984. *Semiotica e filosofia del linguaggio*. Turin: Einaudi. English Trans., *Semiotics and the Philosophy of Language*. Bloomington: Indiana University Press.

Edwards, A. C. 1956. *The Art of Melody*. New York: Philosophical Library.

Ehrenfels, C. V. 1980. Über Gestaltqualitäten. *Vierteljahrschrift für wissenschaftliche Philosophie* 14:249–92.

Ellis, A. J., and A. J. Hipkins. 1884. Tonometrical Observations on Some Existing Nonharmonic Musical Scales. *Proceedings of the Royal Society of London* 37:368–85.

Emmanuel, M. 1926. Le "rythme" d'Euripide à Debussy. In *Premier congrés du rythme* (Geneva, 16–18 August 1926). A. Pfrimmer, ed. Geneva: Institut Jaques-Dalcroze, pp. 103–46.

England, N. 1964. Symposium on Transcription and Analysis. *Ethnomusicology* 8, no. 3:223–77.

Ergo, E. 1912. Über Wagner's Harmonik und Melodik. *Bayreuther Blätter*, no. 35:34–41.

Erickson, E. E. 1969. The Song Trace: Song Styles and the Ethnohistory of Aboriginal America. Ph.D. Diss., Columbia University.

Erpf, H. 1927. *Studien zur Harmonie- und Klangtechnik der neueren Musik*. Leipzig.

Escal, F. 1979. *Espaces sociaux, espaces musicaux*. Paris: Payot.

Falk, J. 1958. *Précis technique de composition musicale théorique et pratique*. Paris: Leduc.

Faure, G. 1962. *Recherche sur les caractères et le rôle des éléments musicaux dans la prononciation anglaise*. Paris: Didier, Études anglaises, no. 10.

Fay, T. 1971. Perceived Hierarchic Structure in Language and Music. *Journal of Music Theory* 15, nos. 1–2:112–37.

Feld, S. 1982. *Sound and Sentiment*. Philadelphia: University of Pennsylvania Press.

Ferchault, G. 1957–1958. Mélodie. *Larousse de la Musique*. Paris: Larousse.

Fétis, F.-J. 1844. *Traité complet de la théorie et de la pratique de l'harmonie contenant la doctrine de la science et de l'Art*. Brussels.

Forel, O. L. 1920. Le rythme; étude psychologique. *Jahrschrift für Psychologie und Neurologie*, 26:1–104.

Forte, A. 1959. Schenker's Conception of Musical Structure. *Journal of Music Theory* 3, no. 1:1–30.

———. 1988. New Approaches to the Linear Analysis of Music. *Journal of the American Musicological Society* 41, no. 2:315–48.

Foucault, M. 1969. *L'archéologie du savoir.* Paris: Gallimard.

Fraisse, P. 1956. *Les structures rythmiques; études psychologiques.* Louvain: Publications Universitaires de Louvain.

———. 1974. *Psychologie du rythme.* Paris: Presses Universitaires de France.

Francès, R. 1958. *La perception de la musique.* Paris: Vrin.

Freund, J. 1973. *Les théories des sciences humaines.* Paris: Presses Universitaires de France.

Fubini, E. 1968. *L'estetica musicale dal settecento a oggi.* Turin: Einaudi.

———. 1973. *Musica e linguaggio nell'estetica contemporanea.* Turin: Einaudi.

———. 1976. *L'estetica musicale dall'antichità al settecento.* Turin: Einaudi.

Gadamer, H. G. 1979. *Truth and Method.* 2nd English ed. London: Sheed and Ward.

Gardin, J.-C. 1974. *Les analyses du discours.* Neuchâtel: Delaschaux et Niestlé.

———. 1979. *Une archéologie théorique.* Paris: Hachette.

Geertz, C. 1973. *The Interpretation of Cultures.* New York: Basic Books.

George, G. 1970. *Tonality and Musical Structure.* New York: Praeger.

Gevaert, F.-A. 1875–1881. *Histoire et théorie de la musique de l'Antiquité.* 2 vols. Ghent: Annoot-Braeckman.

Gilson, E. 1958. *Peinture et société.* Paris: Vrin.

———. 1963. *Introduction aux arts du beau.* Paris: Vrin.

Goblot, E. 1901. La musique descriptive. *Revue philosophique* 52:58–77.

Godzich, W. 1978. Rev. of *A Theory of Semiotics,* by U. Eco and *Fondements d'une sémiologie de la musique,* by J.-J. Nattiez, *Journal of Music Theory* 22, no. 1:117–33.

Goethe, W. 1975. *La métamorphose des plantes* (1790). Paris: Triades.

Goetschius, P. 1900. *Exercises in Melody Writing.* New York: Schirmer.

Goldman, R. F. 1965. *Harmony in Western Music.* New York: Norton.

Goodman, N. 1968. *Languages of Art.* Indianapolis, New York, and Kansas City: Bobbs-Merril.

Goody, J. 1977. *The Domestication of the Savage Mind.* Cambridge: Cambridge University Press.

Gostomsky, D. 1975. Immer noch einmal der "Tristan Akkord." *Zeitschrift für Musiktheorie* 6, no. 1:22–27.

Gottwald, C. 1985. De la difficulté d'une théorie de la nouvelle musique. In *Quoi? quand? comment? La recherche musicale.* T. Machover, ed. Paris: Christian Bourgois éditeur.

Gourlay, K. A. 1984. The Non-Universality of Music and the Universality of Non-Music. *The World of Music* 26, no. 2:25–39.

Granger, G. G. 1967. *Pensée formelle et sciences de l'homme.* 2nd ed. Paris: Aubier.

———. 1968. *Essai d'une philosophie du style.* Paris: Colin.

Griaule, M. 1966. *Dieu d'eau*. Paris: Favard.

Gribenski, A. 1975. *L'audition*. Paris: Presses Universitaires de France.

Groot, A. W. de. 1932. Der Rhythmus. *Neophilologus*, vol. 18. pp. 81–98, 177–97, 241–64.

Guillaume, M., 1975. *Le capital et son double*. Paris: Presses Universitaires de France.

Gushee, L. 1977. Lester Young's "Shoeshine Boy." International Musicological Society, *Report of the Twelfth Congress* (Berkeley, 1977). D. Heartz and B. Wade, eds. Kassel and Basel: Bärenreiter, pp. 151–69.

Gut, S. 1981. Encore et toujours: "L'accord de Tristan," *L'avant-scène Opéra*, no. 34–35, "Tristan et Isole," pp. 148–51.

Hanna, J. L. 1979. *To Dance is Human, a Theory of Nonverbal Communication*. Austin and London: University of Texas Press.

———. 1983. *The Performer-Audience Connection: Emotion to Metaphor in Dance and Society*. Austin and London: University of Texas Press.

Hanslick, E. 1854. *Du beau dans la musique*. Paris: Macquet. New edition, Paris: Christian Bourgois éditeur, 1986. English trans., *The Beautiful in Music*, by G. Cohen. New York: Da Capo Press, 1974.

Harnoncourt, N. 1984. *Le discours musical* (1982). Paris: Gallimard.

Harwood, D. 1976. Universals in Music: A Perspective from Cognitive Psychology. *Ethnomusicology* 20, no. 3:521–33.

Hatten, R. 1980. Nattiez's Semiology of Music: Flaws in the New Science. *Semiotica* 31, nos. 1–2:138–55.

Hempholtz, H.L.F. von. 1963. *Die Lehre von den Tonempfindungen als physiologische Grundlage für die Theorie der Musik*. Braunschweig: Vieweg.

Herndon, M. 1974. Analysis: Herding of Sacred Cows? *Ethnomusicology* 28, no. 2:219–62.

———. 1975. Le modèle transformationnel en linguistique: ses implications pour l'étude de la musique. *Semiotica* 15, no. 1:71–82.

Herndon, M., and N. McLeod. 1973. The Use of Nicknames as Evaluators of Personal Competence. *Texas Working Papers in Socio-linguistics*, no. 14.

Herzog, G. 1941. Do Animals Have Music? *Bulletin of the American Musicological Society*, no. 5:3–4.

———. 1949–1950. Song. In *Standard Dictionary of Folklore, Mythology and Legend*. M. Leach and J. Fried, eds. New York: Funk and Wagnalls, pp. 1035–50.

Hindemith, P. 1937. *Unterweisung in Tonsatz*. Mainz: Schott.

———. 1942. *The Craft of Musical Composition*. New York: Associated Music Publishers.

Hirbour-Paquette, L. 1979. Quelques remarques sur la duplication chez Debussy. Chatman-Eco-Klinkenberg, eds., pp. 998–1002.

Hjelmslev, L. 1943. *Omkring sprogteoriens grundlaeggelse*. Copenhagen: Ejnar Munskgaard. *Prolegomen to a Theory of Language*. International Journal of American Linguistics, Memoir 7. Bloomington: Indiana University Press Publications in Anthropology, 1953. *Prolégomènes à une théorie du langage*. Paris: Minuit, 1971.

Holst, I. 1963. *Time. The Structure of Melody*. London: Faber and Faber.

Holton, G. 1981. *L'imagination scientifique*. Paris: Gallimard.

Hood, M. 1977. Universal Attributes of Music. *The World of Music* 19, no. 2:63–69.

Horowicz, B. 1946. *Le théâtre d'opéra*. Paris: Éditions de Flore.

Imberty, M. 1975. Perspectives nouvelles de la sémantique musicale expérimentale. *Musique en Jeu*, no. 17:87–109.

———. 1976. Rev. of *Fondements d'une sémiologie de la musique*, by J.-J. Nattiez. *Revue française de musicologie* 63, no. 2:336–39.

D'Indy, V. 1903. *Cours de composition musicale*, vol. 1. Paris: Durand.

Ingarden, R. 1962. Das Musikwerk. *Untersuchungen zur Ontologie der Kunst, Musik, Architektur, Film*. Tubingen: Niemeyer. English trans., R. Meyer and J. T. Goldschmidt. Athens: Ohio University Press, 1989.

Jacob, P. 1980. *L'empirisme logique, ses antécédents, ses critiques*. Paris: Minuit.

Jadassohn, S. 1899. *Melodik und Harmonik bei R. Wagner*. Berlin.

Jakobson, R. 1963. *Essais de linguistique générale*. Paris: Minuit.

———. 1970. Language in Relation to Other Communication Systems. *Linguaggi nella societa e nella tecnica*. Milan: Edizioni di Communita, pp. 3–16.

———. 1973a. *Essais de linguistique générale II*. Paris: Minuit.

———. 1973b. *Questions de poétique*. Paris: Seuil.

Jaques-Dalcroze, E. 1920. *Le rythme, la musique et l'éducation*. Paris: Fischbacher.

Jauss, H. R. 1972. *Kleine Apologie der ästhetischen Erfahrung*. Constance: Verlagsanstalt.

———. 1974. *Literaturgeschichte als Provokation*. Frankfurt am Main: Suhrkamp.

———. 1975. *Rezeptionsästhetik*. Munich: Wilhelm Fink Verlag.

Karg-Elert, S. 1931. *Polaristische Klang und Tonalitätlehre*. Leipzig.

Karkoschka, E. 1966. *Das Schriftsbild der neuen Musik*. Celle: Moeck.

Katz, A. 1945. *Challenge to Musical Tradition. A New Concept to Tonality*. New York: Knopf.

Keil, C. 1979. *Tiv Song*. Chicago: University of Chicago Press.

Keller, H. 1958. Wordless Functional Analysis: the First Year, *The Musical Review*, 19:192

———. 1985. Functional Analysis of Mozart's G Minor Quintet, *Musical Analysis*, 4, nos. 1–2:73–94.

Kirnberger, J.-P. 1771–1779. *Die Kunst des reinen Satzes in der Musik*. Leiden: Brill.

Kistler, C. 1879. *Harmonielehre für Lehrer und Lernende*. Munich.

Knorr, I. 1915. Stellvertretende Akkorde. *Jahresbericht des Hochschen Konservatorium*. Frankfurt am Main.

Koechlin, C. 1928–1930. *Traité de l'harmonie*. Paris: Eschig.

Kolinski, M. 1956. The Structure of Melodic Movement, A New Method of Analysis. *Miscelanea de Estudios Dedicados al Dr. Fernando Oritz*, vol 2. Havanna: Sociedad Economica de Amigos del Pais, pp. 879–918.

———. 1961. Classification of Tonal Structures. *Studies in Ethnomusicology* 1:38–76.

Kolinski, M. 1965a. The General Direction of Melodic Movement. *Ethnomusicology* 9, no. 3:240–64.

———. 1965b. The Structure of Melodic Movement. *Studies in Ethnomusicology* 2:95–120.

———. 1973. How About "Multisonance"? *Ethnomusicology* 17, no. 2:279.

Kundera, M. 1984. The Tragedy of Central Europe. *The New York Review of Books* 31, no. 17 (26 April 1984):33–38.

———. 1986. *L'art du roman*. Paris: Gallimard.

Kunst, J. 1950. *Metre, Rhythm, Multi-part Music*. Leiden: Brill.

Kurth, E. 1920. *Romantische Harmonik und ihre Krise in Wagners "Tristan."* Bern and Leipzig.

Lakoff, G., and M. Johnson, 1980. *Metaphors We Live By*. Chicago and London: University of Chicago Press.

Lalande, A. 1956. *Vocabulaire technique et critique de la philosophie*. Paris: Presses Universitaires de France.

Laloy, L. 1902. Sur deux accords. *Revue musicale*. Reprinted in *La musique retrouvée*. Paris: Plon, 1928, pp. 115–18.

Langer, S. K. 1941. *Philosophy in a New Key*. Cambridge: Harvard University Press.

Laske, O. 1977. Towards a Musicology for the Twentieth Century. *Perspectives of New Music* 15, no. 2:220–25.

Lavignac, A. 1942. *La musique et les musiciens*. Paris: Delagrave.

Leibowitz, R. 1951. *L'évolution de la musique, de Bach à Schönberg*. Paris: Corréa.

———. 1971a. Pelléas et Mélisande ou les fantômes de la réalité. *Les Temps Modernes*, no. 305:891–922.

———. 1971b. *Le compositeur et son double*. Paris: Gallimard.

Leroi-Gourhan, A. 1965. *Le geste et la parole, vol. 2: La mémoire et les rythmes*. Paris: Ablin Michel.

Lévi-Strauss, C. 1958. *Anthropologie structurale*. Paris: Plon.

———. 1971. *L'homme nu*. Paris: Plon.

Lidov, D. 1975. *On Musical Phrase*. Monographies de sémiologie et d'analyses musicales, no. 1, Groupe de recherches en sémiologie musicale, Université de Montréal.

———. 1978. Nattiez's Semiotics of Music. *Canadian Journal of Research in Semiotics* 5, no. 2:13–54.

———. 1980. *Musical Structure and Musical Significance*. Toronto: Toronto Semiotic Circle, Monographs, Working Papers and Prepublications, 1980, no. 1.

List, G. 1963. The Boundaries of Speech and Song. *Ethnomusicology* 7, no. 1:1–16.

Lomax, A. 1959. Folksong Style. *American Anthropologist* 61:927–54.

———. 1968. *Folk Song Style and Culture*. Washington: American Association for the Advancement of Science.

Lorenz, A. 1926. *Der musikalische Aufbau von R. Wagners "Tristan und Isolde."* Tutzing: Schneider.

Lortat-Jacob, B. 1976. Rev. of *Fondements d'une sémiologie de la musique*, by J.-J. Nattiez. *Musique en jeu*, no. 24:104–7.

———. 1987. Improvisation: le modèle et ses réalisations. In *L'improvisation dans les musiques de tradition orale*. B. Lortat-Jacob, ed. Paris: S.E.L.A.F., 1987, pp. 45–59.

———, ed. 1987. *L'improvisation dans les musiques de tradition orale*. Paris: S.E.L.A.F.

Louis, R., and L. Thuille. 1907. *Harmonielehre*. Stuttgart.

Lowe, G.-E. 1942. What Is Musical Rhythm? *Musical Times* 13:43–52.

Lussy, M. 1874. *Traité de l'expresssion musicale. Accents nuances et mouvements dans la musique vocale et instrumentale*. Paris: Berger-Levrault et Fischbacher.

Lussy, M. 1883. *Le rythme musical, son origine, sa fonction, son accentuation*. Paris: Heugel.

McAllester, D. 1954. *Enemy Way Music*. Cambridge: Harvard University Press.

———, ed. 1971. *Readings in Ethnomusicology*. New York and London: Johnson Reprint Corp.

McDougall, R. 1902. The Relation of Auditory Rhythm to Nervous Discharge. *Psychological Review* 9:460–80.

McLean, M. 1966. A New Method of Melodic Interval Analysis as Applied to Maori Chant. *Ethnomusicology* 20, no. 2:174–90.

McLeod, N. 1966. Some Techniques of Analysis for Non-Western Music. Ph.D. Diss., Northwestern University.

Mâche, F.-B. 1969. Langage et musique. *N.R.F.*, no. 196:586–94.

———. 1983. *Musique, mythe, nature, ou les Dauphins d'Arion*. Paris: Klincksieck.

Machover, T., ed. 1985. *Quoi? quand? comment? La recherche musicale*. Paris: Christian Bourgois éditeur.

Macpherson, S., n.d. *Form in Music*. London: J. Williams.

Malson, L. 1975. Comment "parle" la musique si elle parle . . . *Le Monde* (22 April 1976):17.

Maneveau, G. 1977. *Musique et éducation*. Aix-en-Provence: Edisud.

Marshall, C. 1982. Towards a Comparative Aesthetics of Music. In *Cross-Cultural Perspective on Music*. R. Fack and T. Rice, eds. Toronto: University of Toronto Press, pp. 162–73.

Martinet, A. 1967. Connotations, poésie et culture. In *To Honour Roman Jakobson*, vol. 2. The Hague: Mouton, pp. 1288–94.

Marx, A. B. 1839. *Allgemeine Musiklehre. Ein Hülfsbuch für Lehrer und Lernende in jedem Zweige musikalischer Unterweisung*. 3rd ed. Leipzig: Breitkopf und Härtel, 1841.

Matras, J.-J. 1948. *Le son*. Paris: Presses Universitaires de France.

Mayrberger, K. 1881. *Die Harmonik Richard Wagner's an den Leitmotiven aus "Tristan und Isolde,"* Bayreuther Patronatverein.

Menger, P. M. 1983. *Le paradoxe du musicien*. Paris: Flamarion.

Merkelbach, C. 1977. Rev. of *Fondements d'une sémiologie de la musique*, by J.-J. Nattiez. *Zomar* (Feb.–March 1977):46–47.

Merriam, A. 1964. *The Anthropology of Music*. Evanston: Northwestern University Press.

———. 1967. *Ethnomusicology of the Flathead Indians*. Chicago: Adline Publishing Co.

Meumann, E. 1894. Untersuchungen zur Psychology und Aesthetik des Rhythmus. *Philosophische Studien*, vol. 10, pp. 249–322 and 393–430.

Meyer, L. B. 1956. *Emotion and Meaning in Music*. Chicago: University of Chicago Press.

———. 1960. Universalism and Relativism in the Study of Ethnic Music. *Ethnomusicology* 4, no. 2:49–54. Reprinted in *Readings in Ethnomusicology*. D. McAllester, ed. New York and London: Johnson Reprint Corp., 1971.

———. 1967. *Music, the Arts, and Ideas*. Chicago: University of Chicago Press.

———. 1973. *Explaining Music*. Berkeley: University of California Press.

———. 1979. Toward a Theory of Style. In *The Concept of Style*. 2nd ed. B. Land, ed. Philadelphia: University of Philadelphia Press, pp. 3–44 1987.

———. 1989. *Style and Music: Theory, History, and Ideology*. Philadelphia: University of Pennsylvania Press.

Mies, P. 1924. *Zwei Skizzenbücher von Beethoven*. Leipzig.

———. 1929. *Beethoven's Sketches, An Analysis of His Style Based on a Study of His Sketch-Books*. Oxford University Press. New edition, New York: Dover, 1974.

Mitchell, W. J. 1967. The Tristan Prelude, Techniques and Stucture. *The Music Forum*. New York: Columbia University Press, pp. 162–203.

Molino, J. 1969. Sur la méthode de Roland Barthes. *La linguistique*, no. 2:141–54.

———. 1975a. Fait musical et sémiologie de la musique. *Musique en Jeu*, no. 17:37–62.

———. 1975b. Les maiximes de La Rochefoucauld. Conférence à la Faculté de musique de l'Université de Montréal (12 March 1975). Unpublished.

———. 1978. Sur la situation du symbolique. *L'Arc*, no. 72:20–25, 31.

———. 1979a. Métaphores, modéles, et analogies dans les sciences. *Languages*, no. 54:83–102.

———. 1979b. Anthropologie et métaphore. *Langages*, no. 54:5–40, 83–102, and 103–25.

———. 1981. Le symbole et les trois fonctions, *Georges Dumézil*, "Cahiers pour un temps." Aix-en-Provence: Centre Georges Pompidou/Pandora, pp. 73–82.

———. 1982. Un discours n'est pas vrai ou faux, c'est une contruction symbolique. *L'Opinion* (Marocco, 8 and 15 Jan. 1982). Reprinted in *Outil, symbole, idéologie*. A. Bensmain, ed. Rabat: Productions-Media, 1987, pp. 77–127.

————. 1984a. Rythme. In *Dictionaire des poétiques* Y. Bonnefoy, ed. Paris: Flammarion.

————. 1984b. Esquisse d'une sémiologie de la poésie. *La petite revue de philosophie* (Montréal) 6, no. 1:1–36.

————. 1984c. Vers une nouvelle anthropologie de l'art de la musique: à propos d'un ouvrage de Steven Feld: *Sound and Sentiment. Revue de musique des universités canadiennes*, no. 5:269–312.

Molino, J., et al. 1974. Sur les titres des romans de Jean Bruce. *Languages*, no. 35:87–116.

Molino, J., and J. M. Martin. 1981. Introduction à l'analyse sémiologique des Maximes de la Rochefoucault. In *La logique du plausible, essais d'épistémologie pratique*. J. C. Gardin et al., eds. Paris: Éditions de la Maison des sciences de l'homme, pp. 147–238.

Molino, J., F. Soublin, and J. Tamine 1979. Problems de la métaphore. *Languages*, no. 54:5–40.

Molino, J. and J. Tamine. 1981. La construction du poème. *Recherches sémiotiques/Semiotic Inquiry* 1, no. 4:343–92.

————. 1982. *Introduction à l'analyse linguistique de la poésie*. Paris: Presses Universitaires de France. Reprinted under the title *Introduction à l'analyse de la poésie, I—Vers et figures*, 1987.

————. 1988. *Introduction à l'analyse de la poésie, II—De la strophe à la construction du poeme*. Paris: Presses Universitaires de France.

Monod, E. 1912. *Mathis Lussy et le rythme musical*. Neuchâtel: Attinger.

Morris, C. 1938. Foundations of the Theory of Signs. *International Encyclopedia of Unified Sciences*, vol. 1, no. 2. Chicago: University of Chicago Press.

Mounin, G. 1970. *Introduction à la sémiologie*. Paris: Minuit.

Murdock, G. P. 1962–1967. Ethnographic Atlas. *Ethnology*, vols. 1–5.

Murray Schafer, R. 1977. *The Tuning of the World*. Toronto: Knopf. New York: McClelland and Steward.

Mursell, J.-L. 1937. *The Psychology of Music*. New York: Norton.

Narveson, P. R. 1984. *Theory of Melody*. Lanham, New York, and London: University Press of America.

Nattiez, J.-J. 1971. Situation de la sémiologie musicale. *Musique en Jeu*, no. 5:3–17. English trans. Musicology and Linguistics: The First Stage of Musical Semiotics. *Journal canadien de Recherche sémiotique* 3, no. 1 (Autumn 1975):51–71.

————. 1972a. La linguistique, voie nouvelle pour l'analyse musicale? *Cahiers canadiens de musique*, no. 4:101–15. English trans. *International Review of the Aesthetics and Sociology of Music* 4, no. 1 (1973):55–67.

————. 1972b. Is a Description of Semiotics of Music Possible? *Language Sciences*, no. 23:1–7.

————. 1973a. What Can Structuralism Do for Musicology? *Journal of Symbolic Anthropology*, no. 1:59–74.

————. 1973b. Trois modèles linguistiques pour l'analyse musicale. *Musique en Jeu*, no. 10:3–11.

Nattiez, J.-J. 1974. La sémiologie musicale. *Encyclopedia Universalis*, vol. 17, Organon, pp. 560–63.

———. 1975a. *Fondements d'une sémiologie de la musique*. Paris: Union générale d'éditions.

———. 1975b. *"Densité 21.5" de Varèse: essai d'analyse sémiologique*. Montréal: Université de Montréal, Groupe de Recherches en Sémiologie musicale, Monographies de Sémiologie et d'Analyse musicales, no. 2.

———. 1976. Le statut sémiologique de l'objet sonore. *Cahiers Recherche/Musique*, no. 2:91–106.

———. 1977a. A quelles conditions peut-on parler d'universaux de la musique. (In French and English.) *Le monde de la musique* 19, nos. 1–2:92–105, 106–17.

———. 1977b. Armonia. *Enciclopedia Einaudi*, vol. 1. Turin: Einaudi, 1977, pp. 841–67.

———. 1978. Le problème de la classification des signes: sémiologie de la sémiologie. *Journal canadien de recherche sémiotique* 6, no. 1:113–26. Reprinted in Nattiez 1987, Chapter 9.

———. 1979. Melodia. *Enciclopedia Einaudi*, vol. 8. Turin: Einaudi, pp. 1042–67.

———. 1979–1980. Le fondements théoriques de la notion d'interprétant en sémiologie musicale. *Journal canadien de Recherche sémiotique*, 7 no. 2:1–19. Reprinted in Nattiez, 1987, Chapter 8.

———. 1981a. Ritmica/Metrica. *Enciclopedia Einaudi*, vol. 12. Turin: Einaudi, 1981, pp. 151–84.

———. 1981b. Suono/Rumore. *Enciclopedia Einaudi*, vol. 13. Turin: Einaudi, pp. 833–49.

———. 1981c. Tonale/atonale. *Enciclopedia Einaudi*, vol. 14. Turin: Einaudi, pp. 318–43.

———. 1981d. Paroles d'informateurs et propos de musiciens: quelques remarques sur la place du discours dans la connaissance de la musique. *Yearbook for Traditional Music* 13:48–59.

———. 1982a. Tonale/atonale. [postface] *Enciclopedia Einaudi*, vol. 15. Turin: Einaudi, pp. 696–702.

———. 1982b. Varèse's "Density 21.5": A Study in Semiological Analysis. *Music Analysis* 1, no. 3, pp. 243–340. (Translated and revised version of Nattiez 1975b.)

———. 1983a. *Tétralogies (Wagner, Boulez, Chéreau), essai sur l'infidélité*. Paris: Christian Bourgois éditeur.

———. 1983b. Problèmes de la poïétique en sémiologie musicale: quelques réflexions à propos du "De Natura Sonorum" de Bernard Parmegiani. In *L'envers d'une oeuvre*. P. Mion, J.-J. Nattiez, and J. C. Thomas, eds. Paris: Buchet-Chastel, pp. 159–91.

———. 1983c. Le beau et le primitif [title supplied by the editor]. *Le Monde de la musique*, no. 60:25–27.

———. 1984. *Proust musicien*. Paris: Christian Bourgois éditeur. English trans. by Derrick Puffett, *Proust as Musician*. Cambridge: Cambridge University Press, 1989.

——. 1985. La relation oblique entre le musicoloque et le compositeur. In T. Machover (ed.), 1985, pp. 121–34.

——. 1986. Introduction à l'esthétique de Hanslick. Preface to the French edition of E. Hanslick, *Du beau dans la musique*. Paris: Christian Bourgois éditeur, pp. 11–51.

——. 1987. *De la sémiologie à la musique*. Montréal: Cahiers du départment d'études littéraires de l'Université du Québec à Montréal, no. 10.

——. 1990. *Wagner androgyne*. Paris: Christian Bourgois éditeur.

Nattiez, J.-J., and L. Hirbour-Paquette. 1973. Analyse musicale et sémiologie: à propos du Prélude de *Pelléas*. *Musique en Jeu*, no. 10:42–69.

Nettl, B. 1954. *North American Indian Musical Styles*. Philadelphia: American Folklore Society.

——. 1956. *Music in Primitive Culture*. Cambridge: Harvard University Press.

——. 1964. *Theory and Method in Ethnomusicology*. Glencoe: Free Press.

——. 1977. On the Question of Universals. *The World of Music* 19, no. 1:1–2, 2–6.

——. 1983. *The Study of Ethnomusicology*. Urbana, Chicago, and London: University of Illinois Press.

Nietzsche, F. 1974. *Généalogie de la morale* (1887). Paris: Union générale d'Éditions.

Norton, R. 1984. *Tonality in Western Culture*. University Park and London: The Pennsylvania State University Press.

Noske, F. 1979. Rev. of *Fondements d'une sémiologie de la musique*, by J.-J. Nattiez. *Ethnomusicology* 23, no. 1:144–48.

——. 1981. Melodic Determinants in Tonal Structure. *Musicological Annual* 17, no. 1:111–120.

Nwachukwu, C. 1981. Taxonomy of Musical Instruments of Mbaise, Nigeria. M.A. thesis, The Queen's University of Belfast.

Ogden, C. K., and I. A. Richards. 1970. *The Meaning of "Meaning"* (1923). New York: Harcourt, Brace and World.

Osgood, C., G. J. Suci, and P. H. Tannenbaum. 1957. *The Measurement of Meaning*. Urbana: University of Illinois Press.

Osmond-Smith, D. 1975. Introduction générale à une méthode d'analyse sémiotique formelle de la musique. *La musique en projet*. Paris: Gallimard, pp. 173–88.

Panofsky, E. 1955. *Meaning in the Visual Arts*. Woodstock: Overlook Press.

Paulus, J. 1969. *La fonction symbolique et le langage*. Brussels: Dessart.

Perle, G. 1977. The Secret Programme of the Lyric Suite. *Musical Times* 148 (Aug.–Oct. 1977):629–32, 709–13, 809–13.

Person, P., ed. 1981. Proceedings of a Symposium on the Neurological Basis of Signs in Communication Processes. *Monographs, Working Papers and Prepublications of the Toronto Semiotic Circle*. Victoria University, 1981, nos. 2–3.

Peirce, C. S. 1931–1935. *Collected Papers*, vols. 1–6. L. Hartshorne and R. Weiss, eds. Cambridge: Harvard University Press.

———. 1931–1935. *Collected Papers*, vols. 7 and 8. T. Burks, ed. Cambridge: Harvard University Press.

Pierret, M. 1969. *Entretiens avec Pierre Schaeffer*. Paris: Belfond.

Pirandello, L. 1972. *Uno, nessuno e centomila*. Milano: Mondadori.

Piston, W. 1941. *Harmony*. New York: Norton.

Popper, K. 1981. *La quête inachevée* (1974). Paris: Calmann-Lévy.

Pousseur, H. 1957. *Introduction aux "Écrits" d'Alban Berg*. Monaco: Éditions du Rocher.

———. 1981. Schumann ist der Dichter. *Revue de musique des universités canadiennes*, no. 2:94–113.

Powers, W. K. 1980. Oglala Song Terminology. *Selected Reports in Ethnomusicology* 3, no. 2:23–41.

Pratt, C. C. 1930. The Spatial Character of High and Low Tones. *Journal of Experimental Psychology* 13:278–85.

Quine, W. V. 1961. *From a Logical Point of View*. Cambridge: Harvard University Press.

Rameau, J. P. 1722. *Traité de l'harmonie réduite à ses principes naturels*. Paris: Ballard.

———. 1737. *Génération harmonique, ou Traité de musique théorique et pratique*. Paris: Prault.

———. 1750. *Démonstration du principe de l'harmonie*. Paris: Durand.

Ratner, L.-G. 1956. Eighteenth-Century Theories of Musical Period Structure. *The Musical Quarterly* 42, no. 4:439–54.

Reber, N. H. 1842. *Traité d'harmonie*. Paris: Colombier.

Régnier, A. 1974. *La crise du langage scientifique*. Paris: Anthropos.

Reicha, A. 1814. *Traité de mélodie, abstraction faite de ses rapports avec l'harmonie*. Paris: Scherff.

Réti, R. 1951. *The Thematic Process in Music*. New York: Macmillan.

———. 1958. *Tonality, Atonality, Pantonality. A Study of Some Trends in Twentieth Century Music*. London: Rockliff.

Ricoeur, P. 1965. *De l'interprétation*. Paris: Seuil.

Riemann, H. 1887. *Handbuch der Harmonielehre*. Leipzig: Breitkopf und Härtel.

———. 1903. *System der musikalischen Rhythmik und Metrik*. Leipzig: Breitkopf und Härtel.

———. 1909. Klangschlüssel. *Musiklexikon*. 7th ed. Leipzig.

———. 1931. Mélodie. *Dictionnaire de musique*. 3rd ed. Paris: Payot, pp. 829–30.

Riepel, J. 1752–1754. *Anfangsgründe zur musikalischen Setzkunst*. 5 vols. Frankfurt am Main: Lotter.

Riffaterre, M. 1978. *Semiotics of Poetry*. Bloomington and London: Indiana University Press.

———. 1979. *La production du texte*. Paris: Seuil.

Roberts, H. H. 1936. *Musical Areas in Aboriginal North America*. New Haven: Yale University Publications in Anthropology, no. 12.

————. 1955. Songs of the Nootka Indians of West Vancouver Island. *Transactions of the American Philosophical Society* 45.

Robertson-De Carbo, C. E. 1976. *Tayil* as Category and Communication among the Argentine Mapuche: A Methodological Suggestion. *1976 Yearbook of the International Folk Music Council*, 8, pp. 35–42.

Roland-Manuel (ed.), 1960. *Histoire de la musique*, tome 1. Paris: Gallimard, Encyclopédie de la Pléiade.

Roland-Manuel, 1963. Le classicisme française et le problème de l'expression musicale. *Histoire de la musique*, vol. 2. Paris: Gallimard, Encyclopédie de la Pléiade, pp. 82–93.

Rosen, C. 1971. *The Classical Style*. New York: Norton.

————. 1975. *Schoenberg*. New York: The Viking Press.

————. 1980. *Sonata Forms*. New York: Norton.

Rouget, G. 1968. L'ethnomusicologie. In *Ethnologie générale*. M. Poirier, ed. Paris: Gallimard, pp. 333–48.

Rousseau, J.-J. 1767. Bruit. *Dictionnaire de musique*. Paris: Duchesne, pp. 59–60.

Ruckmick, C. A. 1927. The Rhythmical Experience from the Systematic Point of View. *American Journal of Psychology* 39:355–66.

Russolo, L. 1954. *L'art des bruits. Manifeste futuriste de 1913*. Introduction by M. Lemaître. Paris: Richard-Masse. English trans. B. Brown. New York: Pendragon Press, Monographs in Musicology, 1986.

————. 1975. *L'art des bruits* (1913). Preface by Giovanni Lista. Lausanne: L'âge d'homme.

Ruwet, N. 1966. Méthodes d'analyse en musicologie. *Revue belge de musicologie* 20:65–90. Reprinted in Ruwet, 1972, pp. 100–34. English trans. M. Everist. *Music Analysis* 6, nos. 1–2 (March–July 1987):4–39.

———— 1967. Musicologie et linguistique. *Revue international des sciences sociales* 19, no. 1:85–93.

————1972. *Langage, musique, poésie*. Paris: Seuil.

———— 1975a. Théorie et Méthodes dans les études musicales: quelques remarques rétrospectives et préliminaires. *Musique en Jeu*, no. 17:11–36.

———— 1975b. Parallélismes et déviations en poésie. In *Langue, discours, société*. J. Kristeva, J. C. Milner, and N. Ruwet, eds. Paris: Seuil, pp. 307–51.

Sachs, C. 1938. Towards a Prehistory of European Music. *Music Quarterly* 24:147–52.

————. 1953. *Rhythm and Tempo, A Study in Music History*. New York: Norton.

————. 1962. *The Wellsprings of Music*. The Hague: Nijhoff.

Sadaï, Y. 1980. *Harmony in its Systemic and Phenomenological Aspects*. Jerusalem: Yanetz.

Sakata, L. 1983. *Music in the Mind, The Concepts of Music and Musician in Afghanistan*. Kent: Kent State University Press.

Salzer, F. 1952. *Structural Hearing*. New York: Dover.

Samson, J. 1975. Pour une approche sémiologique de la bande dessinée. *La Barre du Jour* (Winter 1975):241–61.

Samson, J. 1977. *Music in Transition. A Study of Tonal Expansion and Atonality, 1900–1925*. New York: Norton.

Sapir, E. 1969. Diola-Fogny Funeral Songs and the Native Critic. *African Language Review*, no. 8:176–91.

———. 1971. *Anthropologie*. Paris: Seuil.

Sartre, J.-P. 1964. *Qu'est-ce que la littérature?* Paris: Gallimard. English trans. B. Frechtman. London: Methuen and Co, Ltd, 1978.

Saussure, F. de. 1922. *Cours de linguistique générale*. Paris: Payot. Critical edition by Rudolph Engler, Wiesbaden: Harassowitz, 1968.

Scarpetta, G. 1985. *L'impureté*. Paris: Grasset.

Schaeffer, P. 1957. Lettre à Albert Richard. *La Revue musicale*, no. 236:3–16.

———. 1966. *Traité des objets musicaux*. Paris: Seuil.

———. 1967a. *La musique concrète*. Paris: Presses Universitaires de France.

———. 1967b. *Solfège de l'objet sonore* (3 sound discs with pamphlet for Schaeffer 1966). Paris: Seuil.

———. 1968. La sévère mission de la musique. *Revue d'esthétique* 21, nos. 2–4:253–91.

Schenker, H. 1925–1930. *Das Meisterwerk in der Musik*. 3 vols. Munich, Vienna, and Berlin: Drei Masken Verlag.

———. 1935. *Der freie Satz*. Vienna: Universal Edition.

———. 1973. *Harmony* (1906). Edited and annotated by Oswald Jonas. Cambridge and London: MIT Press.

Schérer, J. 1957. *Le "Livre" de Mallarmé*. Paris: Gallimard.

Schering, A. 1935. Musikalische Symbolkunde. *Jahrbuch der Musikbibliothek Peters* 42:15–30.

Schneider, M. 1980. *Semiotik der Musik, Darstellung und Kritik*. Munich: Fink Verlag.

Schoenberg, A. 1911. *Harmonielehre*. Leipzig and Vienna: Universal Edition.

———. 1950. *Style and Idea*. New York: Philosophical Library.

———. 1954. *Structural Functions of Harmony*. New York: Norton.

Schreyer, J. 1905. *Lehrbuch der Harmonie und der Elementarkomposition*. Dresden.

Schubart, C.F.D. 1806. *Ideen zur einer Aesthetik der Tonkunst*. Vienna.

Scruton, R. 1978. The Semiology of Music. *The Cambridge Review* (2 June 1978):173–76.

Searle, H. 1966. *The Music of Liszt*. New York: Dover.

Seeger, C. 1960. On the Moods of a Music Logic. *Journal of the American Musicology Society* 13:224–61. Reprinted in Seeger 1977, pp. 64–101.

———. 1958. Prescriptive and Descriptive Music Writing. *Musical Quarterly* 44, no. 2:184–95.

———. 1976. Tractatus Esthetico-Semioticus. In *Current Thought in Musicology*. J. W. Grubbs, ed. Austin and London: University of Texas Press, pp. 1–39.

———. 1977. *Studies in Musicology (1935–1975)*. Berkeley, Los Angeles, and London: University of California Press.

Servien, P. 1930. *Les rythmes comme introduction physique à l'Esthétique*. Paris.

Sessions, R. 1962. *The Musical Experience of Composer, Performer, Listener* (1950). New York: Atheneum.

Siegmeister, E. 1965. *Harmony and Melody*. Belmont: Wadsworth.

Simms, B. 1975. Choron, Fétis and the Theory of Tonality. *Journal of Music Theory* 19, no. 1:112–39.

Siohan, R. 1955. Le fantastique musical. *Revue d'esthétique* 8, no. 2:113–34.

———. 1962. La musique comme signe. *Colloque sur le signe et les systèmes de signes*. Royaumont, 12–15 April 1962, E.P.H.E. 6th section, 9, typescript summary.

Simonis, Y. 1968. *Lévi-Strauss ou la passion de l'inceste*. Paris: Aubier-Montaigne.

Smith, S. 1982. The Constituents of Music Ethnocentry: An Example from the Kuna of Panama. In *Ethnotheory*. M. Herndon, ed. Dorby: Norwood Editions.

Smits van Waesberghe, J. 1955. *Theory of Melody*. Rome: American Institute of Musicology.

Souris, A. 1961. Mélodie (A). *Encyclopédie de la musique*, vol. 3. Paris: Fasquelle.

———. 1976. *Conditions de la musique et autres écrits*. Paris and Brussels: CNRS-Université de Bruxelles.

Stefani, G. 1974. Progetto semiotico di una musicologica sistematica. *International Review of the Aesthetics and Sociology of Music*, no. 2:277–89.

———. 1980. Rev. of *Fondements d'une sémiologie de la musique*, by J.-J. Nattiez. *Nuova Rivista Musicale Italiana*, no. 2:269–71.

Stein, L. 1962. *Structure and Style*. Evanston: Sumy-Birchard Co.

Stockhausen, K. 1963. Struktur und Erlebniszeit. *Texte*, vol. 1. Cologne: Du Mont Dokumente, pp. 86–98.

———. 1970–1971. Interview et déclaration. *V.H. 101*, no. 4:110–18.

Stockmann, D. 1970. Musik als kommunikatives System. Informations-und zeichentheoretische Aspekte insbesondere bei der Erforschung mundlich tradierter Musik. *Deutsches Jahrbuch der Musikwissenschaft für 1969* 14:76–95.

Stone, R. M. 1981. Toward a Kapelle Conceptualization of Music Performance. *Journal of American Folklore* 94, no. 372:188–206.

Stravinsky, I. 1971. *Chroniques de ma vie*. Paris: Médiations-Gonthier.

Subotnik, R. R. 1976. Rev. of *Fondements d'une sémiologie de la musique*, by J.-J. Nattiez. *Journal of Aesthetics and Art Criticism* 35, no. 2:240–42.

Supičic, I. 1975. Contemporary Aesthetics of Music and Musicology. *Acta Musicologica* 28, no. 2:193–207.

Tarrab, G. 1976. Le discours de la musique. *La Presse* (16 October 1976).

Tedlock, B. 1980. Songs of the Zuni Kachina Society: Composition, Rehearsal and Performance. In *Southwestern Indian Ritual Drama*. C. Frisbie, ed. Albuquerque: University of New Mexico Press, pp. 7–35.

Thibaud, P. 1983. La notion peircéenne d'interprétant. *Dialectica* 37, no. 1:3–33.

Thomas, E., ed. 1966. Form in der neuen Musik. *Darmstädter Beiträge zur neuen Musik*. Mainz: Schott.

Thomson, W. 1970. Style Analysis, or the Perils of Pigeonholes. *Journal of Music Theory* 14, no. 2:191–208.

Tiessen, H. 1948. Zwei Streitfragen der Musiktheorie. *Stimmen*, no. 1:307–20.

Tovey, D. F. 1978. *Essays in Musical Analysis, 1. Symphonies I* (1935). London: Oxford University Press.

Treitler, L. 1967. On Historical Criticism. *The Musical Quarterly* 53, no. 2:188–205.

Tran van Khe. 1977. Le pentatonique est-il universel? Quelques réflexions sur le pentatonisme. *The World of Music* 19, nos. 1–2:85–91. (English trans. pp. 76–84.)

Valery, P. 1945. Leçon inaugurale du cours de poétique au Collège de France. *Variétés V*. Paris: Gallimard, pp. 297–322.

Van Appledorn, M.-J. 1966. Stylistic Study of Claude Debussy's Opera *Pelléas et Mélisande*. Ph.D. Diss., Eastman School of Music.

Vanasse, F. 1983. Glossolalie: oeuvre ouverte. *Revue de Musique des universités canadiennes*, no. 4:95–124.

Varèse, E. 1937. Modern Percussion Masterpiece Illustrates Composer's Lecture. *Santa Fe Mexican* (9 September 1937):3.

———. 1968. Edgar Varèse on Music and Art: A Conversation Between Varèse and Alcopley. *Leonardo* 1, no. 2:187–95.

———. 1983. *Écrits*. Paris: Christian Bourgois éditeur.

Verrier, P.-I. 1912. L'isochronisme en musique et en poésie. *Journal de psychologie normale et pathologique* 9:212–32.

Veyne, P. 1971. *Comment on écrit l'histoire*. Paris: Seuil. English trans. M. Moore-Rinvolucri. Middletown: Wesleyan University Press, 1984.

———. 1979. Foucault révolutionne l'histoire. *Comment on écrit l'histoire*. Paris: Seuil, pp. 203–42.

———. 1983. *Les Grecs ont-ils cru à leur mythes?* Paris: Seuil.

Vogel, M. 1962. *Der Tristan-Akkord und die Krise der modernen Harmonielehre*. Düsseldorf: Gesellschaft zur Forderung der systematischen Musikwissenschaft.

Vuillermoz, E. 1957. *Claude Debussy*. Geneva: Kister.

Wagner, R. 1879. Über die Anwendung der Musik auf das Drama. *Gesammelte Schriften und Dichtungen*, vol. 10, 176–93.

Warburton, A. O. 1952. *Melody Writing and Analysis*. London: Longmans.

Ward, W. R. 1970. *Examples for the Study of Musical Style*. Dubuque: Brown.

Warren, H. C., ed. 1934. *Dictionary of Psychology*. Boston and New York: Houghton Mifflin.

Weber, G. 1817–1821. *Versuch einer geordneten Theorie der Tonsetzkunst*. 3 vols. Mainz: Schott.

Webern, A. V. 1933. *Chemin de la nouvelle musique*. Paris: Lattès, 1980.

Wehinger, R. 1970. *Artikulationen, de Ligeti*. Hörpartitur. Mainz: Schott.

Westernhagen, C. V. 1973. *Die Enstehung des "Ring."* Zürich and Freiburg: Atlantis.

Willems, E. 1954. *Le rythme musical.* (Rythme-Rythmique-Métrique). Paris: Presses Universitaires de France.

Wiora, W. 1963. *Les quatre âges de la musique.* Paris: Payot. English trans. M. D. Hector Norton. New York: Norton, 1965.

Yeston, M. 1976. *The Stratification of Musical Rhythm.* New Haven and London: Yale University Press.

Zemp, H. 1978. "Are" are Classification of Musical Types and Instruments. *Ethnomusicology* 22, no. 1:37–67.

―――. 1979. Aspects of "Are" are Musical Theory. *Ethnomusicology* 23, no. 1:6–48.

―――. 1981. Melanesian Solo Polyphonic Panpipe Music. *Ethnomusicology* 25, no. 3:383–418.

Index

261

Tamine, J., 195

Tarski, J., 133n

taxonomial stock in harmony, 203, 221

tayil, 55–56, 60

Tchaikovsky, P. I., *Pathétique Symphony*, 121

Tedlock, B., 186n

theme, 158, 195

theory: current definition of, 188; and metaphor, 106; as symbolic construction, 201–38

Thibaud, P., 7n

Thomas, J.-C., 104n, 191

Thomson, W., 137

thread of musical discourse, 100–101

throat-game. See *katajjaq*

Tibetans (musical culture of the), 65

tonality, Norton's conception of, 145–46; as a style, 136, 210n

total social fact, ix, 34n, 42, 143. *See also* Mauss

Tovey, D., 162–63, 165

trace, as neutral level, 12, 15, 16

Tran van Khe, 63

transcendent principles: behind analyses, 175–76, 201; Chailley's, 206; Goldman's, 208–9; and harmonic analysis, 223; and harmonic theories, 202–4, 212

transcription: and analysis of electro-acoustic music, 81–82; and music of the oral tradition, 64, 73; as symbolic substitute, 72; and tripartition, 81–82

tripartition: and analysis, 153; and analysis of electro-acoustic music, 81–82, 91–101; and analysis of open work, 86–87; as analytical situation, 136–38, 230–32; in Boulez's writings, 138n; and cartoon strip, 14–15; and communication, 17–18; (six) components of, 139–43; and critics, 175n; and definitions of music, 41; and formalized models, 166–67; and Hanslick's aesthetics, 110; and harmonic theories, 212–16; and history of musical analysis, 137–38; and history of parameters, 146–47; and improvisation, 89–90; and Ingarden's conception of work, 69–70; and interpretation, 75–77; and metalanguage, 134; in Molino's semiol-

ogy, 10–16, 28–32; and plots, 204–12; and Schaeffer's *Traité des objets musicaux*, 91–97; and semiology, 10–16, 29; and sound object, 91–101; and symbolic forms, 17; and transcription, 81–82, 91–101; and universals, 62–67; and Wagner's *Ring*, 74–77

truth, in analysis, 77, 202, 233–38; in musical interpretation, 77; in musician's discourse, 189, 195–96. *See also* facts

Two-Crows, 192

types, of musical analysis: analysis as an aural genre, 154; classification of analyses, 160–64; classificatory analysis, 163–64; analysis by composers, 183–85; formalized analysis, 163–64; global models of, 163–64; graphics in, 165; hermeneutic readings, 162–63; impressionistic analyses, 161; intermediary models, 165–67; linear models, 164; non-formalized analysis, 161; paraphrases, 162; analysis by traits, 163. *See also* analysis (musical)

units: in the analysis of electro-acoustic music, 80; defining vs. segmenting discrete units, 81n, 164

universals: and behaviors, 65–67; and esthesic, 66; and etic/emic, 62, 65; and immanent structures, 62–64; and pentatonicism, 62; and poietic, 65–66; and strategies, 65–67

Upopo, 71

Uzbek, 195

Valéry, P., 12

value, 5

Van Appledorn, M. J., 175

Vanasse, F., 87n

Varèse, E., 48, 51–53, 92, 108; *Density 21.5*, 152; *Ionization*, 52

variables: autonomization of, 143–49; control of, 194; in harmonic analysis, 201, 222; in the history of music, 148; in Meyer's theory of style, 146; in musical analysis, 143–49. *See also* Boulez; Meyer; Molino; parameters

Variationstrieb, 87

Venda (musical culture of the), 64–65